MW00799970

SERMONS FOR CHRISTIAN FAMILIES

Property of Peggy Staples

July 12, 2015

OTHER SOLID GROUND TITLES

We recently celebrated our eighth anniversary of uncovering buried treasure to the glory of God. During these eight years we have produced over 225 volumes. A sample is listed below:

Biblical & Theological Studies: *Addresses to Commemorate the 100ᵗʰ Anniversary of Princeton Theological Seminary in 1912* by Allis, Machen, Wilson, Vos, Warfield and many more.

Notes on Galatians by J. Gresham Machen

The Origin of Paul's Religion by J. Gresham Machen

A Scientific Investigation of the Old Testament by R.D. Wilson

Theology on Fire: *Sermons from Joseph A. Alexander*

Evangelical Truth: *Sermons for the Family* by Archibald Alexander

A Shepherd's Heart: *Pastoral Sermons of James W. Alexander*

Grace & Glory: *Sermons from Princeton Chapel* by Geerhardus Vos

The Lord of Glory by Benjamin B. Warfield

The Person & Work of the Holy Spirit by Benjamin B. Warfield

The Power of God unto Salvation by Benjamin B. Warfield

Calvin Memorial Addresses by Warfield, Johnson, Orr, Webb...

The Five Points of Calvinism by Robert Lewis Dabney

Annals of the American Presbyterian Pulpit by W.B. Sprague

The Word & Prayer: *Classic Devotions from the Pen of John Calvin*

A Body of Divinity: *Sum and Substance of Christian Doctrine* by Ussher

The Complete Works of Thomas Manton (in 22 volumes)

A Puritan New Testament Commentary by John Trapp

Exposition of the Epistle to the Hebrews by William Gouge

Exposition of the Epistle of Jude by William Jenkyn

Lectures on the Book of Esther by Thomas M'Crie

Lectures on the Book of Acts by John Dick

To order any of our titles please contact us in one of three ways:

Call us at **1-866-789-7423**
Email us at **sgcb@charter.net**
Visit our website at **www.solid-ground-books.com**

SERMONS

FOR

CHRISTIAN FAMILIES

ON THE MOST IMPORTANT

RELATIVE DUTIES

EDWARD PAYSON

SOLID GROUND CHRISTIAN BOOKS
BIRMINGHAM, ALABAMA USA

Solid Ground Christian Books
PO Box 660132
Vestavia Hills AL 35266
205-443-0311
sgcb@charter.net
solid-ground-books.com

Sermons for Christian Families
by Edward Payson (1783 – 1827)
Edited by Asa Cummings (1791 – 1856)

First Solid Ground Edition July 2009

Taken from the 1832 edition published by
Crocker and Brewster, Boston, MA

Cover design by Borgo Design, Tuscaloosa, AL

Cover image is entitled *Family Worship* and was taken from the book
entitled *A Guide to Family Devotion* by Alexander Fletcher

SPECIAL THANKS to Jim Cote of Westbrook, Maine for sending a
photocopy of this book along with a strong encouragement to bring
this back into print.

ISBN: 978-159925-216-2

PREFACE

The cultivation of *domestic* piety and morality is the surest means of elevating the character of our species, and of advancing their welfare both for this world and that which is to come. The good father cannot be a bad citizen; and the child, trained to habits of subordination and duty in the family, will be likely to carry these habits with him into the extended relations of mature life. The rule and measure of human duty is the law of God. A character formed on any other basis, or shaped by any other model, than the Word of God, must be essentially defective. Deep piety constitutes the only sure foundation of a pure morality; and any system of education which overlooks this, and provides only for a reputable passage through the present world, consults for the infancy only of our being. No system is complete, which does not recognize man as the creature of God, and destined to an immortal existence. Still, the duties of the domestic and social relations constitute a highly important and indispensable part of true religion—a part which is greatly undervalued, but without which the most imposing pretensions to piety are "as sounding brass and tinkling cymbals."

If children are to become worthy subjects of the State, or citizens of the Heavenly Zion, the process of training them cannot be commenced too early, nor conducted with too much circumspection, nor followed out with too much perseverance. Every effort, suited to produce and fasten conviction of this kind in the minds of parents, to waken a sense of parental responsibility, and excite to duty;—or to check existing tendencies,—resulting from the pageantry that characterizes much of the religion of the age,—which conspire to divert attention from the noiseless, retired, every day duties of the domestic state, is entitled to serious and grateful regard. Such is the little work, herewith offered to the public. It is designed for a *family* book. It delineates character, enforces obligations, and inculcates duties, by the observance of which, with the blessing of God, families become nurseries of the church of Christ. The few sermons in this selection, which are of a less specific character, will nevertheless be found to have an important bearing on the principal design of the publication.

Christian fathers, the members of maternal associations, all pious mothers indeed, will find it a welcome companion, a faithful monitor and friend. That such a work is greatly needed, there is but too much evidence in the prevailing laxity of family government and discipline. That it may be instrumental of reviving *family religion*,—of "turning the heart of the fathers unto the children, and the heart of the children unto their fathers, and thus of averting the curse of God from our land,"—is the prayer of the Editor.

June 1832
Asa Cummings, Editor

TABLE OF CONTENTS

SERMON I

CHRIST, GOD'S BEST GIFT TO MAN.

Thanks be unto God for his unspeakable gift.—2 CORINTHIANS IX. 15.

PERHAPS there is nothing which would more powerfully tend to convince us how little we resemble the primitive Christians, than a comparison of our views and feelings respecting the gospel of Christ, with those which they express in their writings. While we naturally discover in it nothing wonderful or excellent, listen to it with indifference, treat it with neglect, and perhaps consider it as little better than foolishness; they can scarcely mention or allude to it without feeling the strongest emotions, and breaking forth into the most rapturous expressions of gratitude, admiration, wonder and love. They style it the glorious gospel of the blessed God, speak of it as the most wonderful of all his wondrous works, and represent it as containing things unutterable and unsearchable, things into which even angels desire to look. An example of the glowing and energetic language which they were accustomed to employ in speaking of the subject, we have in our text; in which the apostle, reflecting on the goodness of God in giving his Son to die for us, exclaims in the fulness of his heart, Thanks be unto God for his unspeakable gift!

My friends, in obedience to long established custom, and to the voice of our civil rulers, we have this day assembled to give thanks to God. Perhaps some are ready to say, For what shall we thank him? Our fathers, who established this custom, had reason to praise him, for they were favored with peace and prosperity. We too had formerly reason to praise him, for we once enjoyed the same blessings. But those days are past. Peace and prosperity are gone. We are involved in a war, of which we cannot foresee the termination. Our country is torn in pieces by political dissensions, and contending parties seem almost prepared to imbrue their hands in each other's blood. Our private sufferings and embarrassments are also great. Our commerce is destroyed, our business interrupted, our property, acquired in better days, taken from us; our families look to us for bread, which we shall soon be unable to give them; the prospect before us is dark and cheerless, and we fear that these days are but the beginning of sorrows. For what, then, should we thank God, or how attune our voices to joy and praise?

I answer, were our situation more deplorable than it really is, were we stripped of every earthly blessing, we should still have cause for joy and thankfulness; still have reason to praise God. We ought to rejoice that the Lord reigns, and we ought to praise him that we are not treated as we deserve, that we are not in the mansions of despair, that we are yet prisoners of hope. Above all, we ought to praise him for the unspeakable gift of his Son, and we shall do it if we possess the smallest portion of the apostle's temper. His situation was, in a temporal view, incomparably worse than that of any person in this assembly. Speaking of himself and his fellow disciples, he says, Even to the present hour, we both hunger and thirst, and are naked, and buffeted, and reviled and persecuted. We are made as the filth of the world, and the off-scouring of all things, unto this day. Yet in this distressed, oppressed condition, destitute of all the good things of life, and liable every day to lose life itself, he could still cry, Thanks be unto God for his unspeakable gift. Nay, more; while he lay in the gloomy dungeon of Philippi, his body torn with scourges, and his feet fast in the stocks, we find him still thanking God for the gospel of his Son, and causing his prison, even at midnight, to resound with his songs of joy and praise.

And can we then, with justice, pretend that we have no reason to be thankful? Ought not we, as well as the apostle, to bless God for the gospel of Christ? Is it not to us, as it was to him, the gospel of salvation? Let us then banish from our minds every ungrateful feeling, every murmuring thought, and unitedly cry with the apostle, Thanks be unto God for his unspeakable gift. That you may be induced to do this, I shall attempt to show,

That Jesus Christ is the Gift of God to men : a Gift which may be justly called *unspeakable* : a Gift for which we should thank him with the most lively gratitude.

I. Jesus Christ is the Gift of God to men.

It can scarcely be necessary to remind you that a gift, or present, is something valuable freely offered to persons who have no claim to it, without receiving anything in return, and without any expectation that it will be restored. It must be something valuable ; for a thing of no value cannot properly be considered as a gift. It must be offered freely, or voluntarily ; for if we are obliged to offer it, it is merely the discharge of an obligation. It must be offered to persons who have no claim to it; for to those who can justly deserve it, it is not a gift, but only their due. If they claim it as a recompense for some injury which we have done them, it is restitution. If they claim it in return for services which they have performed, or favors which they have bestowed, it is a debt. It must be offered without expecting anything in return ; for if we expect something equally valuable in return, it is an exchange; if we expect some lawful service to be performed, it is wages; if we expect anything unlawful, it is a bribe. Finally, it must be offered without any expectation that it will be restored to us ; for otherwise it is a loan, and not a gift.

Now a moment's reflection will convince us that, in all these respects, Jesus Christ is, strictly speaking, a gift of God to man. Christ is something valuable; for, as we shall soon attempt to show, his worth is unspeakable. He is offered to us freely, or voluntarily ; for God was under no kind of obligation to make us such an offer. He is offered to persons who have no claim to such a favor, for we can justly claim nothing at the hand of God but destruction. We cannot claim the offer of Christ as a recompense for injuries received from God, for he has never injured us, but has done us good and not evil all the days of our lives. Neither can we claim it in return for services performed, or favors bestowed · for we have never done any thing for God, or bestowed the smallest favor upon him. On the contrary, we have done him all the injury in our power. Nor does God offer his Son with the expectation of receiving any thing in return, for we and all that we possess are already his; and if we were not, we could give him nothing; for even if we are righteous, what do we give him, or what receiveth he at our hands? When we have done all in our power, we are but unprofitable servants, and have done no more than it was our duty to do. Nor, finally, does God offer us his Son with any intention of resuming the gift; for, says the apostle, the gifts of God are without repentance, that is, irrevocable; he offers us his Son to be ours forever. Jesus Christ is, therefore, in the most strict and proper sense of the term, the gift, the free, unmerited gift of God to men.

I am not ignorant, however, that some deny this. I am aware that it is thought and urged by some, that God was under obligations to provide a Saviour for mankind, and that it would have been cruel and unjust for him to create beings who he knew would fall, had he not previously intended to give his Son for their redemption, or to open a way for their restoration, by some other means. These persons then pretend, that the law of God, which requires perfect obedience, on pain of death, is much too strict and severe, for such weak, fallen creatures, as we are; that it is unreasonable and unjust to require perfection of us, or to punish us for falling short of it; and that God, finding he had enacted a law too severe, was obliged to send his Son to bear its curse, deliver us from its authority, and introduce a milder law, which should allow us to sin a little, provided we would not sin much.

It is true, indeed, that few are to be found, who dare openly and directly avow such sentiments; but, they are the sentiments of every unrenewed heart; all men naturally consider the gospel as a kind of remedy for the too great severity of the law; and hence it is, in their view, little better than foolishness. And if this view of the gospel were correct, it would indeed be foolishness in the extreme; and God would no longer deserve our admiration, reverence, gratitude, or love. It would then appear that God was the offending, and we the injured party; that Christ died, not to make satisfaction for our transgression against God, but for God's too great severity to us; that he is offered to us not as a free, unmerited gift, but as a recompense for the injuries we have received from our Maker, in his suffering us to fall, and threatening to punish us for our sins. Farewell, then, all the glory and grace of the gospel. Farewell, all ascriptions of praise to God, for his goodness, mercy and love. The wondrous plan of redeeming love, the unspeakable gift of God's eternal Son, dwindles down to the mere payment of a debt, a satisfaction for injury.

But is this indeed the glorious gospel of the blessed God? Is this that mystery, into which angels desire to look; is this the wonderful scheme which filled the breasts of the apostles with admiration, love and gratitude; and in which they professed to discover such heights and depths, such unutterable and unsearchable things? No, my friends, this is not the gospel; these are not the good tidings of great joy which angels delighted to bring from heaven. God's offer of his Son to guilty men is not the payment of a debt, or a recompense for injuries done them. No, it is a gift, a free, unmerited gift, an unspeakable gift, the worth of which we can neither describe nor conceive. God was under no obligation to provide a Saviour for our ruined race. He provided none for the fallen angels, nor was he any more obliged to provide one for us. With the most perfect justice, and without the smallest impeachment of his goodness, he might have left us all to perish; and peopled the earth and filled heaven, with a new and holy race of beings. Agreeably, the Scriptures every where represent the plan of salvation as entirely of grace, free, sovereign, wondrous grace, from its commencement to its termination. They tell us, that Jesus Christ is the gift of God; that he freely delivered him up for us all; that when we were his enemies Christ died for us; and that God so loved the world that he gave his only begotten Son, that whosoever believeth in him should not perish. Here is nothing said of the payment of a debt, or of recompense for injury. Nor do the blessed spirits of the just made perfect in heaven, view their salvation as flowing from anything but the most astonishing love and grace. Not unto us, they cry, not unto us, but to thy name give glory. Blessing and glory and honor and power be unto him that sitteth on the throne, and to the Lamb forever and ever.

If, therefore, the apostles on earth or saints in heaven, or the Holy Spirit himself, knew anything of the plan of salvation,

Jesus Christ is in every respect the free gift of God to man. And why was such a gift necessary? Because we are children of ignorance, and needed a Divine teacher; because we are children of disobedience, and need a Divine sanctifier; because we are children of wrath, and need a Divine redeemer, to make an atonement for our sins. We have insisted the longer on this part of our subject, because until we are fully convinced that Christ is such a gift, we cannot prize the gospel as we ought, nor truly thank God for this or any other blessing.

II. I proceed to show, that this gift may be justly styled unspeakable.

With this view we observe,

1. That the love which led God to bestow such a gift upon us, must have been unspeakably great. This our Saviour, when speaking of it, plainly intimates. Though he spoke as never man spake, yet even he could not describe it except by its effects. God, says he, so loved the world that he gave his only begotten Son, that whosoever believeth on him should not perish, but have everlasting life. He does not say, God loved the world fervently, greatly, immeasurably; for none of these expressions were sufficient to show the extent of his love. Nor does he say, God so loved the world that he preserves, supports, and fills it with his blessings; for these proofs of his goodness, though great, are comparatively nothing. But he says, God so loved the world that he gave his only begotten Son; thus intimating that his love could not be described, and leaving us to judge of its greatness by its effects. And, judging by this rule, how great must his love have been! Say, ye who are parents, how must you love a person, before you could freely consent, for his sake, to give up an only son, to a cruel and ignominious death? But as high as the heavens are above the earth, as far as God excels his creatures, so far does his love for his Son surpass that which the most affectionate parent feels for his offspring. We are told that God is love, and we find that he can even love his enemies, so as to load them with favors; for he causes his sun to shine, and his showers to descend on the evil and unthankful. If then he can thus love his enemies, how infinitely must he love his innocent, holy, only-begotten Son, who is in the bosom of his Father, and always does those things that please him! And how must he love the world, since, for its redemption, he gave up

this beloved Son to such agonies as Christ endured. But in vain do we attempt to give you any idea of this love. We sink under the weight of our subject. We cannot describe what is indescribable. We can only say, with the apostle, What manner of love is this? Well may it be called an unspeakable love!

2. The gift of Jesus Christ may be justly called unspeakable, because his worth and excellence are unspeakably great. He is the pearl of. great, of inestimable price. He is not only precious, but preciousness itself. In him are hid all the treasures of wisdom, and knowledge, and grace; so that as the apostle informs us, his riches are unsearchable. Nay more, in him dwells all fulness, even all the fulness of the Godhead. In giving us Christ, therefore, God has given us himself and all that he possesses; and hence, those who receive this gift, are said to be filled with the fulness of God. Had God given us a thousand angels to guard and attend us, or ten thousand worlds for our portion, it would have been comparatively nothing. It would have been nothing for him to give, for he could have created them with a single word. It would have been nothing for us to receive; for what are worlds, or angels, in comparison with the Creator of all worlds, and the Lord of angels. Nor is this all. In giving us Christ, God gave us all the other blessings which we enjoy. We are told, that every good and perfect gift is from above, and cometh down from the Father of lights. We are also taught, that all these gifts come in and through Christ; so that he may be justly called, not only a gift, but *the* gift of God, that is, the gift which includes all others. If the earth is full of the riches of God's goodness, if its inhabitants are preserved, fed, and clothed, if God gives them rain from heaven and fruitful seasons, filling their hearts with peace and gladness, if they derive any pleasure from children, friends and social intercourse, if they are permitted to hope for still greater blessings beyond the grave,—in a word, if any happiness is or has been enjoyed on earth, more than in hell, it was all given by God, when he gave us Christ to be the Saviour of the world. In this sense it is, that Christ is said to be the Saviour of all men, including those who do not believe. He pleads for them as the dresser of the vineyard did for the barren fig tree, that it might not be immediately cut down as a cumberer of the ground. Thus he saves them from instantly suffering the agonies of death

and the pains of hell. He saves them from many of the present effects and consequences of sin; he gives them to enjoy the day and means of grace, keeps back the curse which is every moment ready to blast them, and loads them with innumerable temporal and spiritual favors. Since then Christ is inestimably precious in himself, and since in him are included all the other gifts which God has ever bestowed on our race, he may be justly called an unspeakable gift.

3. Unspeakable as is the intrinsic value of Christ, he is, if possible, still more unspeakably valuable to us. You need not be told, that the value of a gift to the person who receives it, depends much on his circumstances. A sum of money may be a valuable present to any one; but to a man on the point of being dragged to prison for debt, it is much more so. Medicine, or food may be valuable in itself; but when given to a man ready to perish with sickness or hunger, its value is very greatly increased. So Christ is unspeakably precious in himself, and had God given him to the angels as their portion, it would have justly been called an unspeakable gift. But how unspeakably more valuable is such a gift to us, who were on the point of perishing forever. Would you know the worth of the gift to creatures in our situation? Go and contemplate the fallen angels in the mansions of despair. See them enveloped in the blackness of darkness, bound in eternal chains, reserved unto the judgment of the great day, and expecting nothing but an eternity of unutterable, and constantly increasing wretchedness, beyond it. Would the gift of an almighty Saviour, to redeem them from this situation, be to them unspeakably precious? If so, Christ is an unspeakably precious gift to us; for what they are suffering was our just doom, a doom which would have been inevitable, were it not for the gift of Christ. A wretched and hopeless life, a still more wretched and despairing death, and an inconceivably more wretched eternity, were all that we could expect; for, being children of disobedience, we were children of wrath; the fire prepared for the devil and his angels burnt to devour us; the broken law of God had pronounced the sentence of our everlasting condemnation, and nothing but the gift of such a Saviour as Christ, could have prevented our suffering it; for the word of truth declares, that he who believeth not the Son of God is condemned already; that he shall never see life,

and that the wrath of God abideth on him. But from this curse Christ has redeemed those who receive God's offered gift, by being made a curse for them, and they are delivered from wrath through him. Well then may the gift of such a Saviour to creatures in our situation, be called an *unspeakable gift.*

Lastly, the gift of Christ may be justly called an unspeakable gift, on account of the spiritual blessings which are enjoyed by those who receive him. We have already observed, that even those who reject him are favored for his sake, with many temporal mercies; but these are nothing compared with spiritual and eternal blessings which he imparts to those who thankfully accept the unspeakable gift of God. He gives them the pardon of all their sins, and accepts them as if they had never sinned. He brings them out of darkness and ignorance into his marvellous light, and imparts to them that knowledge of God and himself which is eternal life. He instamps the holy image of God on their souls, and makes them partakers of a divine nature. He delivers them from sin and guilt, from fear and anxiety, and thus prepares them to enjoy peace of conscience, and favor with God. He withholds from them no good thing, and causes all things, without exception, to work together for their good. He gives them exceeding great and precious promises, and provides for them strong consolation, to support them under the evils of life. He suffers them to fear no evil, in their last hours, and enables them to sing the song of victory over death and the grave. He receives and welcomes their departing spirits in the eternal world, raises their bodies incorruptible, glorious and immortal; acquits, acknowledges and rewards them, at the judgment day, and presents them, perfect in knowledge, in holiness and happiness, before the throne of his Father, with whom they shall live and reign forever and ever. In one word, he makes them heirs of God, and consequently heirs of all things; exerts to the utmost all the infinite perfections of the Godhead, to perfect, perpetuate and increase their happiness. And, my friends, what could he do more? What could any being do more? What can creatures desire more? Should they employ their minds, through eternity, they would be unable to wish for, or conceive of any thing which the gift of Christ does not include. Who then can deny that it may be justly called an unspeakable gift; since it raises those who accept it from the lowest depth of

wretchedness to which a creature can sink, to the highest pitch
of glory and felicity which creatures can reach ?

III. This is a gift for which we ought to thank God with the
most lively gratitude.

But, my friends, is it necessary to prove this? Is it not
already evident ? The principal circumstances which render a
gift deserving of thankfulness, are the motives which occasion
it, its intrinsic value, its being adapted to our circumstances,
and the benefits which we derive from it. But we have already
shown that the love which induced God to offer us the gift of
Christ, his own intrinsic value, our perishing need of such a
Saviour, and the benefits which he bestows on those who accept
him, are alike unspeakably great. It therefore necessarily
follows, that our gratitude to God for this gift should be unspeakable. The gratitude of just men made perfect is so. Never
have they been able, never will they be able, to express all the
gratitude which they feel to God, for the gift of his Son. It is
an inexhaustible fountain which flows, and ever will flow, in
ceaseless praises and thanksgivings, throughout eternity. If
then we possess any thing of the temper of heaven, if we hope
ever to join in the employments of heaven, if we, in the smallest
degree, resemble the apostle, we shall unitedly join with him in
exclaiming, Thanks be unto God for his unspeakable gift ! We
shall partake of the food which God this day provides for our
refreshment, with feelings in some measure similar to those with
which the spirits of the just feast on the bread and water of life,
at the marriage supper of the Lamb in heaven, and our whole
future lives will be one continued day of thanksgiving to God.

If any still feel unconvinced, that we ought to thank God for
the gift of his Son, we would ask them whether God can do
anything for which his creatures ought to thank him. Can he
bestow upon them any favor which shall entitle him to their
gratitude ? If so, he has done it already, in giving us his Son ;
for he can do nothing greater for any creature, he can give us
nothing more precious than this. In giving us Christ, he has
given us himself, and all that he possesses, so that he may now
justly say to us, Unthankful, obstinate creatures ! what shall I
do to excite your gratitude ; how shall I purchase that place in
your affections, which ought to be mine, without purchase ? I
had but one Son ; him I have freely given for your redemption ;

and now I have nothing more to offer. To purchase your gratitude and love, I have made myself poor; I have given you all I possessed, and if this is not sufficient, I can only come to you as a suppliant, and beseech you, for my sake, for my Son's sake, for your own sakes, to be reconciled to your heavenly Father, and accept with thankfulness my offered grace. Such is, in effect, the language of your gracious, condescending God; yet, astonishing to tell, there are hearts so hard as to be unaffected with this language, so stubbornly ungrateful as to refuse to thank him for the unspeakable gift.

My friends, are not some of your hearts of this description? Are there not some among you who have, through life, requited God evil for good? Are there not some present, who never sincerely thanked God for the gift of his Son, and who would feel more joy and gratitude for the gift of a few thousands of pounds, than they have ever felt while hearing the good news of a Saviour? If there be any present of this description, let me entreat them to consider what they have done, what they are now doing. How hateful, how inexcusable, must such ingratitude appear in the sight of God! How widely do you differ from him who uttered the words of our text, and from all holy beings! How impossible is it for you, with such a temper, to join in the praises of heaven, or derive any advantage from the gift of Christ. The gift is indeed offered to all, but it will benefit none but those who thankfully receive it. Be persuaded then, this day, to receive it with thankfulness, and let the goodness of God lead you to repentance. While you feast on the bounties of Providence, remember that they were purchased by the blood of Christ. Should you do this, this will indeed be a thanksgiving day, the beginning of an eternal thanksgiving in heaven.

SERMON II

THE BLAMELESS PAIR.

AND they were both righteous before God, walking in all the commandments
and ordinances of the Lord blameless. — LUKE i. 6.

THE persons of whom the Holy Ghost has borne this honorable testimony are Zacharias and Elizabeth, the parents of John
the Baptist. The character here ascribed to them, so excellent
and desirable in itself, is especially deserving the regard and
imitation of all who are united by conjugal ties. As this union
is the source and basis of all the social relations, the character
of those who "are no more twain but one flesh" must necessarily exert a powerful influence, not only over the domestic circle,
but through all the ramifications of human society. It will be
the object of this discourse,

I. To consider and illustrate the character described in the
text; and,

II. To present some reasons why all who have entered the
marriage state should endeavor to make it their own.

I. The first thing which demands attention in the character
of this truly excellent and happy pair, is, that they were righteous before God. This, my hearers, is a great thing. It is,
indeed, very easy to be righteous in our own estimation; nor is
it very difficult to be righteous in the estimation of our fellow
creatures; but it is by no means equally easy to be righteous in
the estimation of God. He is constantly with us; he sees our

whole conduct; nay more, he reads our hearts. To be righteous before him, then, is to be really, inwardly, and uniformly righteous. It is to be the same persons in every situation, and on all occasions; the same at home, and abroad, in solitude and in society. But much less than this will suffice to make us righteous in the estimation of our fellow creatures. They are not always with us; they do not see the whole of our conduct; and of our hearts, our motives, they know almost nothing. Of course, they know very little of our real characters. How little, for instance, do the nearest neighbors really know of each other. How many characters, which now stand fair, would be blasted in a moment, were every part of their outward conduct only, laid open to public view? And how many husbands and wives, who are generally supposed to live happily together, would be found mutual tormentors, were they fully known to the world! How wretchedly then are those persons deceived, who flatter themselves that they are righteous before God, merely because their characters stand fair in the estimation of men. And yet how many flatter themselves in this manner. How many feel and act, as if they were to be judged by men only, and not by the heart-searching God;—as if that part of their conduct only, which is known to the world, was to be brought into judgment; and not every secret action, thought, and feeling.

My hearers, permit me to warn you against this ruinous delusion. Remember that, in order to be really righteous, you must be righteous before God. Remember, that no man, who would not be thought righteous by his fellow creatures, if his whole conduct and his whole heart were laid open to them, is righteous before God. Do you start at this assertion? A moment's reflection will convince you that it is strictly true. The whole conduct, and the whole heart of every man, is perfectly known to God. Now if God, knowing a man thus perfectly, judges him to be righteous, then his fellow creatures, did they know him as perfectly, would judge him to be righteous. Hence it follows, that every man is unrighteous, whom his fellow creatures would judge to be unrighteous, were they perfectly acquainted with his conduct and with his heart. Try yourselves by this rule. Would men think you righteous, did they know you as perfectly as God knows you? Then you are righteous. Would men think you unrighteous, did they know you thus

perfectly? Then you are unrighteous. It may, however, be
necessary to remark, that in making these assertions, I proceed
on the supposition, that men should judge of you by the rule of
God's Word, the rule by which God himself judges of your
character. With this qualification, the truth of these assertions
must, I conceive, appear evident to all.

And is it not, to some of you at least, an alarming thought,
that if men, did they know you perfectly, would think you unrighteous, then God certainly does think you so? And that he
will treat you accordingly, unless you repent? If this thought
does alarm any one, let me entreat him not to dismiss it hastily.
Keep it in mind, make use of it to regulate your conduct, and
to try your character; and when your heart and life become
such, that an impartial jury of your fellow creatures, perfectly
acquainted with both, and judging of them by the rules of
God's Word, would pronounce you truly righteous, then, and
not till then, may you venture to hope that you are righteous
before God.

But the opinion of men, if they knew us perfectly, and judged
us by the Word of God, would be according to truth; and, of
course, deserve our regard. Yet while they know so little of us,
as they actually do, their good opinion can prove nothing in our
favor, except it be, that our outward conduct, so far as it comes
under their notice, is correct. Still less can our own opinion
that we are righteous prove us to be so. Agreeably, we find
St. Paul saying, It is a very small thing with me to be judged
of man's judgment, yea, I judge not mine own self; but he
that judgeth me is the Lord. And is it not wonderful, my
hearers, that every man who believes there is a God, does not,
like the apostle, feel as if the opinions of other beings respecting
him were of very little consequence? — that many, who acknowledge there is a God, should think so little of his judgment,
and so much of the approbation of their fellow creatures? We
do not feel and act thus in other similar cases. If we perform
any work which requires the exertion of mental abilities, or of
manual skill, we do not much desire or regard the applause of
ignorant, incompetent judges. But we wish to know what
judicious men, men of taste and information, think of it; and
we value the approbation of one such man more than that of
hundreds of inferior stamp. And were there one man in the

world, whose taste and judgment were infallible, and whose decision would fix forever the character of our work, we should prefer his approbation to that of all the world beside. Why, then, do we not thus supremely prize, and labor to obtain the approbation of God, the only being who really knows us ; whose judgment is infallible, on whom our destiny depends, and whose sentence will stamp our characters with a mark, which can never, never be effaced! Thus did the pious pair, whose example we are contemplating. They studied to approve themselves to God; and he declared, in return, that they were righteous before him; and had the whole world known them as perfectly as he did, the whole world would have assented, with one voice, to the truth of this declaration.

Again: This pair walked in all God's commandments and ordinances blameless. I do not, however, mention this, nor do I conceive the inspired writer mentioned it, as something different or distinct from being righteous before God. It is rather mentioned as an effect and a proof of their being righteous. To be righteous, is to be conformed to the rule of right; and the only rule of right is the will of God, as expressed in his commandments and ordinances. These two words, though nearly synonymous, are not perfectly so. The commands of God are his moral precepts, or those precepts which are designed to regulate our temper and conduct on all occasions. By his ordinances are meant those religious rites and institutions, which he has directed us to observe. Repent, believe the gospel, be holy, —are commands; religious worship, baptism, and the Lord's supper, are ordinances. He that is righteous before God will observe both. In this respect many fail. Some pretend to obey God's commands, while they neglect his ordinances. Others visibly observe his ordinances, but neglect his commands. The truly righteous esteem all God's precepts concerning all things to be right, and observe them, not on occasions only, when it suits their convenience, but habitually. Thus did the persons whose character we are considering. They walked in God's commandments and ordinances, as in a path which they never forsook. The term walk signifies a course of life. To walk in God's commandments and ordinances, is to have the heart and life constantly regulated by them. It is not to step occasionally into the path of duty, and then take many steps in a different path; but it is to pursue this path with undeviating steadiness and perseverance, without turning aside either to the right hand or to the left. Nor was it a part only of God's commandments and ordinances that this pious pair observed; for we are told, that they walked in them all. They did not select such as were easy, or reputable, and neglect others. Nor did they observe those only, which they had little temptation to omit; but to use the language of the psalmist, they had respect to all God's commandments. Hence their characters and conduct were blameless, or irreproachable. Not that they were absolutely perfect. Some imperfection, doubtless, attended all their moral and religious performances; but there was nothing particularly blameable, no allowed insincerity or neglect. In the sight of men, their characters were spotless; and in the sight of God they possessed that simplicity and godly sincerity, which entitled them to the honorable appellation of Israelites indeed, in whom was no guile.

Such is the example here presented for the imitation of all, especially heads of families. But in order that the example should produce its full effect, it is necessary to show, more particularly, what is now, under the Christian dispensation, implied in walking in all the ordinances and commandments of the Lord blamelessly.

1. It implies the exercise of repentance toward God, and faith in our Lord Jesus Christ. These are the two first and great commands of the gospel, on obeying which our obedience to all other commands, and our acceptable observance of all Christian ordinances depends. This was the sum of St. Paul's preaching; these were the first duties which our Saviour directed his disciples to press upon all their hearers; and which he himself inculcates upon all. When the Jews asked him, What shall we do, that we may work the work of God? his answer was, This is the work of God, that ye believe on him whom he hath sent. Until we begin to perform these duties, we cannot be righteous before God, nor walk in any of his commandments or ordinances; for inspiration hath declared, without faith it is impossible to please him.

2. Walking in all God's commandments and ordinances blamelessly, implies great diligence in seeking a knowledge of them. No man can regulate his conduct by a rule, with which he is unacquainted. No man can walk in all God's command-

ments and ordinances, unless he knows what they are; nor can any man know what they are, unless he is familiarly acquainted with the Scriptures. As well might a mariner find his way to a distant port, without ever looking to his chart or compass. And the commands and ordinances of God are so numerous, that without daily and long continued attention, we shall certainly forget or overlook some of them ; shall never obtain such a clear, systematic view of our duty, as is necessary to its performance. That copy of the Old Testament, which Zacharias and Elizabeth possessed, was doubtless worn with frequent use. It must have been their daily counsellor and guide.

3. Walking in all God's commandments and ordinances blamelessly, implies a careful performance of all the duties which husbands and wives owe each other. These duties are summarily comprehended in the marriage covenant, in which the husband solemnly promises, before God and men, that he will love, provide for, and be faithful to his wife; and the wife, that she will obey, love, and be faithful to her husband. This covenant has the nature of an oath, and as such involves all who violate it in the guilt of perjury. The duties which they thus solemnly bind themselves to perform, are no more than God requires of them in his Word. He there commands husbands to love their wives, even as they love themselves, and wives to be subject in all things to their husbands. He commands them to make this union resemble that which subsists between Christ and his church. Husbands, love your wives, even as Christ loved the church, and gave himself for it. Wives, be subject to your husbands, as the church is subject to Christ. There must be but one will in a family, but every act of that one will must be prompted by love, love like that which Christ displays for his church. In no family are all God's commands obeyed, in which this love on the one part, and this submission on the other, are not found.

4. Walking in all the commandments and ordinances of God blamelessly, implies a careful performance, on the part of parents, of all the parental duties which he has enjoined. He requires us to give them a religious education, to bring them up in the nurture and admonition of the Lord; to teach them diligently his revealed will, speaking to them of it, in the house, and by the way, when we lie down and when we rise up; and to re-

strain them when they would pursue vicious courses. We have also reason to believe that he requires parents to dedicate their children to him in baptism. That they ought to be dedicated to God, and presented to Christ for his blessing, all Christians are agreed, though our Baptist brethren do not think them proper subjects of baptism. But our Saviour's command, Suffer little children to come unto me, or to be brought to me, and forbid them not, — certainly makes it the duty of every Christian parent to present his children to Christ, and to pray for his blessing upon them, whatever may be his opinion respecting infant baptism. Nor can Christ fail to be displeased with those parents, who, by neglecting to bring their children, do, in effect, forbid them to come. And no Christian parent, who believes infant baptism to be an ordinance of God, can pretend that he walks in all God's ordinances, while he neglects it. Indeed, while any of you, my professing hearers, neglect it, you are violating your own express covenant engagements.

5. Walking in all God's ordinances and commandments blamelessly, implies the maintaining of the worship of God in the family. It is acknowledged, that there is no command which, in so many words, says, worship God in your families, or, maintain family prayer. Yet that this is a duty incumbent on heads of families, is, perhaps, as clearly taught in the Scriptures, as if it were the subject of an express command. We have, for instance, the example of good men in favor of it. God expresses full confidence that Abraham would maintain religion in his family. Joshua's resolution was, As for me and my house, we will serve the Lord. David, after the public exercises of religion were finished, returned to bless his household; that is, to unite with them in an act of worship; and our Saviour often prayed with his little family of disciples. Families that call not upon God's name are classed among the heathen, and it is intimated that God will pour out his fury upon them. Besides, we are commanded to pray always on all occasions, and in all circumstances; of course, in our families. And St. Peter exhorts husbands and wives to live together as heirs of the grace of life, that their prayers may not be hindered, — an expression which evidently refers to united prayers, and intimates that he thought it very important that such prayers should not be hindered; and that he took it for granted that Christian families

would offer such prayers. Besides, the reasonableness, the propriety, and the happy effects of family worship, show it to be a duty. It is reasonable and proper, for families have mercies in common to ask for, and they receive favors in common for which they should unite in expressing their gratitude. And the happy effects which result from a right performance of this duty, are innumerable and inestimable. It has a happy effect upon the head of the family himself. It tends to make him circumspect, to produce watchfulness over his temper and conduct through the day; for how can he indulge sin or give vent to angry passions in presence of the family, when he recollects that he is a priest in his own house; that he prayed with them in the morning; and that he will again be called to pray with them at night? He cannot but feel, that, if the rest of his conduct is not of a piece with this, his own children and servants will despise him for his inconsistency. This practice has also a most salutary influence upon the happiness of domestic life. If any unpleasant feelings arise between members of the same household, such feelings can scarcely outlive the return of the next season for family devotion. Affection and peace must return, when they next meet around the family altar, unless one or the other is a hypocrite. Thus dissensions are prevented, and domestic peace and harmony are perpetuated. I may add, that it always tends to produce, and often does produce, the most happy effects upon the children of the family. At least, it is certain that a much larger proportion of children are moral, and become pious, in families, where this duty is properly performed, than in those where it is wholly neglected, or only occasionally attended to.

6. Walking in all the commandments and ordinances of the Lord blamelessly, implies a suitable concern for the present and future happiness of servants, apprentices and dependents. Their health must be regarded. More labor should not be exacted of them, than we would be willing should be exacted of our own children, were they placed in similar circumstances. Their rights must be held sacred. We are commanded to give unto our servants that which is equal and right, remembering that we have a Master in heaven. Their feelings must not be trifled with. If they are faulty, let them be told of their faults with mildness; but passionate, contemptuous language should never

be addressed to them. Ye masters, forbear threatening, is the command of Jehovah.

7. Walking in the commandments and ordinances of the Lord blamelessly, implies a careful performance of all the duties which we owe our neighbors. Our Saviour has taught us to include in this class all our fellow men, to whom we have opportunity of doing good. He that is righteous before God will ever be a good neighbor. The present and future happiness of all his fellow creatures will be dear to him, and he will promote it as far as his ability extends. Of course, he will never knowingly injure them in their persons, reputation, or estate. And in receiving and returning their visits, he will be governed, not by the sinful or foolish customs, which the fashionable world has adopted, but by a regard to God's glory and their best good.

8. Walking in all the commandments and ordinances of the Lord blamelessly, implies a proper use of the temporal good things which are entrusted to our care. Nothing should be wasted, for God will require an account of all. Nothing should be employed to gratify the lust of the flesh, the lust of the eye, or the pride of life; for property so employed is much worse than wasted. We must use the world as not abusing it, and employ every portion of our property in a manner which God will approve, and to the purpose for· which it was given. He that wastes his possessions, wastes God's property, and the poor's patrimony; he that consumes them upon his lusts, gives them to swine.

Lastly; Walking in all the commandments and ordinances of the Lord blamelessly, implies a sacred observance of the Sabbath, a diligent attendance on the public worship of God, and a commemoration of Christ at his table. All these things are God's ordinances, and, if we except baptism, they are perhaps the only ordinances which he has appointed under the Christian dispensation. Heads of families, who neglect either of them, cannot be said to walk in all God's ordinances blamelessly.

Having thus considered and illustrated the character brought to view in the text, I proceed, as was proposed,

II. To state some reasons, why all who have entered the marriage state should endeavor to make it their own. But is this necessary? Can any of you, my hearers, need reasons or motives to persuade you to the acquisition of such a character? Does it not commend itself at once to the understanding, and to the conscience of every man who is possessed of either? If, however, any of you need such reasons, they can easily be assigned.

1. God approves, and requires you to possess, such a character. He commands you to be righteous before him. His language is, I am the Almighty God; walk before me, and be thou perfect. All the commandments and ordinances which have been mentioned are his. They are sanctioned by his authority; a neglect of them will be punished by his power; a performance of them will be rewarded by his grace. The curse of the Lord, we are told, is in the house of the wicked; but he loveth and blesseth the habitation of the righteous. And is it not reasonable that we should obey his commands? Is it not desirable to avert his curse from our dwellings, and to have his blessing in our habitations? Who, that believes there is a God, would not have his family one of the few faithful families, on which God looks with approbation? Who would not wish that the eye of God should discover in it nothing displeasing to him?

2. Consider how much it would promote your present happiness to possess such a character. Where can happiness be found on earth, if not in such a family as has now been described? Mutual affection and harmony, peace and contentment would dwell in it. All the gifts of Providence would be enjoyed with a double relish, because they would be received as the gifts of a Father, and be sanctified by his word and prayer. Almost every cause of domestic unhappiness would be excluded. There would be no room for anxiety, uneasiness, and alarm; for such a family could cheerfully trust in God to supply all its real wants, and to shield it from all real evils. Even if afflictions came, they would come as mercies, and deprived of their stings. In short, such a family would be of one heart and of one soul; that heart and that soul would be devoted to God, and God in return would devote himself to them. And O, how pleasant, how soothing, how refreshing, would it be to the husband, the father, to return at evening to such a house, after the labors and fatigues of the day, to be greeted with affectionate smiles, and to return them; to shut out the world with its follies and cares,

and to feel, while rejoicing in the circle of those whom he loved, that God was looking down upon them with approbation and delight; that an unseen Saviour was rejoicing in the midst of them, to see the happiness which he had purchased, and which his religion bestowed! How sweet, to close an evening thus pleasant, and a day spent in the service of God, by uniting around the family altar in an offering of prayer and praise to their great Benefactor, and then lie down to rest with that feeling of sincerity and safety, which filial confidence in heaven inspires! Some may, perhaps, choose to call this representation, religious romance; but it is sober reality; it is no more than has been actually enjoyed; and if we see few families in which it is realized, it is only because there are few, in which both heads of the family walk in all the commandments and ordinances of the Lord blameless.

3. Permit me to remind you how greatly such a family would honor God and adorn religion. It would, indeed, in such a world as this, be like one of those ever verdant islands, which rise amidst the wide ocean of Arabian sands, and whose constant verdure leads the weary and thirsty traveler to seek for the hidden spring which produces it. It is, perhaps, impossible for an insulated individual to exhibit all the beauty and excellence of Christianity; because much of it consists in the right performance of those relative duties, which he has no opportunity to perform. But in a religious family, a family where both husband and wife are evidently pious, religion may be displayed in all its parts, and in the fulness of its glory and beauty; and one such family will do more to recommend it, and to soften the prejudices of its enemies, than can be effected by the most powerful and persuasive sermon.

The subject is very far from being exhausted. Many more powerful arguments and motives in favor of imitating the character here recommended might easily be urged; but the unexpected length to which the preceding remarks have been extended, compels me to omit them, and to close with a short address by way of application.

Permit me to commence this address by asking each married pair in this assembly, whether their family is such as has now been described? whether they resemble the parents of John the Baptist? Are you both righteous before God? and do you walk in all his ordinances and commands blameless? If not, whose fault is it? Is it the husband's? or the wife's? or the fault of both? In some families, doubtless both are in fault; neither is righteous. Alas, that there should be such families, and so many of them among us! Alas, that persons should ever enter the married state, so totally unqualified to discharge all its most important duties; that immortal souls should be committed to the care of those who know not their worth, and who will do nothing to effect their salvation! Is this the character of any fathers and mothers present? and if so, shall it continue such? Remember, ye who are in this state, especially ye who have just entered it, that, however happy you may now be, affliction will come, sickness will come, death will come; and what will you then do, ye who have made no provision for such events, ye who have no God to support and comfort you? Be assured, the time will arrive, even in the present life, when you will feel the need of religion; feel that everything besides is comparatively worthless. Remember, too, ye who now love and rejoice in each other, that you must meet in another world; and that the fate of each in that world will depend much upon the conduct of the other. If you now encourage each other in neglecting religion, you will then meet as the bitterest of enemies, and load each other with reproaches and execrations. Each one will then say, O, that we had never met! Had I not been connected with you, had I possessed a religious partner, I might now have been happy. But you tempted and encouraged me to live without God, and to neglect my Saviour; and now I must, in consequence, be miserable forever! On the contrary, should either of you now become truly religious, you may be instrumental in effecting the salvation of the other; and then with what joy will you both meet in heaven! O then, live together in such a manner, that you may hereafter meet with joy; live as it becomes two immortal beings traveling hand in hand to judgment and eternity. Live together in this world as heirs of the grace of life, and you shall live together in heaven, as happy participants of its bliss.

But there are probably other families in which the fault lies on one only of the partners. Perhaps, O husband, it is your fault, that both are not religious. You have a pious partner, one whom you cannot but acknowledge is pious. But you refuse to unite with her in making your habitation a temple of God, the abode of religion, of peace and happiness. You do not, perhaps, oppose her; but you afford her no assistance in her journey to heaven. In this respect she is a widow. She is deprived of one of the greatest blessings which a wife has a right to expect from a husband; and must pursue her way solitary, alone. When she rejoices, she cannot impart to you her joys; when she is sad, she cannot make you understand the cause of her sadness, nor receive from you any consolation or relief. Nay more, you are the chief cause of her sorrows. She mourns with a heart almost broken, because she is compelled to leave you behind, to fear that you will perish forever; and the more kind you are in other respects, so much the more does her grief increase. Yet she, probably, does not express it, lest she should give offence, and be reproached for indulging needless apprehensions. And while you give all this pain to her, of what happiness do you deprive yourself; happiness here, and happiness hereafter! O, then, let it no longer be your fault, that religion is not enthroned, and adorned, and enjoyed in your families; but now, while the Spirit and the bride invite, come and taste of the water of life freely.

In other cases it is, perhaps, the fault of the wife; and if so, how great a fault! What hardness of heart, what inexcusable obstinacy, does it evince, to stand out not only against the authority of God, and the invitations of the Saviour, but the arguments, persuasions, and entreaties of her nearest earthly friend! What cruel unkindness, to plant thorns in the breast of him, who looks to you for his chief earthly consolation; to seal up his lips when he wishes to give vent to the feelings of his heart; to compel him to feel that, when he prays in his family, he prays alone; and to see that his labors for the salvation of his children are rendered almost fruitless for want of a partner to assist him. O, then, let no wife, no mother, in this assembly, be so unmindful of what she owes to her husband, her children, her Saviour, her God, as to continue in an irreligious state. And wherever either partner is pious, let both become so; and then shall the voice of joy and rejoicing be heard in your habitation, as it is in the tabernacles of the righteous.

Blessed be God, there are some such families among us, — families, in which, as we have reason to hope, both the husband

and wife resemble the parents of John the Baptist. Let those who are thus highly favored show their gratitude to God, by striving to become eminently pious. Let them quicken and assist each other in the good work, and be mutual helpers of each other's faith and joy. When you return to your habitations, consult together, and inquire, whether there is any commandment or ordinance of God, in which you are not both walking; any duty which you are neglecting; any thing in your families which is displeasing to Christ. If any thing of this kind is discovered, put it from you instantly, however dear. Thus you will each have increasing reason to bless God through eternity, for giving you a pious partner; and when you meet in heaven, you will love each other with pure and immortal affection, as instruments employed by God to fit each other for that world, where they neither marry nor are given in marriage, but are like the angels of God.

SERMON III

CHILDREN TO BE EDUCATED FOR GOD.

Take this child and nurse it for me, and I will give thee thy wages.
Exodus ii. 9.

These words were addressed by Pharaoh's daughter to the mother of Moses. Of the circumstances which occasioned them, it can scarcely be necessary to inform you. You need not be told, that, soon after the birth of this future leader of Israel, his parents were compelled by the cruelty of the Egyptian king to expose him in an ark of bulrushes, on the banks of the Nile. In this situation he was found by the daughter of Pharaoh; and so powerfully did his infantile cries excite her compassion, that she determined not only to rescue him from a watery grave, but to adopt and educate him as her own. His sister Miriam, who at a distance, had watched his fate unseen, now came forward like a person entirely unacquainted with the circumstances of his exposure, and on hearing of the princess' determination, offered to procure a Hebrew woman, to take the care of him, until he should be of sufficient age to appear at her father's court. This offer being accepted, she immediately went and called the child's mother, to whose care he was committed by the princess in the words of our text, — Take this child and nurse it for me, and I will give thee thy wages.

In similar language, my friends, does God address parents. To every one, on whom he bestows the blessing of children, he says in his word and by the voice of his Providence, Take this child and educate it for me, and I will give thee thy wages.

From this passage, therefore, we may take occasion to show,

I. What is implied in educating children for God;

II. The reward which he gives to those who perform this duty aright.

I. The first thing implied in educating children for God, is a realizing, heart-felt conviction that they are his property, his children, rather than ours; and that he commits them for a time to our care, merely for the purpose of education, as we place children under the care of human instructers for the same purpose. However carefully we may educate children, yet we cannot be said to educate them for God, unless we feel that they are his; for if we feel that they were ours exclusively, we shall and must educate them for ourselves and not for him. To know that they are his, is to feel a cordial operative conviction that he has a sovereign right to dispose of them as he pleases, and to take them from us whenever he thinks fit. That they are his, and that he possesses this right, is evident from innumerable passages in the inspired writings. We are there told that God is the former of our bodies, and the father of our spirits; that we are all his offspring, and that consequently we are not our own but his. We are also assured that, as the soul of the parent, so also the souls of the children are his; and God, once and again severely reproves and threatens the Jews, because they sacrificed his children in the fire, to Moloch. Yet plain and explicit as these passages are, how few parents appear to feel their force. How few appear to feel and act as if conscious that they and theirs were the absolute property of God; that they were merely the foster-parents of their children, and that, in all which they do for them, they are, or ought to be, acting for God. But it is evident that they must feel this before they can bring up their children for Him; for how can they educate their children for a being whose existence they do not realize, whose right to them they do not acknowledge, and whose character they do not love?

Nearly connected with this is a second thing implied in educating children for God,—namely, a cordial and solemn dedication or surrender of them to him, to be his forever. We have already shown that they are his property and not ours; and by dedicating them to him, we mean nothing more than an explicit acknowledgment of this truth; or an acknowledgment that we consider them as entirely his; and that we unreservedly surrender them to him for time and eternity. This, my friends, is a reasonable service. The apostle beseeches Christians by the tender mercies of God, to present themselves as living sacrifices to him, holy and acceptable, and to glorify God in their bodies and spirits which are his. But the same considerations which render it right and reasonable that we should dedicate ourselves to God, render it equally right and reasonable, that to him we should also dedicate our children. If we refuse to give them to God, how can we be said to educate them for him?

In the third place, if we would educate children for God, we must do all that we do for them from right motives. Almost the only motive which the Scriptures allow to be right, is a regard for the glory of God, and a disinterested desire to promote it; and they consider nothing as really done for God, which does not flow from this source. Without this, however exemplary we may be, we do but bring forth fruit to ourselves, and are no better than empty vines. We must, therefore, be governed by this motive in the education of our children, if we would educate them for God. and not for ourselves. In all our cares, labors and sufferings for them, a regard to the divine glory must be the main spring which moves us. If we act merely from parental affection, we act from no higher principle than the irrational animals around us, since many of them evidently appear to love their offspring no less ardently, and to be no less ready to encounter dangers, toils, and sufferings, to promote their happiness, than we are to promote the welfare of ours. But if parental affection can be sanctified by the grace of God, and parental duties hallowed by a wish to promote his glory, then we rise above the irrational world, to our proper station, and may be said to educate our children for God; and here, my friends, we may observe that true religion, when it prevails in the heart, sanctifies every thing, renders even the most common actions of life acceptable to God, and gives them a dignity and importance which, of themselves, they by no means deserve. What, for instance, can be more common or trifling, than the daily reception of food for the support of the body? Yet even this may be done, and ought to be done, to the glory of God; and when this is the case, instead of a trifling, unimportant action, it becomes an important religious duty; Whether ye eat or drink, do all to the glory of God. Thus the care and education of children, however trifling it may be thought by some, ought to be attended to from a regard to the divine glory; and when this is done, it becomes an important part of true religion.

In the fourth place, if we would educate our children for God, we must educate them for his service. The three preceding particulars which we have mentioned, refer principally to ourselves and our motives; but this has more immediate relation to our children themselves. With a view to show with all possible clearness what we mean by educating our children for the service of God, permit me to make the following supposition. Suppose that any of you had a young and numerous family, for which you felt yourselves unable to provide. Suppose, farther, that some benevolent, rich and powerful monarch should condescendingly offer to support them and yourselves, during your lives, and at your death to adopt your children as his own, and raise them to the highest honors and employments in his kingdom, provided that they should be found on examination, any way qualified for his service. Suppose also, that he furnished you with the clearest and fullest instructions respecting the qualifications of every kind which he should require of them, and offered you every necessary assistance, to enable you to instruct and qualify them aright.

Now it is evident, that if you should think proper to embrace his offers, you would educate your children entirely for his service; this would be your sole object respecting them; to this every thing else would be made to give place, and you would feel, and endeavor to make them feel, that every thing which did not tend, either directly or indirectly, to prepare them for the examination through which they must pass, was of no use or consequence to them, however important or pleasant it might be in itself. In order to qualify yourselves for the right instruction of your children, you would diligently study the directions given you, and ascertain as nearly as possible, the qualifications which would be necessary to prepare your children for the honors and employments designed for them. In the next place, as soon as your children were capable of understanding you, you would inform them of every thing relative to their situation and prospects. You would tell them that you were poor, and unable to make provision for their future support; that you must soon die and leave them friendless, destitute and forlorn; and that they would then indispensably need some kind and powerful friend to provide for and protect them. When they began to feel their need of such a friend, you would proceed to tell them of the condescending offers which the king had made, to adopt and provide for them as his own; of the qualifications which his service required, and of the assistance which he was ready to give them in acquiring these qualifications. You would tell them of his power, majesty, riches and goodness; of all the favors he had bestowed on you, of the great importance of securing his favor, and of the dangerous consequences of losing it. You would early begin to teach them the language of the country for which they were destined, and the laws, customs, and dispositions of its inhabitants; you would frequently remind them of the honors and employments before them, and of the folly of degrading themselves by frivolous pursuits, trifling amusements, and unworthy conduct; you would carefully guard against their associating with such companions as would tend to render their taste, their disposition, their conversation and deportment unsuitable to the exalted situation for which they were preparing. You would frequently seek for them the promised assistance of the king; warn them of the fatal effects of indolence and delay, and press them in every possible way, and by every motive which you could conceive of, to persevering diligence and active exertion. In a word, you would so conduct and converse with your children, as most clearly to show them that you considered their preparation for the examination through which they were to pass, as the great object of their lives, the one thing and the only thing really needful; and so to turn their thoughts, desires, words and actions into one channel, and direct them to this one end. You would be careful never to say or do any thing, which should lead them to think of any other friend or protector than the one whom you had chosen for them; of any other kind of honor or happiness than that which would result from his favor; or of any disgrace or misery comparable to the loss of it. Such, in brief, is the manner in which you would probably conduct in the circumstances we have supposed.

My friends, this supposition is not very far from the truth; and you may easily learn from it what is implied in educating your children for God. Like the parents mentioned above, you are in a spiritual sense poor, unable to provide for the happiness of your children in this world, and much more so in the next. God, the King of kings, and Lord of lords, condescendingly offers to adopt them into his own family, cause all things to work together for their good, and make them heirs of a heavenly inheritance, incorruptible, undefiled, and that fadeth not away, provided they are properly qualified to serve and enjoy him. He has also, in his Word, given you the fullest and clearest instruction, respecting the qualifications, which he requires in his servants, and offers you the influence of his Spirit, to impart these qualifications to your children, and assist you in educating them aright. Now if you think proper to accept these offers, and educate your children for the service of God, or to be his servants, you will conduct in a manner very similar to that described above.

In the first place, in order to qualify yourselves for instructing and preparing your children for God's service, you diligently study his Word, to ascertain what he requires of them, and frequently pray for the assistance of his Spirit, both for them and yourselves. In the next place, as soon as they arrive at a suitable age, which is much earlier than is generally supposed, you will begin to tell them of your own inability to preserve them from misery, and render them happy either in this world or the next; of their indispensable need of some other friend and protector, of the gracious offers and invitations of their heavenly Father, of the infinite importance of securing his favor, and the inconceivably dreadful consequences of incurring his displeasure. You will also early begin to teach them the language of heaven, the dispositions, employments and enjoyments of its inhabitants, and the qualifications which are necessary to prepare them for it. You will tell them that God is able and willing to impart these qualifications to all who come to him in the name of Christ; that he has already conferred on them ten thousand favors; that he is the greatest, wisest, and best of beings, and that his Son Jesus Christ is the friend of children, and the Saviour of sinners. You will diligently caution them against all those sinful tempers and practices which are inconsistent with the favor of

God, labor to form them to his image, and prevent them so far
as possible, from associating with companions, who might poison
their principles, corrupt their morals or weaken their sense of
the infinite importance of religion. In a word, you will carefully guard against saying or doing any thing which may, either
directly or indirectly, lead them to consider religion as an object
of secondary importance; on the contrary you will constantly
labor to impress upon their minds a conviction, that you consider religion as the great business of life; the favor of God, as
the only proper object of pursuit, and the enjoyment of him
hereafter, as the only happiness; while every thing else is comparatively of no consequence, however important it may otherwise be.

Such, my friends, in brief, is the manner in which we must
educate children, if we would educate them for the service of
God; and the reasonableness of this, we presume no one will
deny. No one would think of qualifying a child for a physician,
without giving him some knowledge of diseases and their rem-
edies; or for a counsellor without putting him upon the study of
the law; or for a divine, without making him acquainted with
theology. Equally necessary is it, if we would educate children
for God, thus to attempt to qualify them for his service. And
this, we may farther observe, implies three things. It implies,

1. That we pay more attention to the soul than the body.
We do not mean that the body is to be neglected; but the soul
must be considered as the superior part, and the body merely as
its servant. In this respect multitudes of parents fail. They
are extremly attentive to the bodies of their children, their
health, their beauty, the elegance of their form, and the grace-
fulness of their deportment; but seem entirely to forget that
they have a soul, a mind, a heart, that deserves attention. If
the slightest illness affects their children, they are alarmed; but
they feel neither concern nor anxiety on account of the diseases
of their minds. They would be unspeakably distressed should
their children be distorted or deformed, and would use every
possible means to correct or remove the deformity; but their
minds may be deformed, and their tempers distorted by a thous-
and evil passions, without giving them any disturbance. They
would be extremely mortified to see their children awkward,
rude and unpolished in their behavior to their fellow-creatures;

but seem to think it of no consequence with how much indecent rudeness and impiety, they treat their Creator. But surely this is not educating children for God. If mankind indeed were mere animals, devoid of reason, such a mode of education would be proper for them; but surely there ought to be some difference between the education of rational and irrational beings.

2. Educating children for the service of God implies, that we pay more attention to the heart or disposition, than to the mind. You will not surely suspect me of thinking that the mind, or, in other words, our rational faculties, should be neglected; or that the cultivation of it is not of very great importance. We only mean to assert that it is of far less importance than the cultivation of the heart. This, few, if any, will deny; for it is evident that, though our minds should be cultivated in the highest possible degree, and stored with every kind of human literature and science; yet if our hearts are neglected, if our passions, appetites and dispositions continue depraved, we can neither feel nor communicate happiness; but shall only be wretched ourselves, and occasion unhappiness to others, even in this world, much more in the world to come. It is notorious that many of the individuals, whose agency has been productive of the greatest mischief both in the moral and political world, were persons whose mental powers had been carefully cultivated, while their tempers and dispositions were neglected. On the contrary, the most ignorant person, if his heart be right, will be happy himself, both here and hereafter; and may be the means of communicating much happiness and doing much good to others; though not so much, we allow, as he might accomplish with an educated mind. It is therefore evident, that although both are important, yet the cultivation of the heart is more so than that of the understanding. It is highly desirable that our children should possess both the wisdom of the serpent and the harmlessness of the dove; but if they cannot have both, the latter is certainly to be preferred.

But this many parents appear to forget. They are sufficiently attentive to the minds of their children, and spare no pains or expense, to give them the best education in their power to bestow. Every kind of knowledge, and every accomplishment, whether useful or not, which is fashionable, must be acquired by them. But meanwhile their hearts and dispositions are, in a great measure, or entirely, neglected. No means are employed to teach them the most important of all sciences, the knowledge of themselves, of God, and of his Son, Jesus Christ, whom to know aright is life eternal. On the contrary, they are suffered to grow up, almost as perfect strangers to the very first principles of the oracles of God, as if there were no such book, or as if they were inhabitants of a heathen country. Surely, my brethren, these things ought not so to be. This cannot be educating children for God.

3. Educating children for the service of God implies, that we educate them for eternity, rather than for time; for a future world, rather than for this. You need not be told, my friends, that a different education is necessary to prepare us for different situations. For instance, if a parent designs one of his children for the navy, another for the counting house, a third for the bar, and a fourth for the desk, he will give them in some respects a different education; an education suited to their respective destined employments. So he who educates his children for this world, will, in many respects, educate them very differently from one who educates them for the next. The first will confine his views to the present life, and be anxious to teach his children only those things which are necessary to qualify them for acquiring riches, or honors, or applauses here. But the other will extend his views to eternity, and be principally, though not entirely concerned, to give his children that knowledge which will be useful to them beyond the grave. Here, again, multitudes fail. How few parents, my friends, educate their children in such a manner as would lead a stranger to conclude that they believed in God, or a future state; that they viewed their children as immortal beings, in a state of probation for eternity, and candidates for everlasting happiness or misery. He would see many anxious for the success of their children here, rising early, and late taking rest, and eating the bread of carefulness, to promote their temporal welfare; while no anxiety is manifested respecting the destiny of their undying souls.

Thus, my friends, have we endeavored to give you a concise view of what is implied in educating children for God. Let it be observed, in addition, that all this must be done in such a manner, as to convince your children, that you are sincere, that you are in earnest, that the promotion of their spiritual and eternal welfare is the great, the absorbing concern of your souls. We proceed now, as was proposed,

II. To consider the reward which God usually bestows on those who thus educate their children for him. Though God is the Creator and sovereign Lord of all things, and might therefore, with the most perfect justice, have required us to obey all his commands without any compensation, yet he has been graciously pleased to attach a reward to the performance of every duty, and of this among the rest. This reward consists,

1. In the pleasure which attends every attempt to educate children for God. However strong parental affection may be, it is rarely, if ever, sufficient to render the various cares, anxieties, and duties which attend a numerous family, delightful or even pleasant. There is reason to believe, that, in many instances, these cares and troubles are productive of fretfulness, impatience, and discontent; and not only embitter the lives, but sour the tempers of parents. Even Christian parents, who do not recollect that they are, or ought to be, educating their children for God, are prone to murmur at the frequent interruption which they meet with in the hours set apart for devotion, and the little time which the cares of their families allow them, for reading, meditation and, prayer. But did they realize that they are encountering all these cares and troubles for God, that they are educating his children, and that whatever they do or suffer for them, if performed from right motives, will be considered and rewarded as done for him, how greatly would it lessen their sorrows, and alleviate the cares and perplexities attending a family. How easy would it be to spend wearisome days, and sleepless nights, for their children, could they feel that they are acting and suffering for God; and that he looks on, and approves their conduct. This alone, were there no other, would be a sufficient reward to the Christian for bringing up his children for God.

2. Another part of the reward which God bestows on those who educate their children for him, is the happiness which they enjoy, when they see their labors crowned with success. This happiness will usually, if not always, be enjoyed by those who educate their children in the manner above described, and seek with proper earnestness and perseverance, the blessing of God to render their exertions effectual. I am warranted to make

this assertion by the authority of Scripture. We are there expressly assured, that if we train up a child in the way he should go, when he is old, he will not depart from it. In addition to this, God's language to every believing parent, to every child of Abraham is, I will be a God to thee and to thy seed after thee. These passages are abundantly sufficient to warrant a belief, that God will save, at least, some of the seed of every believer, who, like Abraham, teaches and commands his children and his household after him, to keep the way of the Lord; for were it true, that God does not promise to be a God to all the children of such parents, yet he does promise that he will be a God to some of them; and we dare challenge any person to produce a single instance, in which all the offspring of believing parents who educate their children for God, in the manner above described, died without giving evidence of hopeful piety. We know, indeed, that many children of parents undoubtedly pious, far from imitating their example, have been notoriously wicked; but we know also that many parents, really pious, do not educate their children, by any means as they ought. We know also that all the means and endeavors which parents can use, will avail nothing, without the sovereign grace of God; but we likewise know that God usually works by means, and converts those children whose parents labor and pray most earnestly for their conversion. The labors of ministers for their people are no more effectual, without the grace of God, than those of parents for their children; yet St. Paul assures Timothy, that if he took heed to himself and to his doctrine, and continued in them, he should in so doing, both save himself, and them that heard him. Why then may we not with equal reason conclude, that if parents take heed to themselves, to their conduct, and the doctrines of Christ, and continue in them, they shall save, not only themselves, but their children? We cannot at present insist any longer on this part of our subject; but we are, I think, sufficiently warranted to conclude, that God will bestow on every parent who educates children for him, the pleasure of seeing, at least some of them, walking in the truth.

My friends, what a reward is this! How must it relieve the anxiety of a parent's heart, how soothing, how delightful must it be, to see his children safe in the arms of the great Shepherd, happy in the enjoyment of God's love; and to feel assured that

all things shall work together for their good, and that they are
heirs of a heavenly inheritance. What music can be more
sweet, more ravishing to a parent's ear, than the accents of a
beloved and affectionate child exulting in hope of the glory of
God, and gratefully declaring that to the prayers, labors and
pious example of his parents, he is indebted, under God, for all
his present happiness and future hopes. How must it alleviate
the pangs of separation, when death arrives, to know that we
leave our children under the care of an infinitely good, wise,
and powerful being, who will do for them all that they need to
have done, and watch over them with more than parental tenderness; to know too that they will soon follow us to the mansions of eternal rest. Or if they are called to go before us, how
easy must it be to part with them, when we know that they are
going to be with Christ, which is far better, and that we shall
soon be reunited to them in his presence to part no more. And
hereafter, when we meet them in the abodes of the blessed,
when we hear them praising God, for giving them such parents,
when we lead them on to the throne of God and the Lamb,
saying, Behold, here are we and the children whom thou hast
given us; and to hear him greet us with, Well done, good and
faithful servants, enter ye into the joy of your Lord; — what
will be our feelings? how inconceivable our happiness! how
great the reward of educating children for God! And even
should our endeavors fail of success, still we shall not lose our
reward; still the Judge will own and approve us, before the assembled universe, and call us to enter into his joy; for in his
kingdom, rewards are ever proportioned, not to our success, but
to our zeal and faithfulness.

From what has been said, we infer,

1. That the number of those who educate their children for
God is small, very small indeed. This, my friends, is too evident to require proof; for if it be true that a child trained up in
the way he should go, will not depart from it when he is old;
how few have been thus trained; how few walk in the way
they should go, the strait and narrow way to life! And on the
contrary how many walk in the way they should not go; the
broad way that leadeth to destruction! What multitudes of
parents and children go on together, hand in hand, to eternal
ruin, without once pausing to inquire or reflect, whither they are

going. My friends, of all the melancholy, heart-rending spectacles, which this lost world affords, this is perhaps the worst; and of all the sins which exist among us, none is more prevalent or destroys more immortal souls, than the neglect of educating children for God. It involves the souls both of parents and children in one common ruin. Nor is any sin more destructive to a nation, or detrimental to the peace of society. How can it be expected that children, who were never governed or restrained while young, should prove friends of good order, or useful members of society when old?

My friends, this subject calls loudly for our attention, as citizens, as parents, as Christians; and if we have any love either for our country, our children, our God, or ourselves, we shall learn to give it that attention which it deserves.

2. Permit me to improve this subject by asking every parent present, for whom are you educating your children? We ask not this question, as having authority to call you to an account; we ask it not with a view to pry into the state of your families; we ask it not to condemn you; but we ask it merely with a view to call your attention to the subject, and to lead conscience to give an answer. Say then, my friends, for whom are you educating your children; for God, or for his enemies? Do you consider your children as a sacred gift, intrusted to you only for a short period, and which the Donor expects to be employed in his service, and returned to him more valuable than when it was bestowed? Do you recognise God's right to dispose of them according to his good pleasure, and to take them from you whenever he shall see best? Have you sincerely and solemnly surrendered them to God, and dedicated them to his service? Are you governed by a supreme regard to the glory of God, in all your efforts for their improvement, and in all the labors, cares and sufferings, which you undergo on their account? Do you educate them for the service of the King of kings, daily laboring to convince them of the infinite importance of securing his favor, and of avoiding his displeasure; conducting every part of their education with ultimate reference to this end, endeavoring to cultivate all those tempers and dispositions which are agreeable to his will, and to prepare them, as far as in your power, for the employments of heaven? Do you study the directions which God has given you in his word, and frequently

implore the assistance of his Holy Spirit, in performing your arduous and responsible duties? Do you pay more attention to the souls than to the bodies of your children? Do their spiritual maladies occasion you more distress than any infirmities of body, and are you more pained by observing in them wrong tempers and sinful passions, than by seeing them awkward and unpolished in their intercourse with society? Not only so, do you esteem the education of the heart more important than that of the mind, and labor more earnestly to cherish correct moral feelings and suitable affections than to impart intellectual acquirements? In a word, do your children see in your daily deportment, in your conversation, in your very looks, that all your aims and wishes respecting them, are centered in the one great wish for their conversion; that in comparison with this, you regard no other object as of any importance, and that you would be content to see them poor, despised, and contemned in this world, if they may but secure eternal riches and an unfading crown in that which is to come? If you are not at least attempting to do all this, you are not educating your children for God.

If any feel concerned that they have hitherto neglected this great and important duty, we would improve the subject,

3. By urging them immediately to give it that attention which it merits. Consider the reasonableness of this duty. You are the natural guides, friends, and protectors of your children. They look to you for direction in their yet untrodden path. They are necessarily dependent on others for all the light which can be made to shine on their future course; and their unsuspecting feet will follow wherever you lead the way. How cruel in you to lead them wrong, knowing, as you do, the tremendous and irreparable consequences of such guidance!

This duty may be urged on the ground of justice. You have been instrumental of conveying to your children a depraved nature; and are bound by every principle of justice to do all in your power to eradicate that depravity, and to oppose to its tendencies all the counteracting influences, with which the precepts, the threatenings, the promises, and the Spirit of God supply you; and to add to all the weight of your uniform example and daily prayers.

And let the reward, which God promises to those who educate

their children for him, stimulate you to maintain over them a steady government and salutary discipline; to give them line upon line, and precept upon precept; to talk of their obligations, their duties, and their prospects, when you sit in the house, when you walk by the way, when you rest and when you rise, and on all suitable occasions, — till they shall be taken from under your care, or you removed from them, to enjoy the immediate instruction of the Great Father of our spirits.

SERMON IV

HOW LITTLE CHILDREN ARE PREVENTED FROM COMING TO CHRIST.

But when Jesus saw it, he was much displeased and said unto them, Suffer the little children to come unto me and forbid them not; for of such is the kingdom of God. — MARK x. 14.

In the passage of which these words are a part, we have a beautiful instance of the fulfilment of an ancient prediction respecting Christ, that he should gather the lambs of his flock with his arms, and carry them in his bosom. It appears from the context that some persons, probably believing parents who had felt the efficacy of this blessing themselves, and who were anxious that their infant offspring should enjoy the same privilege, brought to him young children that he might touch them; or, as it is expressed by another Evangelist, that he might lay his hands on them and pray. His disciples, who probably thought these children too young to derive any advantage from Christ, and were apprehensive that he would be interrupted and wearied with their applications, rebuked those who brought them. But our merciful Saviour, more compassionate and less concerned for his own comfort than his disciples, soon gave them to understand, that they must on no account discourage any, however young, from approaching him. When Jesus saw it, he was much displeased, and said unto them, Suffer little children to come unto me, and forbid them not; for of such is the kingdom of God.

My friends, we here see a very unusual sight. We see the meek and lowly Jesus, not only displeased but much displeased; displeased too, not with his opposers or enemies, but with his own disciples. And what had they done to excite his displeasure? Had they been guilty of neglect, unkindess, or a criminal disregard to his comfort or convenience? No; had this been the case, he would have passed it over in silence, or have been the first to make an excuse for their conduct. But they discouraged little children from approaching him; and this was an offence which he could not suffer to pass unreproved. Since Christ is yesterday, to-day, and forever, the same, we may conclude that he still entertains similar feelings towards all who imitate the conduct of his disciples in this respect. From our text, therefore, we may fairly deduce the following proposition.

Christ is much displeased with all who, in any way prevent or discourage little children from approaching him.

With a view to illustrate and establish this proposition, I shall endeavor to show who are guilty of preventing or discouraging little children from coming to Christ; and why Christ is displeased with such persons.

I. Who are guilty of preventing or discouraging children from coming to Christ?

I answer: Persons may be guilty of this sin either directly or indirectly. All are indirectly guilty of it,

1. Who do not come to Christ themselves, and publicly profess obedience to his authority. Man, my friends, is an imitative being. In children the propensity to imitate others is peculiarly strong. They come into the world ignorant and helpless, and naturally look to others for guidance, example, and instruction. Their young and tender minds are ready to receive any impression, and take their complexion in a great degree from surrounding objects. What is done by those who are older, and who ought to be wiser than themselves, they are ready to conclude must be right. Instinctively grasping the first hand that is held out to them, they suffer themselves to be led along without knowing or asking whither they are to go. Did they, during their early years, see all around them flocking to Christ and yielding unreserved obedience to his commands; were they

accustomed from infancy to hear his name frequently mentioned with reverence and affection, and his character described as the perfection of excellence and loveliness; they would, probably in most instances, be led by their imitative propensities under the guidance of the divine Spirit to give him the first place in their hearts, and choose him as their best friend. But alas! how different is the scene which the world presents to their view. They see the great mass of those around them, neglecting and disobeying the Saviour of sinners; they seldom hear his name or that of their heavenly Father mentioned, but in a way of profanation; they see the broad road, of sinful conformity with the world, crowded with travellers eager in the pursuit of pleasure, wealth and honor; every thing, which they see and hear, in short, tends to corrupt their unsuspecting minds, which are of themselves but too prone to choose and follow the downward path. Supposing that what is so generally neglected can not be of much importance, and that, if they are no worse than those around them, their condition is safe, they eagerly plunge into the tumultuous current, and are rapidly swept away to perdition, with the careless multitude whose example they follow, unless divine grace, with resistless arm, snatches them from the gulf to which they are hastening, conveys them to the bosom of Christ, and plants their feet on the Rock of ages.

Such, my friends, are the pernicious effects of bad example on the youthful mind. Now every person, who does not come to Christ and publicly profess obedience to his authority, and conduct in a suitable manner, helps to increase the number and strengthen the force of evil example. He pours the stream of his influence into the fatal torrent which is sweeping away the rising generation into the gulf of eternal ruin. He stands as a way-mark at the entrance of life, to direct infant travelers into the path of ruin. Nor can any one excuse himself by pretending that his example has no influence. There is not, I venture to assert, a person in this assembly whose example does not, in a degree at least, influence the present conduct and future destiny of some young immortal; and if his example be not such as it ought to be, he indirectly prevents children from coming to Christ, and is answerable for all the consequences of his conduct. And if he be a parent, these observations apply to him with ten-fold force. The influence of his example on the minds of his children will be almost omnipotent; we clearly see that nothing short of Omnipotence can prevent it from causing their destruction. A chain in the hand of a demon would not more irresistibly drag them to ruin than the example of an irreligious parent; for to his parents more than to all others, does a child look for direction. During the first years of life, while his character is forming, and most lasting impressions made, he considers their sayings as oracles, their word as law, and their opinions as the dictates of unerring wisdom, and their conduct as the pattern he is to imitate.

How powerfully then must the example of those parents, who neglect to come to Christ themselves, tend to prevent or discourage their children from approaching him : not to mention that by refusing to devote themselves to Christ, they put it out of their power to dedicate their children to him, and thus deprive them of all the blessings which would result from such a dedication made in the exercise of faith.

2. If those, who do not come to Christ, whose example is only negatively bad, are guilty of the sin mentioned in our text, much more are those guilty whose example is positively bad. In this class are included all who profess wrong principles, or openly indulge in vicious practices. The open infidel who denies or calls in question the divine authority of revelation ; the conceited infidel who ridicules or explains away the most important doctrines ; the scoffer or profane swearer who familiarizes the infant ear to the language of impiety, and teaches the untutored tongue to utter it; the sabbath breaker who tramples on the barrier with which God has encircled the sacred day; the liar or slanderer who by his example leads the young to trifle with truth and with the reputation of their fellow crea-tures ; the slave to intemperance and sensuality who seduces them into the paths of dissipation and excess, are all, I will not say indirectly, but directly preventing the young from coming to Christ. Every such character does much to bar up the way of life, is a stumbling block over which many will stumble, and fall to rise no more. And if he be one whose talents, wealth, learning, rank, or vivacity of manner gives him extensive influence in society, the pernicious effects of his example will be incalculable. Under his deadly shade no plants of purity will flourish, no flowers of virtue bloom. He breathes around con-

tagion, pestilence and death, and while he sinks into the abyss of vice and infidelity, the whirlpool which he forms, will ingulf every thing that comes within the sphere of its action.

But if he be a parent what shall we say? If there be a sight on earth at which humanity must shudder, over which angels might weep, it is the sight of a young, a numerous family following with unsuspecting confidence a ruthless fiend, in the shape of a parent, who extends the hand of a guide only to lead them far from him who would gather them in his arms and carry them in his bosom; and betrays the helpless lambs to that roaring lion who goes about seeking whom he may devour.

3. Those are indirectly guilty of preventing their children from coming to Christ, who employ no means to bring them to him, who are careful to educate them for this world but not for the next. That children are prone to imbibe the opinions and imitate the conduct of others, especially of their parents, has already been observed. Especially do they learn from them to estimate the value of different objects. What others neglect or despise they consider as worthless; what others highly prize they esteem as valuable. Hence if those who have the charge of their education treated them as they ought, if they appeared more solicitous for their souls than their bodies, for their spiritual and eternal, than their temporal interests; if they frequently mentioned Christ to them, as the pearl of great price, and spake of an interest in his favor as the one thing needful, compared with which every thing else is worthless, it is highly probable that, by the blessing of God, they might be early led to prize Christ in some measure as he deserves, and to feel unsafe and uneasy till an interest in his favor was obtained. Agreeably, the Scriptures assure us that, if we train up a child in the way he should go, when he is old he will not depart from it. But if children perceive that their parents and others, who are entrusted with their education, are more solicitous to educate them for this world than for the next; more anxious for their present than their future welfare; more desirous to see them prosperous than pious, and more concerned for the health of their bodies than the salvation of their souls, they will inevitably be led to conclude that religion is of little consequence; that to come to Christ is needless; and that to obtain learning, riches, honor and applause, are the great objects for which men were created.

All parents therefore who thus educate their children for this world and not for the next, take the most effectual means to prevent them from coming to Christ, and to cultivate that worldly-mindedness which is directly opposed to the love of God. And, my friends, how great is the number who do this. How many even among the professed people of God are guilty in this respect. If it be true that a child, brought up in the right way, will never forsake it, few indeed are educated as they ought to be; for you need not be told that small is the number who follow the right way to the end of life. My friends, did you take one half the pains, or display one half the concern to educate your children for God that you do for the world, you would most probably see them walking in the truth, and avoid the guilt which you now contract, of preventing their coming to Christ.

Under this branch of my subject I may observe, that if parents feel unwilling or unable to instruct their children themselves, they ought at least to countenance and assist those who are willing to do it. Yet many will not even do this. Most gladly, my friends, would we do all in our power to bring these lambs of the flock to Christ, and store their minds with religious truth, would you give us an opportunity of doing it. That many do this we acknowledge with thankfulness and pleasure. But we are compelled to add, that many do not. No one can suppose that more than half the children of this society, who are of a suitable age, have at any time attended on those catechetical instructions which are communicated in this place after divine service. Yet a very slight exertion of parental authority would secure their attendance. If this exertion is withheld, what must your children think? They see you sparing no pains or expense to give them that knowledge which is necessary for them in this world. They know that you require their attendance at school, and pay masters for instructing them. Yet when they have an opportunity of acquiring religious knowledge without expense, you do not require them to improve it. Must they not suppose that you view religious knowledge as a thing of no consequence; and religion itself as something which you do not wish them to acquire? And does not this negligence powerfully tend to prevent them from coming to Christ? We would however indulge the hope, that when the

return of a milder season shall permit us to resume our labors
with the rising generation, we shall find that this negligence
proceeded rather from inattention to the subject, than from a
wish to deprive your children of religious instruction.

4. If those, who neglect to give their children a religious education, are guilty of indirectly preventing them from coming
to Christ, much more so are they who give them an education
which is positively bad, and which tends to foster and strength-
en the evil propensities of their nature; propensities which must
be eradicated before they can embrace the Saviour. Yet such
an education there is reason to fear that not a few parents give
their children, though probably without intending it. How often, for instance, do parents encourage a spirit of revenge in
their infant children by teaching them to strike any inanimate
object which may have accidentally hurt them. How often do
they speak of dress, ornaments, or personal beauty, in a way
which is calculated to render children proud and vain of these
frivolous and perishing distinctions! How often do they, by
praise injudiciously bestowed, foster a spirit of envy and false
ambition, and encourage that emulation which the apostle expressly mentions among the works of the flesh. How often do they
humor and indulge them in such a manner as is calculated to
make them peevish and discontented through life, and to render
their wills unmanageably stubborn and perverse. These are
but a few of the evil propensities which the education, received
by many children, tends to strengthen and increase. Yet these
propensities are diametrically opposed to the religion of
Christ, and tend to prevent children from embracing it. All
therefore who foster and encourage them must be considered as
guilty of the fault we have been describing.

Still more forcibly do these observations apply to such as endeavor to discourage their children from attending to religion,
lest it should render them melancholy or singular; or who speak
of its friends and institutions, in their presence, with disrespect
or contempt. Children begin to listen to conversation and to
receive impressions from it, at a much earlier age than is com-
monly supposed; and their first impressions are not only most
easily made, but are generally most deep and lasting. Almost
every seed, which is then sown in the mind, will take root and
produce fruit in abundance through life and often through eter-

nity. There have been many well authenticated instances in which the recollection, in after life, of some word or sentence, dropped by a pious parent, has proved the means of bringing persons, first to reflection, and finally to Christ; and hence we may conclude that at the judgment day, when the secrets of all hearts are laid open, it will appear that a jest, a sneer, or sarcastic observation, respecting the friends or institutions of religion, uttered in the presence of children, and recollected by them at some future day, has, in many instances, been the means of prejudicing them against it, and leading them far from Christ, from heaven and happiness. The heathen philosophers had a maxim which was, " Great is the reverence due to children." The import and design of this maxim, as understood by them, was, that great care and attention should be shown in guarding against every thing in our conduct and conversation, which tended to corrupt the infant or youthful mind. But if the heathen, who knew nothing of the worth or immortality of the soul, felt the necessity of adopting this maxim, how much more deeply should it be felt by us, to whom life and immortality are brought to light, and who are taught to know the unspeakable worth of the soul by the price which Christ paid for its redemption.

Having thus attempted to show who are guilty of preventing children from coming to Christ, I proceed to show, as was proposed,

II.   Why Christ is displeased with such persons.

1. Christ is displeased with such as prevent children from approaching him, because in doing it they display a temper which he greatly dislikes, and which is diametrically opposite to his own. The temper of Christ is emphatically a temper of love for the souls of men and of compassion for sinners. Of the existence and strength of this temper he has given the strongest and most unequivocal proofs. His object in coming into our world, the object of all his labors, of his sufferings and death, was to seek and to save those who are lost. But it is a long established maxim, that like rejoices in like. Christ, therefore, cannot but be pleased with those who discover a temper similar to his own; and unite their exertions with his in promoting the salvation of sinners. And on the contrary, he cannot but be displeased with such as possess a temper directly the reverse of

his own, and exhibit no love or compassion for perishing immortal beings; no desire to bring them to the knowledge of him, who alone can give them salvation. Still more must he be displeased with those who discourage or prevent any from approaching him; for this is the very temper of evil spirits whose whole desire and employment it is, to seduce men into the paths of sin, and prevent them from coming to the knowledge of Christ.

2. Christ is displeased with those who prevent or endeavor to discourage children from coming to him, because in so doing they oppose his will; and so far as they are able, frustrate his grand design, a design in which he feels most deeply interested. It is his will that not one of these little ones should perish. It is his will that all men should come to the knowledge of the truth and be saved. It is his will that all men should be fellow workers with him in bringing about this great, and to him, most desirable event. To oppose the accomplishment of this event, therefore, is opposing his will. It is touching him on the most tender point. It is like touching the very apple of his eye. He can bear any thing better than this. When his disciples manifested the most inexcusable unbelief, he gently rebuked them. When they ungratefully slept instead of watching with him in his last agonies, he made an excuse for them. When Peter once and again denied that he knew him, he turned and brought him to repentance by a look. But when these very disciples discouraged parents from bringing to him their children he was much displeased. Nay more, when Peter endeavored to dissuade him from dying for sinners, he turned and said to him, get thee behind me, satan; thou art an offence to me. These instances plainly show how deeply the heart of Christ is engaged and interested in the great work of saving sinners; and why nothing displeases him so much, as attempts to oppose or hinder its accomplishment.

3. Christ is angry with those who prevent children from approaching him, because it tends to rob him of a part of his reward. This reward principally consists in the pleasure of saving sinners. He participates largely in the joy which is felt in heaven when a sinner repents; and is especially pleased to see the young seek after him; to hear children crying, Hosanna to the Son of David. No praises are more sweet to him

than those which grace produces from the lips of babes. Whenever he hears and sees such things, he sees of the travail of his soul; he sees the fruit of his sufferings, and is satisfied. But those, who prevent or discourage children from approaching him, deprive him of this pleasure, rob him of a part of his reward, and of course excite his displeasure.

4. Christ is displeased with those who are guilty of this conduct, because it evinces a disregard and contempt of those blessings which he died to purchase. Those who discourage others from approaching him, cannot of course believe in him themselves, and the language of their conduct is, an interest in Christ is of no consequence to us, or our children. Temporal prosperity and the favor of the world are much more important; and if our children can but succeed here, we care not what becomes of them hereafter. That Christ is displeased with those who thus disbelieve him, is evident from his conduct while here on earth. We are informed that he looked round about upon his unbelieving hearers, with anger, being grieved for the hardness of their hearts. As he is yesterday, to-day, and forever, the same, he must still feel similar emotions, and is doubtless now looking round with a mixture of grief and anger on those, in this assembly, who do not cordially believe in him themselves, and feel anxious that the rising generation should embrace him.

IMPROVEMENT. 1. This subject may be improved for the purpose of self-examination. For this purpose permit me to ask, my hearers, whether any of you are guilty, either directly or indirectly, by your example, conduct or conversation, of discouraging children from coming to Christ, or of preventing others from bringing them to him. To assist you in answering this question, permit me to remind you, that in this, as in other respects, he that is not with Christ is against him. Your example must be either positively good, or positively bad; and every one, who does not encourage children in coming to Christ, is guilty of indirectly preventing it; and his negligence leads them to suppose that to come is of no consequence. They will generally be more influenced by your example than by the precepts of Christ; and if your example is not good, if you do not enter the way of life yourselves, and invite them to follow, you do in effect prevent them from entering it.

To. illustrate these remarks, permit me to mention a story, Mr. Baxter relates, of a shepherd driving his flock over a high and narrow bridge, built across a torrent. The foremost of the flock, terrified by some accidental occurrence, leaped over the bridge into the flood below; the others, not seeing the danger into which their leaders had fallen, and supposing they might safely follow them, leaped after them, one by one, till all were destroyed. In a similar manner, I suppose, generations of mankind perish. We have all, says the prophet, gone astray like sheep, and turned every one to his own way. The end of this way is destruction. Into this destruction all past sinners, who died impenitent, have already fallen. But we see not the gulf into which they have plunged; and, like the foolish sheep, pursue with headlong impetuosity the same road. Our children, supposing that they may safely follow, where we lead the way, rush after us, and find too late we have guided them to their ruin: while their children in turn, unless grace prevent, will follow them in like manner to perdition. Thus like a river whose waters are successively swallowed up in the ocean, one generation of men after another, is led on blindfold by the influence of example, and plunged into the gulf which has no bottom. Need any thing more be said to show the infinite importance of setting a good example before our children, and leading them after us in the path of life.

2. From this subject parents and others, to whom the care of young immortals is entrusted, may learn the awful responsibility which rests upon them.

Were the guidance and direction of one, two, or more worlds entrusted to you, my friends, would you not feel that yours was a most important and awfully responsible situation? My friends, if you are parents, something infinitely more important than worlds is committed to your care. You have the charge of immortal souls; souls, which our Saviour has taught us are each of them worth more than whole worlds. This charge is committed to you, that you may bring them up in the nurture and admonition of the Lord. And God considers you as answerable for the performance of this duty, and in some measure for the salvation of your children. At least he will consider you as answerable for their destruction, should they perish, unless you do all in your power to prevent it. If you doubt this, hear what he says to his ministers, Son of man I have made thee a watchman ; hear the word at my mouth, and give them warning from me. When I say unto the wicked, Thou shalt surely die ; and thou givest him not warning, he shall die in his iniquity, but his blood will I require at thy hand. But, my friends, parents are at least as much appointed by God to be watchmen over their children, as ministers are to be watchmen over their people. Therefore if parents prove unfaithful, the blood of their children will be required at their hands. If any still doubt, let them hear what God says to his ancient people, who permitted and by example taught their children to worship idols. Thou hast taken, says he, my sons and my daughters whom thou hast borne unto me, and hast sacrificed them unto idols ; and is this a small matter, that thou hast slain my children ? Also in thy skirts is found the blood of the poor innocents ; I have not found it by secret search, but upon them all. My friends, how much reason have many parents to cry, Deliver us from blood guilt-iness. How dreadfully is our whole land stained and polluted by their blood, and how loudly does it call for vengeance ! I am more and more persuaded, that neglecting the religious ed-ucation of children is one of the most crying sins of which we are guilty as a people. If any doubt this, let him recollect the passage already quoted, Train up a child in the way he should go, and he will not depart from it. My friends, these are the words of God, of the God of truth. Look round and see how few are walking in the right way ; hence learn how few have been brought up in the way they should go. Are there any of your children who do not walk in the way they should go ? It must be because they have not been properly educated, and the blessing of God not sufficiently prayed for. And it is perhaps impossible for any one, who is not a real consistent Christian, to educate children properly. None but such can truly dedicate their children to God. None but such can sincerely pray for, or obtain from Christ that wisdom and grace, which are neces-sary to bring them up for God ; and none but such can expect a blessing to follow their exertions. You can readily see that an unbelieving, impenitent man is not qualified to be a minister of Christ, to guide immortal souls to heaven. How then can an impenitent, unbelieving parent bring up his children as he ought, in the nurture and admonition of the Lord ? My friends, what a powerful motive does this afford to induce you to become the real disciples of Christ. Not only your own salvation, but very probably that of your children, depends upon it. If then you love them, if you love yourselves, if you would not sink under the weight of their blood, and hear them cursing you forever, as the authors of their ruin, be persuaded without delay to come to Christ, to bring them with you, to bind yourselves and them to him in an everlasting covenant.

SERMON V

THE CHILDREN OF THE COVENANT, THE SAVIOUR'S FIRST CARE.

Ye are the children of the prophets and of the covenant which God made with our fathers, saying unto Abraham, And in thy seed shall all the kindreds of the earth be blessed. Unto you first, God, having raised up his Son Jesus, sent him to bless you, in turning away every one of you from his iniquities. — ACTS III. 25, 26.

THESE words compose part of a sermon delivered by St. Peter to an assembly of his countrymen; a sermon, on many accounts highly interesting, and especially on account of the success with which it was attended; for it appears from the context, that it was the means of converting some thousands of the hearers. In that part of it which has now been read, the apostle suggests several considerations which were calculated deeply to affect the minds of his audience. He reminds them, that they were descended from pious ancestors; that, in consequence of this, they were the children of the covenant which God had made with their fathers, and especially with Abraham, the illustrious progenitor of their race; and that, from regard to this covenant, God, having raised up his Son Jesus, had sent him first to them, to bless them in turning away every one of them from his iniquities.

My hearers, are there any in this assembly to whom this address of the apostle to his countrymen is applicable? There are. All the baptized persons here present, who have been dedicated to God by believing parents, and who have not cordially embraced the Saviour, are in a situation almost precisely similar to that of the audience whom St. Peter addressed on this occasion. To all such baptized persons present then, to all in this assembly, who have been dedicated to God, by believing parents, in the ordinance of baptism, I say, Ye are the children of the covenant which God made with your parents, and to you first, God having raised up his Son Jesus, now sends him to bless you in turning away every one of you from your iniquities. In discoursing farther on this passage, so interesting to believing parents and to their children, I shall endeavor,

I. To explain and establish the assertion, that all who have been dedicated to God by believing parents, are children of the covenant which God has made with their parents, and especially with Abraham, the great father of the faithful.

With this view I remark, that the blessings of the covenant, which God made with Abraham, were all included in three great promises. The first was, In thy seed shall all the nations of the earth be blessed. The second was, To thee and to thy seed will I give this land; that is, the land of Canaan. The third was, I will be a God to thee and to thy seed after thee. Of these promises the first was made to Abraham as an individual. It merely assured him that the promised seed of the woman, who was to bring blessings to all nations, should descend from him, or be one of his posterity. This promise has long since been fulfilled by the birth of Christ, the promised seed, who was born of a daughter of Abraham. Of course we have nothing to do with it, except to receive the Saviour whose coming it reveals. The second promise was made to Abraham, considered as the progenitor of the Jewish nation, the twelve tribes of Israel; and this promise also has been fulfilled by their being put in possession of Canaan, the promised land. With this promise therefore we have no concern, only so far as it has a typical reference to the heavenly Canaan. The third promise, I will be a God to thee and to thy seed after thee, — was made to Abraham, considered as a believer, in covenant with God; as the great father of the faithful, or of all who should believe with a faith similar to his own. In this promise, the covenant which God made with Abraham principally and essentially consists; in the stipulations which we find in the 17th chapter of Genesis, where God says to him, I will establish my covenant between me and thee and thy seed after thee, for an everlasting covenant, to be a God to thee and to thy seed after thee. It is this covenant, of which circumcision was the seal, with which we are principally concerned, and to which the following discourse refers.

That the Jews were the children of the covenant, it is needless to prove, since it is everywhere asserted by the inspired writers, as well as in our text. In passages too numerous to mention particularly, they are styled God's covenant people, children of the promise, and represented as being born in covenant, and as enjoying covenanted blessings. Speaking of the Jews in his own day, St. Paul says, Who are Israelites, to whom pertaineth the adoption, and the glory, and the covenants, and the giving of the law, and the service of God, and the promises. This covenant, it may be farther remarked, was perfectly distinct from the Mosaic law, and from the covenant which God made with the Jews as a nation, when he brought them out of Egypt, and which was afterwards renewed at Mount Sinai; for the apostle tells us, that it was confirmed of God in Christ four hundred and thirty years before the law was given; and that being thus confirmed it could never be disannulled. Agreeably, we meet with various allusions to this covenant scattered through the Old Testament. The children of thy servants, says the psalmist, shall continue, and their seed shall be established before thee. The Redeemer shall come to Zion, and to them that turn from transgression in Jacob, saith the Lord. And as for me, this is my covenant with them, saith the Lord: my Spirit that is upon thee, and my words that I have put in thy mouth, shall not depart out of thy mouth, nor out of the mouth of thy seed, nor out of the mouth of thy seed's seed, saith the Lord, from henceforth even forever. And again God says, fear not O Jacob my servant, and thou Jeshurun, whom I have chosen, for I will pour water upon him that is thirsty, and floods upon the dry ground; I will pour out my Spirit upon thy seed and my blessing upon thine offspring; and they shall spring up as among grass, and as willows by the water courses. One shall say, I am the Lord's: and another shall call himself by the name of Jacob, and another shall subscribe with his hand unto the Lord, and surname himself by the name of Israel. Since then it cannot be denied, that the Jews were in covenant with God, the only question is, whether the baptized children of professed believers, at the present day, are in the same situation; whether they, like the Jews, are born in covenant, and stand in the same relation to God, which the Jews formerly sustained. With a view to prove that they are so, I observe,

1. It is frequently predicted by the prophets, that in the latter days the Gentiles should, like the Jews, be brought into covenant with God, and share with them in the blessings of the covenant. Thus in the prophecy of Hosea, God says, I will have mercy on them that had not obtained mercy. I will call them my people which were not my people. This passage is quoted by St. Paul, to prove that the Gentiles, or nations, as the word signifies, should be taken into covenant with God, and become his people, as the Jews had formerly been. In many chapters of the prophecy of Isaiah, this event is more particularly predicted and described. The Jewish church is there assured, that the Gentiles shall come to her light, that they shall come bringing her children in their arms, and that these shall supply the place of the children whom she had lost.

2. In the second place, we learn from many passages in the New Testament, that all these promises and predictions were fulfilled. We are there told, that Abraham is the father of all who believe, though they be not circumcised, as were the Jews; that the blessing of Abraham has come upon the Gentiles; that all who belong to Christ are Abraham's seed, and heirs according to the promise. St. Paul, writing to the Ephesian church, says, Wherefore, remember that ye, being in time past Gentiles in the flesh, were at that time without Christ, being aliens from the commonwealth of Israel, and strangers from the covenants of promise, having no hope, and without God in the world. But now ye, who were sometimes afar off, are made nigh by the blood of Christ. Therefore, ye are no more strangers and foreigners, but fellow citizens with the saints, and of the household of God. And in the succeeding chapter he speaks of it as a great mystery, which had not been made known, but which was then revealed, that the Gentiles, or nations should be fellow heirs with the Jews, and of the same body. My hearers, reflect a moment on the import of these passages. They teach us,

that all true believers, all who belong to Christ are Abraham's seed; but if they are Abraham's seed, they must be Abraham's heirs, heirs of the same promises and spiritual privileges, which he enjoyed. But one of the privileges which he enjoyed, was the liberty of bringing his children into covenant with God, and one of the promises which was made to him was, I will be a God to thy seed after thee. If then, Christians are Abraham's heirs, they also have the same privilege of bringing their children into covenant with God, and God's language to every Christian parent is, I will be a God to thee and to thy seed after thee. Agreeably, the same passage tells us, that they are heirs according to the promise, and that they are fellow-heirs with the Jews. It appears then, that Christians stand in the same place, which was formerly occupied by the Jews; we take up what they laid down; we receive the privileges and blessings which they forfeited; the kingdom of God, which was taken from them according to our Saviour's prediction, has been given to us; and therefore if their children were in covenant with God, so, my Christian friends, are ours. This conclusion is confirmed, and the whole subject illustrated by St. Paul in that well known allegorical passage, in which he compares the church to a good olive tree, of which the Jews were the natural branches. But these natural branches, he tells us, were broken off, and Gentile believers grafted in in their room; and these Gentile believers, he adds, now partake of the fatness and sap of the good olive tree; that is, they enjoy those church privileges, which the Jews lost by unbelief; and, of course, the privilege of bringing their children into covenant with God.

That this must be the apostle's meaning, is evident from another passage in the same chapter, in which he says, if the first fruit be holy, the lump is also holy; and if the root be holy, so are the branches. By the root here he evidently means parents, and, by the branches, their children; and the import of his assertion is, that if the parents be holy, so are the children. It must, however, be observed, that he is here speaking, not of personal, but of relative holiness, of that kind of holiness which results from being dedicated to God. In this sense, the vessels of the tabernacle were said to be holy, because they were consecrated to the service of God; and in the same verse, the children of believing parents are holy, because they have been consecrated to God in the ordinance of baptism.

The passages which we have quoted, are scarcely a tenth part of those which might be adduced from the Scriptures on this subject; but they are, I conceive, abundantly sufficient to show that believers are the children and heirs of Abraham; that, like him they are in covenant with God; that the same promise, which was made to him, is now made to them; that they have the same right to dedicate their children to God, as he had; and, consequently, that all the baptized children of believing parents, are, as the Jews formerly, the children of the covenant which God made with their fathers, and especially with Abraham, the great father of the faithful.

If these truths have been established, it follows, that we are authorized to address every baptized child of believing parents in the language of St. Peter in our text; for if such persons are in a situation similar to that of his hearers, we ought to address them in a similar manner. To all such persons then, in this assembly, to all of every age who have believing parents, but who are not themselves believers, I say, To you first God, having raised up his Son Jesus, hath sent him to bless you in turning away every one of you from his iniquities. That you may understand the import of this address, it is necessary to remind you, that one of the privileges which the Jews enjoyed in consequence of being children of the covenant was, the enjoyment of the first offer of that salvation which Christ had accomplished. Thus, when Christ commissioned his disciples to preach the gospel, he charged them to begin at Jerusalem, to preach the glad tidings first to the Jews. Until they should have done this, he forbade them to go to the Gentiles, or to enter into any city of the Samaritans. This command the apostles strictly observed. They preached the gospel at first, we are told, to none but the Jews only; and St. Paul, addressing the Jews at Antioch, says, It was needful that the gospel of Christ should first be preached to you. These remarks will enable you to understand, why St. Peter, in our text, says to his Jewish hearers, to you first God sends his Son to bless you. It is the same at the present day. God sends the offer of salvation first, to the children of believing parents.

In this respect he acts as a wise earthly prince would do, Were such a prince disposed to confer distinguishing favors and privileges upon any person, he would doubtless offer them to the children of his obedient subjects, who had sworn allegiance to him before he offered them to the children of rebels, or of strangers, who had not submitted to his government. Now your parents have sworn allegiance to God, and engaged to submit to his government, as obedient subjects. They have also engaged to use all their influence to induce you to do the same. In token of their readiness to do this, they have solemnly and publicly dedicated you to God, to be his forever; and he has so far accepted this dedication, that he now sends you the first offer of pardon and salvation, through his Son. In his name, then, in the name of your parents' God, of Him into whose adorable name you have been baptised, I now solemnly make you this offer. In his name, I declare that he has sent his Son, in whom all blessings are deposited, and by whom they are conferred, to bless you, to bless every one of you; to bless you with all temporal and spiritual blessings in Christ Jesus. At the same time, I inform you, that he can confer these blessings upon you only by turning you from your iniquities; for so long of you cleave to them, it is impossible that Christ should bless or prove a blessing to you; since between sin and misery there is an inseparable connection. I also inform you that you cannot be turned from your iniquities but by your own consent; for so long as you live and are unwilling to renounce them, it is impossible that you and they should be separated. Christ's language to you is, Turn ye at my reproof, and I will pour out my Spirit upon you, I will make known my words unto you. Come ye out from the ungodly world, and be ye separate, and touch not the unclean thing, and I will receive you, and be a father to you, and ye shall be my sons and my daughters, saith the Lord Almighty. Such are the invitations, such the promises of your heavenly Father and Redeemer. And now I ask every baptized person present, what answer will you return to these invitations? With respect to those of you who have arrived to years of understanding, it is time that your answer was given. It is time that it were known to whom you belong; whether you are for Christ or against him; whether you intend to ratify or to discard what your parents have done in your behalf. While you were infants, God permitted them to act for you; but now you must act for yourselves, and stand or fall by your own choice. And what is that choice? Will you take your parents' God to be your God? Will you give yourselves up to him as you have already been given up by them? Will you take upon yourselves that covenant which they have made in your behalf, and perform its duties, that you may enjoy its blessings? Will you receive Christ as all must do who would receive power from him to become the children of God? and as a proof of your willingness to receive him, will you turn from your iniquities, and renounce the sinful pleasures and pursuits of which you are naturally so fond? Before you reply to these questions, permit me to suggest some considerations, which, by the blessing of God, may induce you to return such an answer as your duty and happiness require. In the first place, permit me to remind you that you are this day to determine whether God or the world shall be your portion, whether Christ or Satan shall be your king. One of these masters you must serve; both you cannot serve, and you are now to decide, in the presence of heaven and earth, which you will serve. Your conduct from this day will show whose servants you intend to be.

In the second place, permit me to remind you, that the choice you make will make a complete discovery of your true characters. If you choose to persist in pursuing worldly objects, and the pleasures of sin, it will prove that you prefer sin to holiness, that you are lovers of pleasure more than lovers of God; nay, it will prove that you are God's enemies, for the Scriptures assure us that the friendship of the world is enmity with God, and that whosoever will love the world is the enemy of God. What is still worse, it will prove that you are irreconcilably God's enemies, that you are so strongly opposed to his character and government, that the tears, entreaties, and example of your parents cannot induce you to love him.

In the third place, remember that your choice is to be made for eternity. You are not to choose whether you will serve sin and Satan in this world, and God in the next; but whether you will be the slaves of sin, and, of course, the enemies of God forever; for what you choose to be in time, you will continue to be through eternity. On the decision which you this day make, it will probably depend whether myriads of ages hence you shall be angels in heaven, or spirits of disobedience in hell; for it becomes you to remember,

In the fourth place, that your choice will decide, not only

your character, but your doom. You must receive the wages
of that master whom you choose to serve. Now the wages of
sin, we read, is death, eternal death; but the gift of God is everlasting life. Be not deceived, God is not mocked; whatsoever
a man soweth, that shall he also reap. They that sow to the
flesh shall of the flesh reap corrruption, etc. In choosing between God and the world then, you are choosing between life
and death, between heaven and hell, between happiness eternal
and ineffable, and misery endless and unutterable. And will
you then, can you then choose death and hell and everlasting
wo? Will you, by your conduct, say to all about you, I am a
wretch so totally devoid of goodness, that I prefer the world to
God, the tempter to Christ, sin to holiness, hell to heaven. If
so, surely your guilt will be no common guilt; for you can
make no excuse. You cannot even plead ignorance; for you
have lived in pious families; you have had a religious education; you have seen the influence of religion upon your parents;
you have had good examples placed before you; you have from
your earliest years heard much of God and of your Saviour;
you have heard many prayers addressed to them; your earthly
parents have united with your Father in heaven, in persuading
you to love him; and his word has been read in your presence,
and placed in your hands. If then you reject your God and
Saviour, you reject him knowingly and voluntarily. You reject a known, and not an unknown God. After seeing the
difference between a life of religion and a life of sin, you de-
liberately choose the latter. Nay more, you reject not only God,
but your parents' God; you violate not only the obligations
which all his creatures are under to love and serve him, but the
peculiar obligations which result from your baptismal dedication to God, and say by your conduct, let us break his bands
asunder, and cast away his cords from us. Your conduct then
dishonors God more than the conduct of a thousand heathen,
who never heard his name; and if they, as the apostle declares,
are without excuse, how totally inexcusable must you be, should
you follow their example. In addition to this, you will be guilty of the most inexcusable ingratitude. In giving you pious
parents, God has conferred on you one of the greatest blessings
which he could bestow. He might have caused your souls to
inhabit bodies among the heathen, where you would never have

heard of a Saviour, where your parents would have dedicated you to false gods, and perhaps have offered you in sacrifice upon their altars! And will you requite him for this favor by practically saying, I regret that my parents were pious, or that they dedicated me to God? Would I had been born in an irreligious family, where I should never have been troubled with religion or prayer, but where I might have indulged in the pursuit of worldy pleasures without interruption or restraint. Will you ungratefully undo all that your parents have done for your salvation, and tear yourselves out of the arms of the Saviour in which they have placed you? Will those of you whose parents have ascended to heaven, do this? If so, remember that as your guilt will be no common guilt, so your punishment will be no common punishment. How awfully aggravated it will be, you may learn from the terrible threatenings denounced against the unbelieving Jews who like you were children of the covenant. Christ declares that the very heathen will rise up against them in the day of judgment and condemn them; that it will be more tolerable for Sodom and Gomorrha in that day than for them, and that while many shall come from the east and the west, and the north and the south, and sit down in the kingdom of God, the children of the kingdom shall be cast into outer darkness, where shall be weeping and gnashing of teeth. In a word, he tells us that they who know their Lord's will and do it not shall be beaten with many stripes. And will you then, by refusing to turn from your iniquities, pull down upon yourselves this terrible fate? Shall all the tears, prayers and exertions of your parents only serve to increase your condemnation? Shall the baptismal water with which you have been sprinkled, be converted into drops of liquid fire? Shall the blessings which Christ was sent to bring, be transformed into curses; and will you, to whom they are first offered, be the first to reject them? You are like Capernaum, raised, as it were, to heaven by your privileges. Will you, by abusing or neglecting them, be yourselves cast down to hell, to the lowest hell? And now I wait for your reply.

What answer shall I return to him that sent me, to him who sends his Son to bless you in turning away every one of you from your iniquities? I suspect that most of you will return no direct answer, but plead for time to deliberate, for a little longer delay. But, my friends, this time cannot be granted. You have already delayed too long. The Jewish children were required to partake of the passover, and appear before God at the solemn feasts, as soon as they arrived at a proper age; and this, as we learn from our Saviour's example, was the age of twelve years. If they refused or delayed to comply, they were doomed to be cut off from among the people; to lose forever the privileges which they slighted. Now a large proportion of those whom I am addressing, have not only reached, but overpast this period of life. Not a few baptized persons present have reached the meridian of life, and some have even advanced beyond it. You ought then long since to have embraced the Saviour, and thus have become prepared to appear at the table of Christ, who, the apostle tells us, is our passover that was sacrificed for us. Already are you liable to be cut off forever from his people, in consequence of delaying to receive him; and will you then talk of a longer delay? It cannot be granted. Soon will you, like the Jews, be broken off as withered branches, because of unbelief. Soon will the kingdom of God be taken from you and given to others. God's language to you is, Now is the accepted time, now is the day of salvation. To-day, if ye will hear my voice, harden not your hearts. This day then, this very day, must you make your choice. This very day must you choose between God and the world, between Christ and the tempter, between heaven and hell. This day, before you leave this house, must you decide the great, the all-important question, whether you will be happy or miserable forever. Heaven and hell are now waiting your answer. Heaven is waiting to rejoice in your repentance. Hell is waiting to exult in your fall. To which then will you give joy? The answer is given. Your hearts have uttered it; God has heard it. It is already recorded in heaven, and your future conduct will soon cause its import to be known on earth. At least, some of you have, I hope, answered as you ought. Some of you, I hope are ready to say to Christ's church, as did Ruth to Naomi, Entreat us not to leave you, nor to return from following after you; for where you go, we will go; where you dwell, we will dwell; your people shall be our people, and your God our God. The Lord do so to us and more also, if aught but death part you and us. Farewell, vain world! farewell, sinful pleasures! farewell, sinful companions! Our Fathers' God calls us, our Saviour invites us, and we have determined to comply with the call, and cast in our lot among his people. And is this your determination? this the sincere language of your hearts? Welcome then, ye once wandering lambs of the flock; welcome to the fold of Christ; welcome to his church, welcome to the good and great Shepherd, who gathers the lambs with his arms and carries them in his bosom. We bid you a thousand and a thousand welcomes to the ark of safety; and while we congratulate you on your happy escape from the snares of the world, and the toils of the tempter, we would unite with you in blessing him who has set your sin-entangled feet at liberty, and inclined you to choose the wise, the better part. You now ratify what your parents have done in your name; you consent to take their God for your God, and to give yourselves up to him in the bonds of his everlasting covenant. Remember then, that from this time, your language must be, What have we to do any more with idols? we have opened our mouths unto the Lord, and we cannot go back. Follow on then, to know the Lord, and you shall know him, and in due time reap, if you faint not.

But have all, to whom, this discourse is addressed, returned such an answer? Fain would I hope this to be the case; yet I cannot but fear, that some of them have not. I cannot but fear that some are still delaying a reply, and saying to the preacher as Felix did to Paul, Go thy way for this time, when I have a convenient season, I will call for thee. But my friends, I cannot depart without a direct and decided answer. Indeed, if you persist in delaying, I have one; for, in this case, to delay, is to refuse. Reflect then, a moment, before you persist in your determination to make a longer delay. Listen to the warning, which God has recently sent you in his providence, as if with a view to add weight and efficacy to the present discourse. Think of the young person whom death, a few weeks since, snatched away from among us. He was, like you, a child of the covenant; he felt the obligation which this privilege imposed upon him, and it is but a few months since you saw him, in this place, publicly ratifying the vows which his parents had previously made in his name. But suppose he had delayed to embrace Christ as you are now intending to do. A delay of only a few months would have been fatal to his everlasting happiness; for he was deprived of his reason by the violence of disease, almost from the moment in which it arrested him. Had not sickness found him prepared, he must have died unprepared. So some of you may have but a few months to live, and delay may be everlasting death. And even should your lives be spared, delay may be equally fatal. God may, and he probably will, take from you his holy Spirit forever, and give you up to final hardness of heart, as he did the Jews. Remember the Jews at Antioch. When Paul offered them salvation and they delayed to accept it, he said to them, It was necessary that the gospel should first be preached to you; but since ye put it from you, and count yourselves unworthy of eternal life, lo, we turn to the Gentiles; for so hath the Lord commanded. My friends, if God commanded his apostle to turn from the children of the covenant, when they rejected his offer, will he not turn from you, if you do the same? Most certainly he will. Beware then, lest there be among you any profane person, as Esau, who for one morsel of meat sold his birthright; for ye know how that afterwards, when he would have inherited the blessing, he was rejected, and found no place for repentance, though he sought it carefully with tears.

My friends, if you, through fear of losing your worldly pleasures, refuse to embrace the Saviour now, you will, like Esau, sell your birthright; and if you do, it will be too late to repent; you will find no place for repentance, though you should carefully and tearfully seek it. But why should I multiply words? I have fulfilled my commission. It was necessary, first, to offer Christ to you, and I have done it. I repeat the offer. I once more assure you, that to you first God sends his Son to bless you, in turning every one of you from his iniquities. Will you then persist in rejecting him, or, what is the same thing, in delaying to accept his offer? If so, your doom is sealed. You have bid farewell, a long, an eternal farewell to God, to Christ, to his church, to your religious friends, to happiness. Your blood be upon you, I am clear. From henceforth I turn to others; to those who have not been dedicated to God.

It was my duty, my friends, first to offer Christ to others This duty I have discharged, and am now at liberty to make the same offer to you. Your heavenly Father, is more careful for your happiness than even your earthly parents. They refused or neglected to give you to him in your infancy, but he has provided a Saviour, through whom you may present yourselves to him and be accepted. The Gentiles accepted Christ, when the children of the covenant rejected him. Will you then imitate their example. Will you give yourselves to that God, whom the children of the covenant neglect? Will you accept the privileges which they despise? If so, the blessing of Abraham will come upon you and your families, as it has on thousands of the Gentiles; and God will make with you an everlasting covenant, as he did with him, to be a God to you. To those of you, who are parents then, this subject is peculiarly interesting. It shows you the reason, why your children are not admitted to the ordinance of baptism. It is because they are not children of the covenant, and they are not children of the covenant, because you have refused to take hold on that covenant, which God offers to make with you. His language to you has long been, Incline your ear, and come unto me; hear and your souls shall live; and I will make with you an everlasting covenant, even the sure mercies of David. But it is evident, that the parent, who will not make a covenant with God for himself, cannot covenant for his children. If he will not give himself to God, he cannot in sincerity give them to God. If he has no faith himself, he cannot present them in faith, and without faith nothing can be done acceptably. But no sooner does a parent become a believer in Christ, and embrace him as the mediator of the new covenant, than he is enabled and entitled to present his children to God through Christ, and claim for them covenanted blessings. This we find was the case under the ancient dispensation. No sooner did one of the Gentiles become a proselyte to the true religion, and receive the seal of the covenant, than his posterity became entitled to share in all the privileges which were enjoyed by the Jews; and to receive the seal of circumcision. It was the same under the New Testament dispensation. When a Jew or a Gentile embraced Christ by faith, not only he, but his household, were baptized, as we see in the case of the jailor, of Lydia, and Stephanus; but never do we find an instance, in which the children of any but professed believers were admitted either to circumcision or to baptism on their parents' account. This then, if you love your children, affords an additional reason why you should, without delay, embrace the Saviour, that you may present them to him for his blessing, and thus render them the children of the covenant. They themselves, if they were acquainted with their best interests, would entreat and beseech you, as soon as they could speak, to dedicate yourselves to God, that you might thus be prepared and entitled to present them.

This subject is also highly interesting to those parents, who are professed believers. I need not tell you, that no promised blessing can become ours, unless it be received by faith; or that without faith it is impossible to please God. It is by faith alone, that we can take hold on the covenant for ourselves; and it is only by faith that we can dedicate our children to God in such a manner, as to be accepted, and obtain for them the most precious blessings of the covenant. But real believers do not always exercise faith, no, not even when they present their children to God. They too often suffer themselves to fall into a cold backsliding state, and then the dedication of their children becomes a mere formality. In addition to this, many professors awfully neglect to fulfil their vows by which they have publicly and solemnly bound themselves to bring up their children in the nurture and admonition of the Lord. By this negligence, they do, in effect, throw themselves out of the covenant, at least so far as their children are concerned. So did not Abraham. I know him, says Jehovah, that he will command his children and his household after him, and they shall keep the way of the Lord, that the Lord may bring upon Abraham that which he hath spoken of him. Here the fulfilment of God's promise to Abraham, is made to depend upon Abraham's performance of the essential duties of the covenant. It is the same at the present day. If you, my professing friends, forget your covenant engagements, God will forget his promises; he will not give the blessings of the covenant to your children.

SERMON VI

DUTY OF THE PRESENT, TO THE COMING
GENERATION.

One generation shall praise thy works to another, and shall declare thy
mighty acts.—Psalm cxlv. 4.

In bringing into existence angels and men,—the only orders
of intelligent creatures with which we are acquainted,—the
all-wise Creator saw fit to adopt two very different methods of
proceeding. The angels, we have reason to believe, were all
created at the same time, and in the full maturity of their intellectual powers. But men are brought into existence successively; and a small part only of the whole race inhabit this
world at the same period. One generation gives birth to another, and then passes off the stage of life, to give place to its descendants. From the mode which God has thus adopted of
bringing mankind into existence in successive generations, many
most important consequences result.

Of these consequences one is, that they all originally possess
the same moral nature; for it seems to be an established law,
and universal so far as this world is concerned, that every thing
which is productive shall produce its own likeness. Again; in
the mode of bringing mankind into existence, all the natural
relations which subsist among them have their origin. No similar relations, it is evident, can subsist among angelic beings.
Among them the titles of parent, child, brother, and other names

expressive of relationship, are not known. Once more; from the mode of bringing mankind into existence, which God has adopted, result most of the social and relative duties which he requires them to perform. Of these duties one of the most important is described in our text. One generation shall praise thy works to another, and shall declare thy mighty acts.

This passage may be understood either as a prediction, or as a command. On the present occasion I shall consider it as a command. Viewed in this light, it prescribes a most important duty to each of the successive generations of mankind; of course, to the present generation, as well as to those which shall follow it. To show in what the duty consists, and to state some reasons why it should be performed, is my design in the present discourse.

With this view I remark, that the duty here enjoined consists of two parts. The first is, to declare, or make known the works of God to succeeding generations, and especially, to that generation which immediately follows us. In other words, it is to inform them what God has done, and what he is now doing. This, it is obvious, embraces a wide field of instruction; for the works of God are both numerous and various.

1. They include his works of creation. These, therefore, we must make known to the generation which follows us. We must declare to them the fact, that in the beginning God created the heavens and the earth, with all which they contain; that, when nothing existed besides himself, — worlds, angels, men and animals came into being at his command. They include,

2. His works of providence. These, therefore, must be made known to the succeeding generation. They must be taught that, in a mysterious, but most powerful and efficacious manner, God preserves and governs every thing which he has made; that all events, from the greatest to the most minute, are under his control; and that what men call the laws of nature are only fixed modes of operation which he has adopted. Their attention must be particularly directed to those great dispensations of providence which respect our whole race; to those which are recorded in the Scriptures; to those of which their country has been the scene or the object; and to those which more immediately affect themselves. In short, they must be taught to

see God's hand in every thing, to view him as the source of all temporal blessings, and the great agent who worketh all in all.

3. God's works include the work of redemption, considered as a whole, together with all those gracious dispensations which are parts of it. This is the great work of works,—the work with reference to which all God's other works are performed. In this work every individual of every generation is deeply interested; and, therefore, this work especially should be made known to all. To make known this work, is to make known all that God has ever done for the salvation of our ruined race, so far as he has revealed it to us. It includes all the preparations which have been made for the coming of Christ; his coming itself, the work which he performed and the sufferings which he endured while on earth, and what he has done since he ascended to heaven. It includes also the revelation which God has given us in the Scriptures; for this is one of his works, though men were employed in effecting it. They wrote, but he dictated. They held the pen, but he moved it. Such are the works of God which one generation should make known to another; and a very little reflection will convince us that, in making known all these works, the whole system of religious truth and duty will be made known; for there is no doctrine, no precept of Christianity, which is not either founded upon some of God's works, or intimately connected with them.

But how, it may be asked, are these works of God to be communicated by one generation to another? I answer,—they are to be communicated, generally speaking, just as a knowledge of other things is communicated by one generation to another. Observation teaches us, that all the knowledge of temporal things which one generation possesses, is usually imparted to the next. This is done in various ways. Parents teach their children, if they are able; and if not, they employ other persons to teach them those things which are necessary to qualify them for active life. Colleges, academies, and schools are founded, and their support provided for, either by the civil powers, or by the munificence of private individuals, on purpose to impart instruction to the rising generation. A great part of the knowledge which every generation possesses is also recorded in books, and thus transmitted to posterity. And we may add, that much useful knowledge is every day imparted casually in conversation, in carrying on the common business of life. Now in all these ways one generation ought to communicate to another a knowledge of the works of God. Parents who possess this knowledge,—and every parent ought to possess it,—must impart it to their children. All who are employed in the instruction of youth should impart it to their pupils. A competent number of well-qualified religious teachers should be provided. Seminaries, if necessary, should be founded and supported for the education of such teachers. All who are qualified to instruct mankind by their writings, should communicate religious knowledge through the medium of the press; and those who are not thus qualified, should embrace every opportunity of imparting it in conversation. In one or another of these various ways, all the religious knowledge which is possessed by one generation must be transmitted to the generation which follows it. This constitutes the first part of the duty enjoined in the text.

The second part is, for one generation to praise God's works to another. While they communicate a knowledge of his works they must speak highly of them. While they tell what he has done, they must add, he has done all things well. When they describe his works of creation, they must extol the wisdom, power and goodness which are displayed in them. While they communicate a knowledge of his works of providence, they must applaud them as infinitely wise, holy, just, and good. And while they exhibit the wonders of redemption, and God's works of grace to the following generation, they must accompany the exhibition with those glowing expressions of admiration, gratitude, love and joy, which this grand display of all God's perfections ought to call forth from those, for whose benefit it was made, and whose everlasting happiness it is designed to promote. In short, the high praises of God must be seduously poured into the ears of the rising generation; all the praise which has come down to us from former generations, or which has resounded from heaven to earth, must be echoed back to them; they must never hear him spoken of, but in just, that is, most exalted terms. They must be convinced that we regard him with the utmost admiration, reverence, gratitude, and love; and be made, if possible, to feel that among the gods there is none like Jehovah, nor any works like his works.

Such is the duty which every generation of mankind is commanded to perform with respect to the generation which immediately follows it.

Should it be thought by any, that the passage under consideration does not enjoin this duty; that it is simply a prediction and not a command; other passages can be easily adduced, in which the duty is explicitly enjoined. The church of God is represented as saying, We will not hide what our fathers have told us, showing to the generation to come the praises of the Lord, and his strength, and his wonderful works which he hath done. For he established a testimony in Jacob, and appointed a law in Israel, which he commanded our fathers, that they should make them known to their children; that the generation to come might know them, and declare them to their children. In this passage the duty of transmitting the knowledge and the praises of God's works from one generation to another, is surely prescribed and enjoined as clearly as language can do it.

Having shown in what the duty consists, I proceed, as was proposed,

II. To state some reasons which should induce us to perform it.

1. One reason may be found in the natural relations which exist between the present and the next generation. These relations are intimate and endearing. The next generation will owe its existence to the present. They will be our descendants, our children. Even those of us who are related to none of them as parents, will be related to them in some other way. In short, there is probably not one individual present, who will have none that are related to him in the next generation. Now in consequence of the relations which exist between this generation and the next, we are its natural guardians, instructors, and guides. To us the education of their bodies, their minds, and their hearts, are entrusted. They have a natural right to look to us for instruction, and to expect that we should teach them every thing which it is necessary for them to know. And is it not necessary that they should know their Creator, their God, the being on whom they depend? Is it not necessary that they should know the Father and his Son Jesus Christ, whom to know is eternal life? Is it not necessary that they should have that knowledge which makes men wise unto salvation?

Again: the rising generation look to us for instruction respecting the real value of objects. In regard to these they are liable to be deceived. They cannot readily distinguish between appearances and reality, between food and poison. They need, and they have a claim to, the benefit of our knowledge and experience. They expect that we will speak to them in high terms of that which is most valuable; that we shall teach them to admire what is most admirable, and to pursue what is most worthy of pursuit. And is there any thing more admirable than the works and perfections of God; any thing more valuable, or more worthy of pursuit, than his favor? We ought then to praise him in their hearing, to speak of him in the highest terms; and to show them by our conduct that our praises are sincere. If we fail to do this, we sin against the relations which we sustain. If he who provides not for his own, especially for those of his own household, is worse than an infidel; what shall be said of him, who communicates to his own children, no knowledge of God, and teaches them neither by precept nor by example to praise him!

2. Another reason for the performance of this duty may be found in the fact, that each of the successive generations of mankind is the natural and rightful heir of the generation which preceded it. This is the appointment of God, the sovereign proprietor of all things. He has granted to each generation of mankind a life-estate only in their temporal possessions; and when the period, for which this grant was made, terminates, their possessions must go to the next generation. The present generation, for instance, can hold their lands, houses, goods, and privileges during life only; and when they pass off the stage, all these things will become the property of the next generation. Since then that generation are, by God's appointment, our natural and rightful heirs; since they will inherit all our other possessions,—it seems right and proper that they should inherit our knowledge of God and of his works. And since we cannot bequeath this knowledge by a will or testament, as we can our other possessions; since all which we do not communicate, while living, will be buried with us and lost forever; it seems necessary that we should impart it while life continues; and also make suitable provision for its preservation and increase. Every one who believes the Scriptures, and indeed every one who

believes that men are accountable, will acknowledge that it
would be cruel to transmit our temporal possessions to posterity,
and yet withhold from them that religious knowledge, which
alone can teach them how to use these possessions, and prevent
them from becoming a snare and a curse, as they certainly will,
if not employed in a right manner. Would not he be thought
greatly deficient, either in prudence or in affection, who should
bequeath to his children a magazine of gunpowder, or a quan-
tity of virulent poison, and yet leave them in ignorance how to
use it in such a manner as would be safe to themselves and
others? My hearers, to bequeath a large portion of wealth, or
of worldly knowledge, or of any other temporal possession to
posterity, without imparting to them a knowledge of God, and
of their duty, and their accountability, is worse than to bequeath
them poison without cautioning them how they use it. How
many have we seen ruined, both for this world and the next, in
consequence of inheriting from their parents a large estate,
without being taught how to use it, or to know that they must
account for it! On the other hand, he who bequeaths posterity
the knowledge and the praises of God, bequeaths a rich inheritance, even should he leave them nothing else.

3. The obligation to perform this duty will appear still more
evident, if we recollect that for the religious knowledge and the
means of acquiring it, which we possess, we are indebted, under
God, to preceding generations. From them we received the
Bible, that grand, inexhaustible depository of religious truth.
From them we have received numberless other volumes, designed to explain and enforce its contents. From them we receive
all the oral religious instruction which was imparted to us in our
early years. To them we are indebted for our religious institutions, for a large proportion of our religious teachers, and for
most of the colleges and other seminaries in which men are
educated for the teacher's office. And all these blessings they
imparted to us, on purpose that we might transmit them to
posterity. It was their design, as it is the will of God, that we
should do this. Our religious knowledge and privileges may,
therefore, be considered as a kind of entailed estate; or an estate which we have no right to alienate, and which we are under obligation to transmit, unimpaired, to posterity. And can
any of you wish, or even consent, to disregard these obligations?

Can you consent that the life-giving streams of that knowledge which makes men wise unto salvation, and which have flowed down from former generations to the present, should here stop, and proceed no further? Can you consent that at the last day, these streams should be traced down to us, and there be found to have disappeared, like a river lost among sands? Can you consent that your descendants should perish for thirst, and through eternity curse you as the cause? Shall they have reason to say, religious knowledge was transmitted and increased until it reached our fathers, but with them it was lost? Let those especially, who were blessed with pious parents, and with early religious instruction, think of these questions. Let them recollect, that they have incurred a debt, which they can discharge only by communicating to the next generation the instruction which they have received from the last. And let all my hearers remember, that there is no country on the face of the globe, in which these remarks should have such weight, as in New England. In no country are the present generation so deeply indebted to their ancestors as in this. O, what a birthright, what an inheritance did the fathers of New England bequeath to their posterity! Their knowledge of God, and their disposition to praise him have long since carried them to heaven; but they have left these blessings to us, that we may be taught and persuaded to follow them. And shall we disappoint their hopes and frustrate their endeavors? Most men are unwilling that an estate which has been for ages in their family shall go out of it. Shall we not then be unwilling that the religion of our fathers, and the blessings connected with it, should go out of the family? Shall we not, instead of selling our birthright, like profane Esau, say with Naboth, God forbid that I should part with the inheritance of my fathers! God forbid that I should fail to transmit to posterity the rich legacy which has descended to me.

4. A still more powerful reason why we should perform this duty, may be found in the fact, that we transmit to our posterity a corrupt and depraved nature, which, unless its influence is counteracted by religion, will render them miserable here and hereafter. It is in vain to deny or conceal the fact. The Scriptures assert it in the plainest terms, and universal observation and experience confirm the assertion. Every generation of man-

kind is an exact counterpart of the generation which preceded it; and exhibits the same moral image, the same sinful propensities, the same disposition to neglect and disobey God. Man was, indeed, first planted a noble vine; but he fell, and in consequence of his fall, men are now the degenerate plants of a strange vine. Nor are the human form and the human countenance more certainly transmitted by them to their posterity, than is a depraved and corrupt nature. Those of you who are parents, and who know any thing of your own hearts, see in your children an exact moral resemblance of yourselves. You are at no loss to determine whence they derive those sinful passions and propensities which they exhibit; you see, full blown in your own hearts, all those evils, the seeds of which you discover in them. Thus from one generation to another the poisonous streams flow down, diffusing moral contagion and death, and threatening to engulf the whole race in remediless sinfulness, wretchedness, and despair. It is no part of my present design to prove the justice of that constitution, which establishes a connection between the moral nature of parents and that of their offspring. That constitution is one of God's works, one of those works which we are required not only to make known, but to praise. Of course, it must be just. But it is more to my present purpose to call your attention to the means which God has graciously appointed for the remedy and prevention of those evils, under which the successive generations of mankind have so long groaned. These means are a faithful performance of the duty enjoined in our text. And we have reason to believe, that if this duty were faithfully and universally attended to, it would be sufficient. Let all the individuals of any one generation acquire the knowledge of God, and exercise those feelings towards his character and his works, which are expressed in praise; and then let them communicate this knowledge and express these feelings to all the individuals of the next generation; and the tide of corruption which now overflows the world would, in a great measure at least, be stopped. I do not mean that any generation, even if every member of it were pious, could convert the next; but I believe, and the Scriptures warrant the belief, that if one generation should faithfully perform its duty, God would bless its exertions and answer its prayers, by rendering the next generation almost universally pious.

And then that generation, in its turn, would perform the same
duty to the next, with similar success; and thus the knowledge
and praises of God would flow down from generation to generation, and fill the earth, even as the waters fill the seas. If any
doubt this, let me request them to suppose that all the present
inhabitants of this town should become judicious, well-informed,
and zealous Christians; that they should all exemplify Christianity in their temper and conduct; that every practice and
amusement inconsistent with pure religion should be banished;
that they should all take as much pains to educate children for
the other world, as they do to educate them for this; that children should never hear God or his works mentioned, but with
admiration, gratitude, and love, and be taught from infancy that
religion is the one thing needful; I say, suppose this to be the
case, and can you doubt that all, or nearly all, the next generation in this town would become Christians; and in their turn
act the same part to the generation which should follow them?
If so, how much more probable is it, that similar consequences
would follow, should all the inhabitants of this country, or of
the world do the same? If any still doubt, let them think of
such passages as these: Train up a child in the way he
should go, and when he is old he will not depart from it. I
know him, says God of Abraham,—that he will command his
children and his household after him. And what will be the
consequence? They shall keep the way of the Lord. Such
language more than intimates, that, if one generation should
perform its duty to the next, the next generation would be pious.
In the millennium it will be so. Men will then be born, as they
are now, with a corrupt nature; but the effects of it will, through
the blessing of God, be prevented by the pious education which
they will receive, and the pious examples which will be every
where set before them. They will see that all who are older
and wiser than themselves do know, and love and praise God,
and value his favor more than life; and the same proneness to
imitate others, which now leads them astray, will then lead
them to seek the good and right way.

And now, parents, let me beseech you to think seriously of
this. You have imparted to your children your own corrupt
nature. That unwillingness to retain God in your knowledge,
that aversion to his service, that dislike of religion, that strong

propensity to pursue this world and neglect the other, which, you cannot but be conscious, exist in yourselves, you have transmitted to them. And in consequence of these evils which they have derived from you, they will perish forever, unless these evils be counteracted. But God has in mercy put into your hands means to counteract them. Make known to them his works and his will. Pour into their ears his praises. Let them see, that you think of nothing, care for nothing, fear nothing, and love nothing, as you do him. Let them see that you care, comparatively, very little what their situation is in this world, provided they receive a Christian's portion in the world to come. Do this, and add fervent persevering prayer; and the corrupt nature which they have derived from you shall be changed by God's grace, a new heart and a right spirit shall be given them, and they shall be thus prepared to perform the same good office for their children, which you have performed for them.

Should it be thought by any, that though the remarks which have been made prove the propriety and necessity of communicating to the next generation a knowledge of God's works,— they do not prove it to be necessary that we should praise him in their hearing; I answer, the former without the latter will be of little, if any, avail. It will answer very little purpose to communicate knowledge of any object to the rising generation, unless they see that we highly prize the object itself, and consider a knowledge of it as exceedingly valuable. It must be evident to every person of observation, that children and youth, in forming their estimate of different objects, are guided almost entirely by the opinions of those who precede them in the journey of life. A child, left to itself, would prefer the smallest coin to a bank note, and a piece of painted glass to the most valuable diamond. And how does he learn to judge more correctly? Simply by observing how objects are valued by those who are older and wiser than himself. In this way, young persons, and even children, soon learn what we think most valuable. And however diligently we may impart to them a knowledge of God and his works, if we do not appear to think highly of him, to love his character, to admire his works, and to prefer him to every other object,—our instructions will have but very little effect. But if they hear us frequently speak of him in the glowing language of gratitude, love, and praise; if they see that

we consider him as all in all; that we regard it as detestable
and base to neglect him; and that the language of our conduct
is, Whom have we in heaven but thee, and what is there on
earth that we desire besides thee?—they will, in all probability,
be insensibly led to adopt, not only our opinions respecting him,
but our feelings towards him. The just, but trite remark, that
if we would speak to the heart, we must speak from the heart,
is especially true with respect to children and youth. Perhaps
one reason why many parents, who are careful to give their
children religious instruction, see very little good effect result
from their labors, is they do not with sufficient frequency and
fervency speak to them in praise of God; do not appear to over-
flow with those emotions which praise expresses; but merely
speak of him in a dry, cold, and formal manner. But to say
nothing of parental efforts, how great, probably, would be the
effect upon the rising generation, were they accustomed from
their childhood to hear our rulers, our legislators, our judges,
our officers, our wise, our learned and wealthy men, all speak
of God and of his works in the highest terms, and utter his
praises with emotion ! if they never heard his name profaned
or religion treated with disrespect! How would such examples
tend to subdue their sinful prejudices, and tear down their opposition to the truth ! To speak God's praises to the rising
generation is then, if possible, even more important than to
impart to them a knowledge of his works. Both, however, are
necessary, and should never be separated.

It would be easy to enlarge on this subject, and to multiply
reasons in favor of the duty before us, to an indefinite extent;
but the undesigned length of the preceding remarks, renders it
necessary to close with a brief improvement.

1. Is it the duty of the present generation to communicate a
knowledge of God's works, and to proclaim his praises to the
generation which will succeed us? Then it is incumbent on all
to qualify themselves for the performance of this duty. It is
incumbent on all to acquire a competent portion of religious
knowledge, and to exercise those devotional feelings, which are
expressed in praise. The man who does not know God, and
who cannot cordially praise his character and his works, is
totally unqualified to discharge one of the most important duties,
which his Maker requires of him and which he is placed in

this world to perform. He is qualified neither to live usefully nor to die happily. My hearers, is not this the character of some of you? Are there not some before me, who know too little of God and his works, to impart a knowledge of either to the rising generation? Are there not a still greater number, who cannot cordially praise the works of God—nay, who are dissatisfied with many of his works, who complain of his law, neglect his gospel, and murmur at the dispensations of his providence? And how can such persons declare God's praises to the next generation? Or what can they teach it, but to neglect him, disobey him, and complain of him? Surely, no such person ought to be a parent, or an instructor of youth. Surely no such person is fit to educate immortal souls.

2. Is it the duty of one generation to declare and praise God's works to another? Then it becomes us all to inquire how far we have performed this duty to the generation which is to succeed us. Let me then ask every one who has reached the age of manhood,—what have you done to impart religious knowledge to the minds, and call forth the praises of God from the hearts, of the rising generation? There are, I know, many present who can reply, We have done something for the promotion of these objects. There are parents who have, in some measure at least, performed this duty to their children. There are some present who have imparted religious instruction to their apprentices, servants, and dependants:—some who have voluntarily labored in our Sabbath schools, to impart this knowledge to children with whom they are not naturally connected, and to call forth from their lips the high praises of God; and some who have contributed to diffuse this knowledge to the ends of the earth. But is there one present, who can truly say, I have done all that was in my power? I have done every thing which I was able to do for the rising generation in my own country, and in other parts of the world; for, be it remembered, the rising generation in other countries, in pagan, Jewish, and Mahomedan lands, have claims upon us, commensurate with our ability. In this, as in other respects, charity begins at home, but it must not end there. And is there one parent present, who can truly say, I have done every thing which I could do for the religious education of my own children? And are there not many, who have done comparatively nothing for any part of the rising

generation, even for the instruction of their own families in religious truths? Are there not some present who, if they were to die this day, would leave behind them no mind upon which they had made the least salutary impression—the slightest proof, that they knew and praised God themselves, or that they had ever taught others to do it? Nay more—are there not some who, as far as they have taught any thing to the rising generation, have taught them to neglect religion, to dishonor God, perhaps to take his name in vain? My hearers, let me beseech you to think seriously of these questions and of the subjects which led to them. If there be any who have performed no part of the duty enjoined in our text, let them immediately begin to perform it. Let those who have already done something, be excited to do more. Let it be remembered, that there is probably not now in New England one half the religion, in proportion to the number of inhabitants, that there was a century and a half since. If our posterity are not to become pagans or infidels, not only something, but much must be done.

3. Is it the duty of this generation to make known God's works and proclaim his praises to the next? Then it is the duty of the rising generation to receive with eagerness the religious instruction which is afforded them, and to drink in the praises of God. Remember, my young friends, we shall soon pass off the stage, and you will take our places. Then a new generation will spring up, whom it will be your duty to instruct. Now is the time to qualify yourselves for the performance of that duty. Now then acquire a knowledge of God and of his works. Now learn to love, admire, and praise him, that you may teach those who will come after you to do the same. Do this; and after you have, like ancient worthies, served God and your generation, you will rest from your labors, your works will follow you, and future generations shall rise up and call you blessed.

Finally. What a happy, glorious world will this be, when our text, considered as a command, shall be universally obeyed; considered as a prediction, shall be universally fulfilled! Whether we obey it or not, this will one day be the case. Then one generation will eagerly transmit the knowledge and praises of God to the next; while that generation will, with alacrity, receive and hand them down to their descendants. Then all shall know God from the eldest to the youngest, from the least to the greatest. Then those things which are an abomination in the sight of God, shall no longer be highly esteemed among men; and the applauses which have been lavished, and the encomiums which have been bestowed upon heroes and conquerers, shall be transferred to the faithful soldiers and martyrs of Jesus Christ; while every knee shall bow to him, and every tongue shall confess him Lord to the glory of the Father. Then every day will be a day of thanksgiving; all nations, tongues, and languages shall join in one universal chorus of praise. Princes and subjects, young men and maidens, old men and children, shall conspire to swell the song. In one immense cloud of incense the grateful offering shall ascend the skies. Heaven shall hear with wonder and delight its own songs sung on earth; and God, the all good and almighty Father of the universe, bending from his eternal throne, shall accept the worship, smile with ineffable benignity and complacency on the worshippers, and shed down upon them, with unsparing hand, his richest blessings. Then death will indeed lose his sting, and cease to be the king of terrors. Easy and pleasant will be the passage from earth to heaven; and those who die will only pass from a world, filled with the glory and the high praises of God, to contemplate brighter glories, and join in louder praises in the world above. This is no poetic fiction, no sick man's dream, but sober truth. Let us all, then, exert ourselves to hasten this glorious consummation. It may not greet our own, or our children's eyes; but our children's children may witness it.

SERMON VII

ANGUISH OF PARENTS AT THE PERVERSENESS OF CHILDREN.

And the king was much moved, and went up to the chamber over the gate, and wept; and as he went, thus he said, O my son Absalom! my son, my son Absalom! would God I had died for thee, O Absalom, my son, my son!—2 Samuel xviii. 33.

With the character of Absalom, his unnatural rebellion, and his untimely, but merited fate, you are all I presume acquainted. You doubtless recollect, that, being defeated in a battle which he fought, with a view to dethrone his father David, he was entangled in his flight among the boughs of an oak, and there, suspended between the heavens and the earth, was slain by his pursuers. In our text, we have an account of the manner in which his father was affected, by the tidings of his death. He was much moved, and retired to his chamber weeping, and exclaiming as he went, O Absalom, my son, my son Absalom! would God I had died for thee, O Absalom, my son, my son!

It cannot I think be doubted, at least no pious parent will doubt, that the grief which David felt on this occasion, was caused principally, though not solely, by an apprehension that his son was unprepared for death, and that of course his soul was lost forever. He knew what had been his character and conduct; he knew that he was suddenly cut off in the midst of his sins, with little or no opportunity for repentance; and he knew, for he tells us in one of his psalms, that all the wicked, and all that forget God, shall be turned into hell. He could not, therefore, but greatly fear, or rather feel almost certain, that this was the portion of his son.

It is probable, also, that the anguish occasioned by this heart-rending thought, was aggravated by the reflection, that in consequence of having neglected to restrain and correct his son, in early life, he had been indirectly the occasion of his ruin. Hence his bitter cries; hence especially his wish that he had died in his son's stead. He was himself prepared for death; and, therefore, it would have been to him a comparatively trifling evil, and he hoped, that, had Absalom lived, he might have repented of his sins, and become prepared for death. Now, all such hopes were blasted at once, and forever.

My hearers, there are two classes of persons in this assembly, to whom some reflections on the subject before us may be profitable. They may be so to the irreligious children of pious parents; and to pious parents themselves.

I. I would call to this subject the attention of every sinner present, who has a pious parent, or parents, still living. I wish to show such persons how much anguish they occasion their parents, by neglecting to prepare for death. Of this anguish such persons think, because they know, very little. It is desirable that they should know more of it because this knowledge may lead them to serious reflection, and perhaps to repentance.

Permit me then to remind those of you whom I am addressing, that the hearts, or feelings of all truly pious persons are very much alike. Every Christian parent in David's situation, would feel, in some measure, as David felt. Every Christian parent feels a similar concern for the souls, the eternal interests of his children. Your parents feel this concern for you. Consequently, your remaining in an irreligious state occasions them much unhappiness; for it is not only over a dead child that such parents weep. No, they are distressed for you now, while you are in the full enjoyment of health.

In the first place, they are distressed by apprehensions that you may be led astray by vicious companions, or become the slaves of some vicious habit, or embrace false and destructive sentiments respecting religion. They have cause to entertain such apprehensions. They have often seen the children of even pious parents fall a prey to these evils; they have seen those who in their youth were amiable, correct, and full of respect for religion, afterwards become enslaved by dissipation, intemperance, and infidelity; they know that your hearts resemble theirs, and that you are exposed to similar temptations. How can they then but be distressed for you? It will be in vain to attempt to relieve their distress by assuring them that you will never forsake the path of rectitude. They know too well, how little human resolutions and promises are worth. They have witnessed the failure of the strongest resolutions, and they have reason to fear that yours will be broken in a similar manner. They know that there is but one being who can hold you up; but one Shepherd who can keep you from wandering, and to this Shepherd they cannot persuade you to come. They have, therefore, no security that you will not become the vilest of the vile. This being the case, their anxiety must be as great as the affection which they feel for you, and as their desire to see you happy. Were these however the only dangers to which you are exposed; were you not immortal, accountable creatures, the distress which your parents feel for you would be comparatively small.

But, in the second place, they are much more distressed by fears that you will perish forever. They believe what God has said respecting the future state of those who die in their sins. They know the terrors of the Lord. They know that unless you repent, you will perish. They know that unless you are born again you cannot see the kingdom of God. They know that God is able to destroy both soul and body in hell, where their worm dieth not, and the fire is not quenched; and that he will thus destroy you, should death come and find you unprepared. Knowing these things, and loving you as they do, how great must be their anguish! How must they feel when such reflections as these crowd into their minds: Perhaps this child, whom I have so often caressed and nourished, over whom I have so often wept, and for whom I have cared and labored so much, will continue an enemy of the God who made him; will live only to fill up the measure of his iniquities, and to treasure up wrath; then die unprepared, and be miserable forever. Hence they often think of you, and weep and pray for you, when you are quietly sleeping. Hence, the more careless and thoughtless you appear, the greater is their anxiety. Hence they earnestly look and wait for some appearances of religious sensibility, notice all such appearances with delight, and feel the most painful disappointment when they vanish. In short, could you know all the sorrows which your parents have suffered since your birth, you would find that a great part of them have been occasioned by anxiety for you, for your immortal interests; and that to the same cause is to be ascribed, a great part of their daily sorrows. You can in some measure conceive what would have been the feelings of Noah, when he saw the flood approaching, had one of his sons, in defiance of all warnings and entreaties, refused to believe its approach, and enter the ark. You can conceive how greatly it would have diminished the happiness which his own safety occasioned, to look from the windows of the ark, and see a child exposed to be swept away with an ungodly world. What then must be the feelings of your parents, how greatly must it diminish the joy which their own safety occasions, to see you out of C'ist, of whom the ark was a type, and hourly exposed to the wrath, which, as a deluge, will come upon the world of the ungodly; to see that all their warnings and entreaties cannot persuade you to fly from this wrath.

The distress which you thus occasion them is further aggravated by the reflection, that if you perish, your doom will be peculiarly terrible. You have enjoyed peculiar privileges. You have been dedicated to God, you were early taught to know his will, you have often been entreated, admonished, and warned, you have enjoyed the benefits of religious example, and have been preserved from many temptations to which the children of irreligious parents are exposed. Now if notwithstanding all these privileges, you live and die without religion, how aggravated will be your guilt!—how terrible your condemnation! Yours will be the doom of one who knew his Lord's will and did it not, and who is therefore deservedly beaten with many stripes; and it will be more tolerable for Sodom and Gomorrah, in the day of judgment, than for you. All this, your parents well know, and they are sometimes almost afraid to address you on religious subjects, lest all their attempts to effect your salvation, should only serve, in consequence of your neglecting them, to aggravate your guilt and wretchedness.

In the third place, if you persist in neglecting religion, the distress which your parents now feel, may be raised to the highest pitch, by seeing you die without hope. Then they will feel as David felt, and wish like him that they could have died for you. Conceive if you can, what his feelings were. He probably recollected the joy which was occasioned by his son's birth, the delight with which the fond parents contemplated his uncommon beauty; the pleasure which they felt, when, with tottering steps he first ventured to pass from one to the other, and which was renewed when he began to lisp their names; the deep interest with which they had watched his progress from infancy up to manhood, and the hopes which they had often indulged that he would prove a comfort to them, in their old age. And now what was the end of all these pleasures and hopes? That son, the son of his affections, his joys, his hopes, endeared to him by all these tender recollections, was dead; and, what was ten thousand times worse, had died in his sins. His mangled body lay buried under a heap of stones, and his soul— O where was his immortal soul?— what was it even then suffering!

But this reflection was too terrible. As often as the agonized father's thoughts attempted to follow his son into the world of spirits, they were met and driven back by horrors of which he shuddered to think, but which he could not banish from his mind. He felt that he should never meet his son again, never —never. They were not only separated, but separated forever. And O how did the father's heart sicken with anguish, while these thoughts swiftly passed and repassed through his mind! And can any of you think, with calmness, of wringing your parents' hearts with such anguish? Yet such anguish they would feel, should they see you die unprepared. To see you die would be a sore trial to them, even though you should die the death of the righteous. It would be a trial under which they would need strong consolation. But this would be nothing, I may say rather, it would be transport, compared with the misery of seeing you die the death of the wicked; of seeing you, like him, driven away in your wickedness.

Will you then by continuing to neglect religion, prepare for that hour, the most painful hour which a parent's heart can know, this additional pang? Will you infuse new bitterness

into that cup, which is of itself sufficiently bitter? Do you reply, perhaps my parents will escape this trial by dying before
me. True; but should it be so, your neglect of religion will
give additional sharpness to their dying pangs. Could they
leave you safe in the love of a Heavenly Father, they might
leave you without a tear. But to leave you in such a world as
this without a protector, to leave you in the broad road to destruction, in that road which leads directly away from the heaven
to which they are going; to leave you uncertain whether you
will ever follow them to glory, — O this will be painful indeed.
Some present have already occasioned this pain to a dying parent. Yes, the last moments of that father, that mother, whom
you still perhaps remember, at times with a sigh or a tear, were
embittered by the thought that they left you without God in the
world, and of course without hope. And O how much more
would their last moments have been embittered, could they have
foreseen that their dying counsels, prayers, and tears would
produce no more effect upon you, and be so soon forgotten.
Will you not from this time begin to cry, God of my parents,
forgive me that I have neglected thee so long; forgive me that
I have paid no more regard to the parting advice of those whom
thou hast taken to thyself.

But to return to those whose parents are still living. You
have heard a little, and words can tell but little, of the distress
which you occasion your parents by neglecting religion. And
now permit me to ask, will you continue to occasion them this
distress? Will you expose them to the additional anguish of
seeing you die, or of dying and leaving you without hope? Is
this the only return which they deserve from you for all that
they have done and suffered for your good? Will you compel
them, after they have spent the day in laboring for your support,
to retire at night, sorrowful, and almost broken-hearted, and
water their pillow with tears? Are any so hardened as to reply,
we do not wish our parents thus to distress themselves on our
account; we see no occasion for all this anxiety. True, you do
not see it, and for this very reason they are the more anxious.
And as long as they love you, they cannot cease to be anxious.
To wish them not to feel distressed on your account, is to wish
them not to love you. Or will any reply, we see nothing in our
parents' conduct which leads us to believe that we occasion

them so much unhappiness. Alas, they dare not tell you all their feelings, nor dare they speak to you on religious subjects as often as they wish, lest it should disgust and harden you. They are aware that you do not love such subjects, and that if they are pressed upon you too frequently, the effect may be hurtful, rather than salutary. Let me then beseech you to lay these things seriously to heart, and to rejoice your parents, to excite joy in heaven, and to save your own souls, by commencing immediately and sincerely a religious life. In pressing you to do this, I seem to myself to come armed with all the efficacy of a parent's numberless prayers. And O that the God at whose feet those prayers have been poured out, may render these considerations efficacious to your salvation, and save your parents from the anguish of seeing you die in despair, and from pouring forth fruitless wishes over your remains, that they had been permitted to die in your stead.

II. I proceed now, as was proposed, to press the subject upon the attention of pious parents; for such parents may learn from it many important truths. In the first place, you may learn from it that no parent, whose children are not all pious, can be certain that they will ever become so, or certain that he shall not be called to weep over some of them, wishing that he had died in their stead. Perhaps most religious parents, when distressed with apprehensions respecting the fate of their children, endeavor to quiet these apprehensions, by hoping that, sooner or later, they will become the subjects of conversion. And sometimes they seem to take it for granted that this will actually be the case. They know that many will perish, but none of their children are to be of that number. We readily allow that if parents are conscious of doing every thing in their power to promote the salvation of their children ; if they educate them, watch over them, pray for them, as they ought, they may, with propriety hope, though they cannot be certain, that they will be converted. But perhaps those parents are most ready to indulge such hopes, who have the least right to entertain them; those I mean, who are most negligent of the souls of their children, and whose religion is in a declining state. The hopes which such parents entertain respecting the future conversion of their children, are of precisely the same nature, with the hope that every impenitent sinner entertains respecting himself. He hopes, though he has no reason for such a hope, that if conversion be necessary, he shall, sometime or other, be converted. And so these parents hope that their children will be converted, though like the sinner, they neglect their duty. But let such parents look at David, and learn that not only good men, but men eminently good, may be called to weep in anguish over a child who has died impenitent. And if this is not sufficient to convince them, let them look at the children of Eli, who were wicked to a proverb; at the sons of Samuel who walked not in his ways, and at the many other instances, mentioned in Scripture, of emienently pious parents whose children proved most abandoned characters. Surely, these instances, as well as daily observation, must convince all, that no parent can be certain that he shall not be called on to weep as David wept.

From this subject, Christian parents may learn, in the second place, the fatal consequences of neglecting their duty to their children. David, though a great man, was guilty of this neglect. It is said of Adonijah, another of his sons, that his father had not at any time displeased him, saying, why hast thou done so? and there seems to be abundant reason to believe that he indulged his other children in the same injudicious and sinful manner. Doubtless he prayed for them, and gave them religious instruction, but he did not restrain and reprove them as he ought to have done. Hence the foul sins which stained his family. Hence the conduct and fate of Absalom. While he indulged, he ruined him, and prepared bitterness for himself. See pious Eli, scourged in an equally terrible manner for the same fault. His sons made themselves vile, and he restrained them not, and therefore God says, I will judge his house forever, nor shall the iniquity of his house be purged by sacrifice or burnt-offering. Christian parents, think often of these instances; for they stand as a pillar of salt, to warn you not to neglect the duty which you owe to your children. Yet as it respects many, they seem to stand and warn almost in vain. A neglect of parental duties, or an injudicious manner of performing them, are among the most prevalent and threatening evils which are to be found among us. There is perhaps no evil which threatens more danger to the cause of religion, or to the church of God, and I may add, to the prosperity of our country. Unless the hearts of children shall be soon turned to their parents, and the hearts of parents to their children, God will certainly come and smite the land with a curse. Do you ask, what is to be done? I answer, the root of the evil, I conceive, lies here. Christian parents do not pray sufficiently for wisdom and grace, to enable them to perform their duty. They pray indeed for these blessings, but they do not pray sufficiently. They feel that ministers ought to be men of prayer; but they do not consider that to educate a family is little if any less difficult, than to perform the duty of a minister. Nay, in some respects, it is more so; for many men have been useful ministers, and yet failed greatly as parents. Even David, though he has for centuries instructed the whole church of God by his writings, failed, you perceive, in this respect. Parents, then, who would avoid this failure, must not only pray, but pray frequently and fervently, for wisdom and grace from on high, as well as for a blessing on their endeavors. If this is neglected, all the anxiety and distress which you may feel for your children will be vain, and you may see them perish.

Can you bear the thought? Look at those of them who are yet infants or in the early part of childhood. See how they depend on you, how they cling to you, in how many engaging, endearing ways, they twine themselves around your hearts. And can you bear to think of their growing up to be vicious or abandoned, to fall a prey to dissipation, debauchery, and intemperance, to live without God, and die without hope, and to become fiends hereafter? In a word, can you bear to think of being in David's situation, when he heard of Absalom's death? If not, O awake seasonably, and exert yourselves diligently. Be assured that you will find it much less difficult and painful to perform your duty, than to bear the consequences of neglecting it. But perhaps religion is in a declining state in your own hearts, and therefore you have little faith or disposition to pray. And is it so? So you remember, it once was with David. He declined, at length he fell openly, and his fall was chastised by a declaration from Jehovah, that the sword should never depart from his house. In a similar manner, your religious declensions may be punished. You may be made to suffer in the persons of your children, and to feel that remorse which David felt, when in the ruin of his son, he saw the consequence of his own folly. Believe me, believe me, Christians, or rather, believe God, you cannot become negligent in religion, without suffering for it; and if the thoughts of your own sufferings are not sufficient to rouse you, O think of your children, and be roused.

I shall conclude with a word to those parents who feel no concern for the conversion or for the souls of their children. Permit me to ask such parents, why they are thus unconcerned? Our Saviour was distressed for the Jews and wept over them. Paul felt great heaviness and continual sorrow of heart, for his unconverted countrymen. The Psalmist could say, I beheld the transgressors, and was grieved; rivers of waters ran down mine eyes, because men keep not thy law. Yet you do not feel for your own children, as they felt even for strangers. And does not this prove conclusively that you do not resemble the Saviour and his disciples, that you have no particle of the spirit which glowed in their breasts? Yes, if any thing can prove this, if any thing can prove that you do not believe the Scriptures, it is your indifference respecting the spiritual, eternal interests of your children. While you feel thus unconcerned respecting their souls, it is evident that you cannot have learned the worth of your own, nor have taken any measures to secure its salvation. But surely, if children at any time, or in any place, need the counsels, example and prayers of pious parents, they need them at such a time, and in such a town, as this. You see what multitudes of children are here growing up. You see what courses many of our youth pursue, what a pitch of wickedness many of them have already reached. Yet you cannot even pray that your children may be preserved from such courses, and the reason is, you have never learned to pray for yourselves. O, then, if you love your own souls, or the souls of your children, learn to pray, that you may go before them in the path to heaven, and perhaps they will follow.

SERMON VIII

THE GUILT AND CONSEQUENCES OF PARENTAL UNFAITHFULNESS.

For I have told him, that I will judge his house forever, for the iniquity which he knoweth: because his sons made themselves vile, and he restrained them not. And therefore I have sworn unto the house of Eli, that the iniquity of Eli's house shall not be purged with sacrifice nor offering forever. — 1 SAMUEL III. 13, 14.

THESE words compose a part of the first revelation which was made by God to his prophet Samuel. This eminent servant of Jehovah was directed to begin his ministry by denouncing God's judgments against a sin which, it seems, was but too common then, as it is now; the sin of neglecting the moral and religious education of children. It was this sin which drew down the most awful threatenings upon the house of Eli. Eli was in many respects an eminently good man; but, like many other good men, he was in this particular grossly deficient. His sons made themselves vile, and he restrained them not. We may be ready to think this a small and very pardonable offence; but God thought otherwise, and he made Eli to know that he did so in a most awful manner. Behold the days come, said he, when I will cut off thine arm, and the arm of thy father's house, that there shall not be an old man in thine house. And the man of thine, whom I shall not cut off, shall be to consume thine eyes, and to grieve thine heart; and all the increase of thy house shall die in the flower of their age. And as for thy two sons, they shall both die in one day. These awful threatenings, addressed to Eli, were farther confirmed by the ministry of Samuel. I have told Eli, that I will judge his house forever, for the iniquity which he knoweth; because his sons made themselves vile, and he restrained them not. Therefore have I sworn unto the house of Eli, that the iniquity of his house shall not be purged with sacrifice nor offering forever.

It may perhaps appear strange to some of you, my friends, that we have chosen such a subject as this for a day of public fasting and prayer. But we are not without hopes that, before we have done with the subject, you will be convinced that we could not have chosen one more important, nor more suitable to the present occasion. We are assembled this day for the purpose of humbling ourselves before God, for our personal and national sins, and praying for public and private prosperity. Now I firmly believe, that no sin is more prevalent among us, more provoking to God, or more destructive of individual, domestic, and national happiness, than that to which we propose to call your attention. Could we trace the public and private evils, which infect our otherwise happy country, to their true source, I doubt not we should find that most of them proceed from a general neglect of the moral and religious education of children. And if our civil and religious institutions should ever be subverted; and this nation should share the fate of many other once flourishing nations of the earth, our destruction, like that of the house of Eli, will have been occasioned by this very sin; a sin, which is the parent of innumerable other sins, and which, consequently, directly tends to draw down upon those nations, among whom it prevails, the judgments of offended heaven. Surely, then, no subject can be more important, or more suited to the purposes for which we are now assembled. In farther discoursing on this subject, we propose to consider the sin mentioned in our text, the punishments denounced on those who are guilty of it, and the reasons why this sin is so provoking to God, as it evidently is.

I. We are to consider the sin here mentioned. Eli's sons made themselves vile, and he restrained them not. It is not said that he set them a bad example. It is evident, on the contrary, that his example was good. Nor is he accused of neglecting to admonish them; for we are told that he reproved them in a very solemn and affectionate manner, and warned them of the danger of continuing to pursue vicious courses. In this respect he was much less culpable than many parents at the present day; for not a few set before their children an example positively bad; and still more entirely neglect to admonish and reprove them. But though Eli admonished, he did not restrain his children. He did not employ the authority with which he was clothed, as a parent, to prevent them from indulging their depraved inclinations. This is the only sin of which he is accused; and yet this was sufficient to bring guilt and misery upon himself, and entail ruin upon his posterity.

Of the same sin those parents are now guilty, who suffer their children to indulge, without restraint, those sinful propensities to which childhood and youth are but too subject; and which, when indulged, render them vile in the sight of God. Among the practices which thus render children vile, are a quarrelsome, malicious disposition, disregard to truth, excessive indulgence of their appetites, neglect of the Bible and religious institutions, profanation of the Sabbath, profane, scurrilous, or indecent language, wilful disobedience, associating with openly vicious company, taking the property of their neighbors, and idleness which naturally leads to every thing bad. From all these practices it is in the power of parents to restrain their children in a very considerable degree, if they employ the proper means; at least, it is in the power of all to make the attempt, and to persevere in it so long as children remain under the paternal roof; and those who neglect to do this, those who know, or who might know, that their children are beginning to practise any of these vices, without steadily and perseveringly using all proper exertions, to restrain and correct them, are guilty of the sin mentioned in the text. Nor will a few occasional reproofs and admonitions, given to children, free parents from the guilt of partaking in their sins. No, they must be restrained; restrained with a mild and prudent, but firm and steady hand; restrained early, while they may be formed to habits of submission, obedience, and diligence; and the reins of government must never, for a moment, be slackened, much less given up into their hands, as is too often the case. Nor will even this excuse those parents who neglect family religion, and the religious instruction of their children, and who do not frequently pray for the blessing of heaven upon their endeavors. If we neglect our duty to our heavenly Father, we surely cannot wonder or complain, if he suffers our children to neglect their duty to us; nor, if we do not ask his blessing, have we any reason to complain should it be withheld. In this, as in all other cases, exertion without prayer, and prayer without exertion are equally vain. To sum up all in a word, every parent who is not as careful of the morals, as he is of the health of his children; every one who takes more care of the literary, than of the moral and religious education of his children, is certainly guilty of the sin mentioned in our text. How much more criminal, then, are those parents who set before their children an irreligious, or vicious example; who join with the great enemy of their peace in tempting them to sin, and thus, instead of restraining, inflame and strengthen their sinful propensities. The parent who starves or poisons his children, is innocent in the sight of God, compared with one who thus entices them into the path of ruin.

Having thus briefly considered the sin mentioned in our text, I proceed to notice,

II. The punishments denounced against those who are guilty of it. It will soon appear, that these punishments, like most of those with which God threatens mankind, are the natural consequences of the sin against which they are denounced.

In our text these punishments are denounced in a general way. I have told Eli, that I will judge his house forever, for the iniquity which he knoweth. The particular judgments here alluded to, are described more at large in the preceding chapter, to which this passage evidently refers. God there declares to Eli,

1. That most of his posterity should die early, and that none of them should live to see old age. The increase of thy house, says he, shall die in the flower of their age, and there shall not be an old man in thine house forever. Now it is too evident to require proof, that the sin, of which Eli was guilty, naturally tends to produce the consequence which is here threatened as a punishment. When youth are permitted to make themselves vile, without restraint, they almost inevitably fall into courses which tend to undermine their constitutions, and shorten their days. It is indeed a well known fact that, in populous towns,

comparatively few live to become aged, and that a much larger proportion of mankind, especially of the male sex who are most exposed to the influence of temptation, die in the flower or meridian of their days, than in the country where parental discipline is less generally neglected, and youth are under greater restraints. If parents wished that their sons should drag out a short life of debility and disease, and die before they reach half the common age of man, they could not adopt measures better calculated to produce this effect, than to cast loose the reins of parental authority, and suffer them to follow their own inclinations, and associate with vicious companions without restraint. We may, therefore, consider the premature death of ungoverned children, as the natural consequence, as well as the usual punishment, of parental neglect.

2. In the second place, God declares to Eli, that such of his children as were spared should prove a grief and vexation, rather than a comfort to him. The man of thine, whom I shall not cut off, shall be to consume thine eyes, and to grieve thine heart. How terribly this threatening was fulfilled in the case of Eli, you need not be told. Nor was it less terribly fulfilled in the family of David. Though he was in many respects an eminently good man, yet with respect to the government of his children he was grossly deficient. We are told respecting one of his children, that his father had not displeased him at any time, saying, Wherefore hast thou done so? We may then conclude that he was equally culpable in his treatment of his other children. And what was the consequence? One of his sons committed incest with his sister, and was in revenge barbarously murdered in cool blood by his brother Absalom. This same Absalom afterwards rebelled against his father, compelled him to fly for his life, and was cut off in the flower of his age, and in the midst of his sins. A third son rebelled against him in his old age, and endeavored to wrest the sceptre from his feeble hands. How keen were the sufferings which this conduct of his children occasioned, we may infer from his bitter lamentation on account of the death of Absalom. O, my son, my son Absalom! would to God I had died for thee, my son, my son! Well therefore might it be said of him that his children were to consume his eyes, and to grieve his heart. The fact is, this part of the threatened punishment, like the former, is the nat-

ural and almost inevitable consequence of the sin, against which it is denounced. If parents indulge their children in infancy and childhood, and do not restrain them when they make themselves vile, it is almost impossible that they should not pursue courses and contract habits, which will render them as bitterness to their fathers, and a sorrow of heart to those that bore them. If such parents are pious, their hearts will probably be grieved, and their eyes consumed with tears, to see their children rebelling against God and plunging into eternal ruin. If they are not pious, and care nothing for the future happiness of their children, they will still probably have the grief of seeing them idle, dissolute, undutiful, bad husbands, bad fathers, and bad members of society; for it can scarcely be expected that he, who is a bad son, will act his part well in any other relation of life. Especially will such parents usually meet with unkindness and neglect from their children, if they live to be dependent on them in their old age. It is in this, as in almost every other instance, the case that, as a man sows, so he must reap. They that sow the seeds of vice in the minds of their children, or who suffer them to be sown by others, and to grow without restraint, will almost invariably be compelled to reap, and to eat with many tears the bitter harvest which those seeds tend to produce.

3. In the third place, God forewarns Eli, that his posterity should be poor and contemptible. They that despise me, says he, shall be lightly esteemed ; and it shall come to pass that every one that is left in thy house shall come and crouch to another for a piece of silver and a morsel of bread. Here again we see the natural consequences of Eli's sin in its punishment. Children who are not well instructed and restrained by their parents, will almost inevitably in such a place as this, contract habits of idleness, instability, and extravagance, which naturally lead to poverty and contempt. Were we well acquainted with the private history of those individuals among us, who are idle, intemperate, unstable and despised, we should probably find that in almost every instance, they were the children of parents who neglected to restrain them when they made themselves vile.

Lastly; God declares that none of the methods thus appointed to obtain the pardon of sin, should avail to procure pardon for the iniquity of his house; I have sworn unto Eli, that the iniquity of his house shall not be purged away by sacrifice nor offering forever. This awful threatening conveyed a plain intimation that his children should die in their sins; and, of course be miserable forever. This too was the natural consequence of his conduct. He had suffered them to follow without restraint those courses which rendered them unfit for heaven, until their day of grace was past, and the door of mercy forever closed against them. They were now given up to a hard heart and reprobate mind. They could not now be brought to repentance; and, of course, no sacrifice or offering could purge away their sins. My friends, it is still the same, and there can be no room to doubt, that there are thousands now in the regions of despair, and thousands more on their way to join them, who will forever curse their parents, as the authors of their misery.

My friends, the terrible punishments denounced against this sin sufficiently show that it is exceedingly displeasing in the sight of God. Let us then inquire as was proposed.

II. Why it is so? To this we answer, it is so,

1. Because it proceeds from very wicked and hateful principles. Actions take their character in the sight of God principally from the motives and dispositions in which they originate. Now there is scarcely any sin which proceeds from worse principles and more hateful dispositions than this. For instance, sometimes it proceeds from the love and the practice of vice. Openly vicious and profligate parents, who do not restrain themselves, cannot, of course, but be ashamed to restrain their children. Such parents, whatever their children may do, dare not reprove them, lest they should hear them reply, Physician, heal thyself. In other instances, this sin is occasioned by secret impiety and infidelity. Those who live without God in the world, who think his power of no consequence, and feel not the force of those motives, which the Scriptures present to us, will be disposed to view the sins of their children with a favorable eye, and consider them as merely the common foibles of youth, which require little censure or restraint, and which they will renounce voluntarily. Even if such parents sometimes restrain the grosser vices of their children, they will give them no religious instruction; they will never pray for them, for they never pray for themselves; and without religious instruction

and prayer, little or nothing effectual can be done. But in religious parents, this sin almost invariably proceeds from indolence and selfishness. They love their own ease too well to employ that constant care and exertion, which are necessary to restrain their children, and educate them as they ought. They cannot bear to correct them, or put them to pain; not because they love their children, but because they love themselves, and are unwilling to endure the pain of inflicting punishment, and of seeing their children suffer; though they cannot but be sensible, that their happiness requires it.

There is also much unbelief, much contempt of God, and much positive disobedience in this sin. Parents are as expressly and as frequently commanded to restrain, to correct, and instruct their children, as to perform any other duty whatever. Great promises are made to the performance of this duty; awful threatenings are denounced against the neglect of it. Yet all these motives prove ineffectual. The commands are disobeyed, the promises and threatenings are disbelieved and disregarded, and thus parents honor their children more than God, and seek their own ease rather than his pleasure, as Eli is said to have done. It appears, then, that this sin proceeds from open wickedness, which renders parents ashamed to restrain their children; or from impiety and infidelity, which causes them to think it needless; or from indolence and selfishness, which make them unwilling to do it. Now these are some of the worst principles of our depraved nature; and therefore we need not wonder that a sin, which proceeds from such sources, is exceedingly displeasing to God.

2. This sin is exceedingly displeasing to God, because, so far as it prevails, it entirely frustrates his design in establishing the family state. We are taught, that he at first formed one man and one woman, and united them in marriage, that he might seek a Godly seed. But this important design is entirely frustrated by those parents who neglect the moral and religious education of their children; and therefore God cannot but be greatly displeased with a sin which renders his benevolent measures for our happiness unavailing.

3. God is greatly displeased with this sin on account of the good which it prevents, and the infinite evil which it produces. He has taught us, that children properly educated will be good

and happy, both here and hereafter. He has also taught us that children, whose education is neglected, will probably be temporally and eternally miserable. At least, it will not be owing to their parents, if they are not. He also compels us to learn from observation and experience, that innumerable evils and miseries do evidently result from this sin; that the happiness of families is destroyed; that the peace of society is disturbed; that the prosperity of nations is subverted, and that immortal souls are ruined by its effects. Now the anger of God against any sin, is in proportion to the evils and the misery which it tends to produce. But it is evident that no sin tends to produce more evils, or greater misery than this. It is the fruitful parent of thousands of other sins, and entails ruin upon our descendants to the third and fourth generation. With no sin, therefore, has God more reason to be angry than with this.

Lastly; this sin is exceedingly displeasing to him, because those who are guilty of it break over the most powerful restraints, and act a most unnatural part. He knew that it would not be safe to entrust such creatures as we are with the education of immortal souls, unless we had powerful inducements to be faithful to the trust. He, therefore, implanted in the hearts of parents a strong and tender affection for their offspring, and a most ardent desire for their happiness, that they might thus be induced to educate them as they ought. But those who neglect to restrain their children, do violence to this powerful operative principle, and may be said to be like the heathen, without natural affection. It is true they may have a kind of blind fondness for their offspring, like that of the irrational animals; but it does not at all resemble a virtuous, enlightened affection, and is altogether unworthy of a rational, and still more of a Christian parent; and, therefore, instead of prompting them to seek the real happiness of their children, it is but too often made an excuse for neglecting it.

Thus, my friends, have we endeavored to describe the sin mentioned in our text, with its punishment, and the reasons why it is so exceedingly displeasing to God. And now let us improve the subject,

1. By inquiring whether the sin does not greatly prevail among ourselves. But inquiry is needless. It most evidently does. I am inclined to believe that it is the greatest and most

provoking sin among us. And, my friends, you must allow that the speaker has had sufficient opportunity to form something of a correct opinion on this subject. He has resided in this place three years as an instructor of youth, and almost nine years as a preacher of the gospel. In this capacity he has had free access to families of every class, in all circumstances, and he has had very considerable opportunities of witnessing the manner in which children are treated; he has felt disposed to avail himself of these opportunities, and he is constrained to declare thus publicly, that he has found but comparatively few families in which there is not a gross and evident neglect of the moral and religious education of children. He has but too often witnessed in his parochial visits attempts to restrain children, while he was present; attempts, which were evidently unusual, and which were of course unsuccessful, and which only proved that the children, and not the parents, ruled. But it is needless to mention these circumstances. Our streets, and the vicious conduct of but too many of our youth are open witnesses against many among us, that their sons make themselves vile and they restrain them not. You well know that it is almost impossible to walk our streets, without having the ear wounded by profane and indecent expressions from lips which have but just learned to speak. You need not be told, at least many of you need not, that there are many haunts of intemperance and every kind of wickedness in this town, to which boys resort to learn and practice the vices of men; where they soon learn to glory in their shame, and to get rid betimes of the troublesome restraints and reproaches of conscience. You need not be told, that our annual days of fasting are, by many of the young, considered and treated as days set apart for sinful and almost riotous amusement, and that the language of their conduct seems to be, We are determined to fill up the measure of our national sins, as fast as our parents empty it. In fact, I suspect that there is more sin committed on our days of fasting, than on almost any other day of the year. But it is needless to enlarge. My very soul sickens to think of the dreadful proofs of youthful wickedness and profligacy, which I almost daily hear or witness. Surely, if it be true, that a child trained up in the way he should go will not depart from it, but few, very few indeed of the rising generation are thus trained. I would not, however, be understood to mean, that all, or even a large proportion of the vicious children in this town are the children of this society. I do not now particularly recollect any one that is so. But, my friends, are there not many, even among us, who are grossly deficient in this respect, many whose sons make themselves vile, many who suffer their children to associate with vile companions and they restrain them not? Are there not many, who have already suffered some of the punishments with which the house of Eli was visited? Are there none, who have reason to fear that their children were cut off by an untimely death, the consequence, at least in some degree, of a neglected education? Are there none, whose children survive only to consume their eyes and grieve their hearts by their misconduct, and cause them bitterly to lament the consequences of their neglect now, when it is too late to repair it? It is indescribably painful to tear open the bleeding wounds of such parents, if such there are; but it must be done, if it be only to bring them to repentance and the enjoyment of pardon. It seems that if any sin calls for repentance, this especially does; and it becomes all of us, who are parents, to humble ourselves before God for our innumerable deficiencies, and to beg that he will not visit our sins upon our children. It may perhaps be too late with many to reform now. The children have become too old to be controlled; they have left the paternal roof, and perhaps gone to the world of spirits. The mischief is done and cannot be remedied. My friends, if any thing can convince you of the need of an atonement, it must be this. Suppose a parent, by neglect or by bad example, has ruined his children; they die in their sins, and go to the judgment seat. After their death, suppose their criminal parent is brought to repentance, what can clear him from guilt? what can wash away his sin? He has destroyed an immortal soul, the soul of his own child; a soul which God committed to his care, and of which he will demand an account. Now what account can such a parent render? What atonement can he make to God for destroying one of his creatures? to that God who declares that he will require blood for blood, life for life, of every one who unlawfully takes away the life of a fellow creature? Will his tears, his repentance restore the dead to life, or save the soul which he has ruined? No; nor would it avail should he offer thousands of rams, or ten thousands of rivers of oil; for God expressly declared that the sin of Eli's house should not be purged with offering nor sacrifice forever. What then can take away the guilt, and procure the pardon of such a parent? Is there any way, or must he perish? There is a way. The blood of Christ cleanseth from all sin; and surely such a parent needs it all, nor could any thing short of this precious atoning blood, make satisfaction for this irreparable mischief which his neglect has occasioned. If then there be any present, who are guilty of this sin, any, who fear that by their bad example, or their neglect, they have occasioned the ruin of an immortal soul, we would point them to Christ for relief and pardon. By his blood even those who have destroyed others may themselves be saved from destruction, if their repentance be sincere; for he has declared that all manner of sin and blasphemy, not committed against the Holy Ghost, shall be forgiven to the penitent. But if any, who are guilty of this sin, do not repent and apply to the Saviour for pardon, the oath of God stands against them, that their iniquity shall not be purged forever. My friends, let all who are parents think of this, and beware of this ruinous, this aggravated, this almost unpardonable sin. Chasten thy son, says the wise man, while there is yet hope, nor let thy soul spare for his crying; for he that spareth correction hateth his son, but he that loveth him will chasten him betimes. Thou shalt scourge him with the rod, and shalt deliver his soul from hell.

2. If there are any children or youth now present, whose parents do not restrain them, and who make themselves vile by indulging in vicious or sinful practices, they may learn from this subject, what will be their fate, unless repentance prevent. Children and youth, I am now speaking to you. You are deeply interested in this subject. Remember the character and the fate of Eli's sons. They made themselves vile, and God slew them. Remember that a quarrelsome temper, disobedience to parents, idleness, neglect of the Sabbath, and the Bible, profane and indecent language, falsehood, and every kind of vicious indulgence, render you vile in the sight of God, and are the high road to poverty and contempt in this world, and everlasting wretchedness in the next. Remember too that, if your parents do not forbid, and punish you for these sins, that will not excuse you in the sight of God. Eli did not restrain his sons, and yet

God destroyed them. But if any of you, who have religious parents, pursue such courses in defiance of their admonitions, your doom will be still worse. There is no more certain fore-runner of ruin in this world and the next, than habitual disregard to the counsels and warnings of such parents. We are told that Eli's sons hearkened not to their father, because the Lord would slay them; and if any children present refuse to obey their parents, it gives reason to fear that God intends, in like manner, to destroy them.

Excellent.
America-wake up
The Sermon is for you!

SERMON IX

THE INIQUITY OF THE FATHERS VISITED UPON THEIR CHILDREN.

Visiting the iniquity of the fathers upon the children, and upon the children's children, unto the third and fourth generation.—Exodus xxxiv. 7.

In this passage we have a part of the name of Jehovah, as proclaimed by himself. In the preceding chapter we find Moses praying for a manifestation of those attributes in which the divine glory essentially consists. I beseech thee, said he, show me thy glory. This request God answered by saying, I will make all my goodness to pass before thee; and will proclaim before thee the name of the Lord. This promise he fulfilled. The Lord, says the inspired penman, descended in a cloud, and proclaimed the name of the Lord. And the Lord passed by before him, and proclaimed, JEHOVAH, JEHOVAH GOD, merciful and gracious, long suffering, and abundant in goodness and truth; keeping mercy for thousands; forgiving iniquity, transgression and sin; and by no means clearing the guilty; visiting the iniquity of the fathers upon the children, and upon the children's children, unto the third and fourth generation. On hearing this adorable name, thus proclaimed, Moses made haste, and bowed his head, and worshipped; thus expressing his cordial acquiescence in all that God had revealed respecting his character, and the maxims of his government. Every one who possesses the temper of Moses, will feel disposed, on hearing

this name, to follow his example. But it is more than probable
that all present do not possess his temper; and that some, on
hearing that part of God's name which has been read as our
text, will rather feel disposed to ask, how can it be just, how
can it be made to appear consistent with our ideas of perfect
rectitude, for God to visit the iniquity of men upon their posterity; or, as the expression evidently means, to punish children,
and children's children, for the sins of their parents? To answer
these questions by stating the true import of the passage, and
showing that the method of proceeding, which it describes, is
perfectly just, is my design in the present discourse.

With this view, I remark,

1. That this passage has no reference whatsoever, to God's
treatment of mankind, in a future state. It does not mean that
God will punish children in a future state for the sins of their
parents; but the visitation or punishment which it threatens, is
exclusively temporal. [This is evident from a passage in the
eighteenth chapter of Ezekiel, when God, speaking of the death
to which his law dooms transgressors, says, The soul that sinneth, it shall die. The son shall not bear the iniquity of the
father, neither shall the father bear the iniquity of the son. In
another passage, he says, The fathers shall not die for their
children, neither shall the children die for the fathers; but every
man shall die for his own sin.) The same truth is clearly taught
in the many passages which assure us, that, at the judgment
day, God will reward every man according to his works. Not,
you will observe, according to the works of his parents, but
according to his own works; nor is the smallest intimation to be
found in the Bible, that, in dispensing eternal rewards and punishments, God will pay any regard to the conduct of a man's
ancestors, whatever it may have been. I remark,

2. That God never visits children even with temporal judgments for the sins of their parents, unless they imitate, and thus
justify their parents' offences. This, he himself declares, in the
most positive and unequivocal manner. The impious Jews,
while suffering the just punishment of their own offences, made
use of this proverb; The fathers have eaten sour grapes, and
the children's teeth are set on edge; that is, our fathers have
sinned, and we, their children, are punished for it. They thus
justified themselves by insinuating that the calamities which

they suffered were not the consequence of their own conduct, and at the same time, accused God of injustice. The ways of the Lord, said they, are not equal, or equitable. For this impious and groundless complaint, God severely reproves them, declares that they shall no more use this proverb, and shows, in the clearest manner, that they had no cause to use it. He assures these murmurers that, if a wicked man has a son who seeth all his father's sins, and considereth and doeth them not, but executeth God's judgments, and walketh in his statutes, he shall not die for the iniquity of his father, but shall surely live. With this assurance, the divine conduct, as described in the Old Testament, corresponds. Hezekiah, Josiah, and many other pious men were the children of exceedingly wicked parents; but as they shunned the sins of their fathers, and were supremely devoted to God, they enjoyed his favor in a very high degree, and were visited with no marks of displeasure on account of their progenitors.

There is, however, one apparent exception to these remarks, which must be noticed. It is evident from facts, that even pious children often suffer in consequence of the wicked conduct of their parents. If a father be idle, or extravagant; if he squander his property by gaming, or intemperance, or destroy his reputation by scandalous crimes, or ruin his constitution by sensual indulgences; his children, and perhaps his children's children, may suffer in consequence; nor will any degree of piety always shield them from such sufferings. Those sufferings ought not, however, to be considered as punishments inflicted by God; but merely as the natural consequences of their parents' misconduct; and even these consequences, though painful, will be overruled for their benefit; for all things work together for good to them that love God. It must, however, be added, that the sinful example and conduct of wicked parents *unsaved* has a most powerful tendency to prevent their children from becoming pious, to induce them to pursue vicious courses, and thus to bring upon them divine judgments. Such parents seldom, if ever, give their children good advice, or a religious education, but suffer them to grow up, almost without restraint, with a bad example in its most influential form, ever before their eyes. Hence, wickedness often descends in families from generation to generation, becoming more deep and inveterate as

it descends, till long delayed vengeance overtakes the guilty
race, and blots their very name from the earth.   I remark,

3. That our text describes God's method of proceeding with
nations, and civil or ecclesiastical communities, rather than with
individuals.   I do not say that it has *no* reference to individuals, but that it refers principally to nations, states and churches.
It seems designed to teach us that God often visits one generation with national judgments, on account of the sins of preceding
generations; or in other words, that in punishing a nation, at
one period of its existence, he has respect to sins of which it
had been guilty during former periods.   For instance, when he
doomed the Canaanites to destruction, he had respect not only
to the sins of that generation which was destroyed, but to all
the sins of which the nation had been guilty, from the commencement of its political existence.   This is evident from his
informing Abraham that the Canaanites could not be immediately destroyed, because their iniquity was not then full; but
that after four generations should have passed away, their measure would be full, and their destruction would be effected.   In
a similar manner he dealt with the Amalekites.   That nation
made a cruel, treacherous, and unprovoked assault upon the
Israelites in the wilderness.   God then declared that he would
punish the nation of Amalek for that offence; but the punishment was deferred for some hundreds of years, and was then
inflicted with awful severity; and the destruction of the Amalekites which then took place, was expressly stated to be on account of the sin committed so many years before, by a preceding
generation.

By similar maxims God was governed, in his dealings with
the Jews.   The Babylonish captivity was designed as a punishment, not only for the sins of that generation, which was
actually carried away, but for the sins of the preceding generation.   And so the present dispersion of the Jews, with all the
calamities which, for eighteen hundred years, have overwhelm-
ed that devoted people, is a continued expression of the divine
displeasure against the sin of which their fathers were guilty, in
crucifying the Son of God, of whom they said, His blood be on
us and on our children.   Our Saviour himself said to that generation, by whom he was crucified, Fill ye up the measure of
your fathers, that upon you may come all the righteous blood,

shed from the foundation of the world; from the blood of righteous Abel to the blood of Zacharias whom ye slew between the temple and the altar. That we may perceive the justice, wisdom and propriety of this method of proceeding, it is necessary to consider the following things.

It is indispensably necessary to the perfection of God's moral government that it should extend to nations and communities, as well as to individuals. This, I conceive, is too evident to require proof; for how could God be considered as the moral governor of the world, if nations and communities were exempt from his government? Again, if God is to exercise a moral government, over nations and communities, by rewarding or punishing them according to their works, the rewards and punishments must evidently be dispensed, in this world; for nations and communities will not exist, as such, in the world to come. In that world, God must deal with men, considered simply as individuals. Further, it seems evidently proper, that communities as well as individuals, should have a time of trial and probation allowed them; that if the first generation prove sinful, the community should not be immediately destroyed, but that the punishment should be suspended, till it be seen whether the nation will prove incorrigible, or whether some succeeding generation will not repent of the national sins, and thus avert national judgments. Now it is evident, that if God thus waits upon nations, as he does upon individuals, and allows them a season of probation, a space for repentance, he cannot destroy them, until many generations of sinners are laid in their graves. Besides, by thus suspending the rod, or the sword over a nation, he presents to it powerful inducements to reform. He appeals to parental feelings, to men's affection for their posterity; and endeavors to deter them from sin, by the assurance that their posterity will suffer for it. In connection with these remarks, we must recollect, what has been already stated, that God never punishes a generation for the sins of its ancestors, unless it imitates their conduct, unless it is guilty of similar or more aggravated offences, and thus justifies the wicked conduct of preceding generations. Besides, as sinful nations, like individuals, if they do not reform, usually become worse, it will ever be found that the last days of a nation, are its worst days, and that the generation which is destroyed, is more abandoned than

all preceding generations.   I will only add, that when God forsakes or destroys a nation, for its national sins, he does not inflict
more upon that generation which is destroyed, than its own sins
deserve, though he punishes them more severely than he would
have done, were it not for the guilt which has been accumula-
ted by the generations which have preceded it.   From these
statements and considerations, I conceive that not only the
justice, but the wisdom and propriety of the divine proceedings,
must appear evident to every calm and unprejudiced mind.   If
doubts respecting it still remain, permit me to attempt their re-
moval by the following statement.

Suppose that from the commencement of our existence as a
nation, some other nation had without provocation treated us in
the most hostile and injurious manner, interrupting our commerce, murdering our fellow-citizens, and finally, forcibly seiz-
ing, and unjustly retaining a part of our territory.   Suppose the
generation by whom these acts of hostility were committed, to
be all laid in their graves, and a new generation to succeed,
who, instead of making any reparation for the injuries we had
sustained from their fathers, should repeat the same injuries,
and retain the territory which they had unjustly acquired :
Should we not feel that we had just cause of complaint against
this new generation ; that they were, in effect, accessaries in
the crimes of their fathers, and deserving of the punishment
due to those crimes ?   And supposing war, in any case, to be
just, should we not feel it just to make war upon that nation,
at any succeeding period of its existence, so long as its offences
were repeated, and the territory which it had unjustly acquired
was retained ?   My hearers, God's visiting the iniquities of the
fathers upon the children, implies no more than is involved in
this supposition.   Who then will deny his method of proceeding
to be just ?

My hearers, the subject we have been considering, would, at
any time, be interesting and instructive, but there is something
in our present situation, which renders it, at this time, peculiarly so.   As a community, we are just entering on a new mode
of political existence.   We are now separated from our parent
State, and have no further concern in its sins or its virtues, except what results from our connection with it, as members of
the Union.   But though we have no other concern with the sins

of which it may hereafter be guilty, it is evident from our subject that we are still deeply interested in the sinfulness and guilt contracted by that State, during the period of our political connection with it.   In that sinfulness we shared; in accumulating that guilt we assisted, and should God visit our parent State for its sins, we must expect to share in the visitation, unless previous repentance and reform prevent.   Had the State, at the period of our separation, been burdened with a debt which it was unable to discharge, we must have been charged with our proportion of it; and the same remark will apply to the debt which is due to divine justice.   It becomes us, then, to look back and inquire of what sins the State was guilty during our connection with it.   With respect to the primitive fathers, or first settlers of the State, it was intimated in the morning, that they were, in a very uncommon degree, devoted to God.   No other nation can boast of such ancestors, to no other nation has so small a share of guilt been transmitted by its founders.   But it is too evident to require proof, that our immediate ancestor have sunk very far below the standard of their forefathers.   The progress of those vices which principally tend to draw down divine judgments upon a people, has been constant, rapid, and highly alarming.   Dissipation, intemperance, profanation of the Sabbath, neglect of divine institutions, and profane language have burst in upon us like an overwhelming flood.   The prevalence of perjury, or false swearing, is, if possible, still more alarming.   To say nothing of the little regard paid, in many cases, to oaths of office, how terribly have our commercial transactions, for some years, been polluted by this crime! Of what palpable perjuries have great numbers of our fellow-citizens been guilty, both at home and in foreign lands; and how largely have those who employed them, participated in the guilt! We may think little of this, and flatter ourselves that customary oaths are trifles; but be assured, my hearers, that when God is, on any occasion, called to bear witness to a transaction, he witnesses it; and wo be to the wretch who calls upon the God of truth to bear witness to a lie.   God will not hold him guiltless who taketh his name in vain; nor will he hold a nation or community guiltless in which this sin prevails.   Even you, my hearers, would think it the greatest of insults should a man impudently call upon you to testify to the truth of a

known lie. With what feelings, then, must the God of truth
hear himself so frequently called upon to bear such testimony?

But to return from what is, perhaps, a digression; — if these
and other sins have grossly prevailed, in our parent State, and
in this part of it, during the period of our political union, then,
unless we repent of these sins; and much more, if we persist
in them, we may be certain that God will, sooner or later, visit
upon us the iniquity of our fathers. We shall commence our
separate existence with our measure of iniquity partly filled,
and our own sins will soon fill it to the brim.

In the second place, this subject will teach us not only to reflect upon the past, but to look forward to the future. If God
in his dealings with civil communities, visits the sins of parents
upon their children, then he will visit our sins upon our children.
We shall suffer for them in the world to come, and they will
suffer for them in this world. We often speak of acting for our
posterity, of providing for their happiness; but in no way can
we promote their happiness so effectually, as by abstaining from
sin; in no way can we do more to destroy it, than by continuing in sin. We profess to have been actuated, partly at least,
if not principally, by a concern for their interest, in seeking the
separation which has taken place. But what will it avail for
them to be a separate State, if we indirectly separate them from
the favor and blessing of heaven? What will it avail to bequeath to them our civil and religious privileges, if the bequest,
in consequence of our sins, is accompanied with heaven's curse?
A measure of iniquity nearly full is a terrible inheritance to
bequeath to posterity. Yet such an inheritance we shall certainly transmit to them, unless a more general reformation,
than there seems any reason to expect, should prevent. May
God have mercy upon our posterity, for I fear we shall have
none.

In the third place, this subject may be interesting and instructive to many of us, not only as members of the community to
which we belong, but as individuals. Are there any present,
who are descended from a long line of irreligious ancestors;
who can scarcely find, among their progenitors, one devoted servant of God? Surely, such have reason to tremble, lest a curse
should be entailed upon a race, which has been so long estran-

ged from God. Are there any whose immediate ancestors have lived without God, in the world? Let such remember that if they would not be visited for the sins of their fathers, they must forsake their fathers' sinful ways. Are there any, who, while their parents remain strangers to God, have been led to know and serve him themselves? What reason have such to bless and adore the sovereign mercy, which, instead of leaving them under the load of derived and personal guilt, has visited them with salvation. Are there parents present, who know not God? It surely becomes them to lay this subject seriously to heart, lest they should treasure up wrath for their descendants. Let me entreat such parents to reflect how soothing, how delightful it must be to be able, in their expiring moments, to bequeath to their children, and their children's children, the blessing of a pious father; to be able, with dying Jacob, to say, The God of my fathers, the God who has fed me all my life long, the Angel who redeemed me from all evil, bless my children, and be their God. Surely, if there be a delightful spectacle on earth, it is that of a dying father, who after having guided his children in the way of peace by his principles and example, expires while the blessing which he bequeaths to them, trembles on his lips. On the other hand, what sight can be more dreadful than that of a dying sinner,—his own gloomy prospect rendered ten-fold more dismal by the reflection that his own children are involved for time, perhaps for eternity, in the consequences of his transgressions.

SERMON X

AN EARLY INTEREST IN GOD'S MERCY ESSENTIAL TO A HAPPY LIFE.

O satisfy us early with thy mercy; that we may rejoice and be glad all our days. — PSALM xc. 14.

My hearers, should all the youth in this assembly express sincerely their secret wishes and inclinations, it can scarcely be doubted, that many of them would say something like this; I should wish to live a long life, to be allowed to spend it in worldly pleasures and pursuits, and then, just before its termination, to be converted, and prepared for death. Such, indeed, it is evident, must be the wishes of every person, who, while he is convinced that religion is necessary, does not love it; for while he does not love religion, while he regards a religious life as a life of unhappiness, he will, of course, wish to defer the commencement of such a life, as long as he can, consistently with his own safety. My youthful hearers, am I wrong in supposing that such are your wishes? Am I wrong in supposing, that if it were submitted to your choice, whether your conversion should take place now, or at the close of life, many, if not most of you, would choose the latter? If such would be your choice, your feelings evidently differ widely from those by which the pious writer of our text was actuated. He exclaims, O satisfy us early with thy mercy, that we may rejoice and be glad all our days.

By the mercy of God is here evidently intended, his pardoning mercy. But God's pardoning mercy is extended, as the psalmist well knew, to none but the penitent, but those who have really commenced a religious life. And he knew that none can obtain such manifestations of this mercy as will satisfy them, except those who pursue a religious course with zeal and diligence. When he said, O satisfy us early with thy mercy, he did, therefore, in effect say, Incline us early to enter on a religious course of life, and to pursue it with such zeal and diligence, as shall afford us satisfactory evidence, that we are indeed the children of God, partakers of his mercy, and heirs of his salvation. The psalmist then, it appears, thought it highly desirable, that men should seek and obtain God's mercy; or, in other words, commence a religious course, in early life,— as early as possible. The reason which he assigns for the opinion is particularly worthy of remark. O satisfy us early with thy mercy; why? that we may be happy hereafter? No; but that we may live happily here; that we may rejoice and be glad all our days. This language evidently and forcibly intimates, that if the young early seek and obtain God's pardoning mercy, the way will be prepared for them to rejoice and be glad all their days. And it intimates with equal clearness, that, if they do not early seek and obtain mercy, joy and gladness cannot attend them. Or, to express the same sentiments in different language, he who in early youth commences and diligently pursues, a religious course, will be happy through life; but he who does not, at that period, commence a religious life, will not live happily, even though he should subsequently become religious. That these intimations are perfectly accordant with truth; that every man who wishes to rejoice and be glad all his days, must early seek and obtain God's pardoning mercy, it is my present design to show. With this view I remark,

1. That a man may live happily, that he may rejoice and be glad all his days, it is necessary that he should be early freed from all fears of death. That a man who is subject to such fears, who regards with dread an event which is constantly approaching, to which he is every moment exposed, and from which it is impossible to escape, cannot be happy, it is needless to prove. But every man who has not sought and obtained God's pardoning mercy is, in a greater or less degree, subject to

such fears. Nor is this any proof of weakness. It is perfectly reasonable that he should entertain such fears, that he should regard death as an evil greatly to be dreaded; for, to such a man, it must be the greatest of all evils, since it will separate him forever from every thing which he values or loves. And the more prosperous he is, the more his honors, friends and possessions increase, the more reason he has to fear an event which will strip him of them all. O death, exclaims an apocryphal writer, how terrible are the thoughts of thee to a man who is at ease in his possessions. Indeed, could we look into the hearts of men, we should probably find that nothing so much embitters life to them, as apprehensions of death. And how is a sinner, who has no interest in God's mercy, to free himself from such apprehensions? Will it be said, he may refuse to think of death? I answer, he cannot always banish this subject from his thoughts in a world like this, where so many things occur which are suited to remind him of it. Scarcely a day passes in which he does not meet with something which forces upon him a conviction, that he is mortal; that he is constantly approaching the grave, and liable every moment to fall into it. But from this cause of unhappiness, the man who early obtains satisfactory evidence that he is a subject of God's pardoning mercy, is entirely free. The Saviour on whom he relies came on purpose to deliver those, who, through fear of death, were all their life time subject to bondage. This deliverance he grants to all who have obtained mercy of the Lord, and enables them triumphantly to exclaim, O death, where is thy sting? O grave, where is thy victory? Thanks be to God, who giveth me the victory, through Jesus Christ my Redeemer. And O, what a cause of unhappiness, what an oppressive load is removed from a man's mind, when he can adopt this language, when he ceases to regard death as an evil to be dreaded!

2. That a man may rejoice and be glad all his days, it is necessary that he should be freed in early life from a guilty conscience, and from apprehensions of God's displeasure. That a man whose conscience troubles him cannot be happy, no one who has a conscience needs be informed. And that apprehensions of God's displeasure and of its terrible consequences, must render men unhappy, is equally obvious. The man who cannot be happy when alone, whose own thoughts are unpleasant com-

panions, who cannot look into his own breast without uneasiness, nor up to heaven without terror, nor toward the eternal world without apprehension, must surely be very far from deserving to be regarded as a happy man. If he ever enjoys any thing like happiness, it can be then only when he forgets that he is an immortal being, and that there is a God to whom he is accountable. But these things no unpardoned sinner can always forget. The recollection of them will return at intervals to disturb his peace; and if he has received much religious instruction, it will return often. The understanding and conscience of such a man cannot but be at war with the temper which he indulges, and with the course which he pursues. And even when they are not actually reproaching him, and when no distinct apprehensions of an offended God, of judgment and eternity press upon his mind, he often feels that indescribable uneasiness, restlessness and dissatisfaction, which are the almost inseparable attendants of all who are not at peace with God. Agreeably, we read that the wicked are like the troubled sea, which cannot rest, whose waters cast up mire and dirt; that they travail with pain all their days; that a dreadful sound is in their ears, that they believe not that they shall return out of darkness. But from these causes of unhappiness the man who is early satisfied with God's pardoning mercy, is free. He knows the blessedness of the man whose iniquities are forgiven, and whose sin is covered. He enjoys peace of conscience and peace with God through our Lord Jesus Christ. He knows that heaven regards with an approving eye the course which he pursues; that God is his friend, heaven his destined home, and everlasting glory and felicity his reward. Hence he can be happy in solitude; nay, in solitude his happiest hours are spent. He is not obliged to rush into company for the sake of escaping from his own thoughts. He is not obliged to walk with his face bent downward to the earth, lest he should catch a glimpse of that glorious sun which shines in heaven, and its brightness should pain his eye. No; he can look up to that sun, not only without pain, but with delight; for he rejoices with joy unspeakable, while contemplating its unsullied and unfading glories. Nor is he obliged carefully to confine his thoughts within the narrow circle around him, lest they should wander into the eternal world, and bring back cause of alarm. On the contrary, he

sends them forward with pleasure to visit that world; he fixes
on it the eye of delighted contemplation, and anticipates the
hour when he shall be permitted to enter it, for he regards it as
the place where the objects of his supreme affections reside, and
where his happiness is to be rendered perfect and complete. In
a word, all those invisible and eternal realities, every thought
which gives pain to the guilty, unpardoned sinner, are to him
sources of happiness. And at the same time, he derives more
pleasure from temporal blessings than they ever afford the sinner,
because he tastes the goodness of God in them, and because his
enjoyment of them is less embittered by fears that they will be
taken away. Surely then the man who wishes to enjoy life, to
rejoice and be glad all his days, should seek to be satisfied early
with God's mercy. .

3. To render a man happy during the whole progress of life,
it is necessary that he should be early freed from care and
anxiety, and especially from apprehensions of losing what he
most loves. A feeling of safety, of security, is indispensably
necessary to our happiness. But it is impossible that an unpardoned sinner should feel perfectly safe, or that he should be free
from care, anxiety, and apprehension. He has no almighty
friend, no father in heaven, on whom he can cast the burden of
his cares. He cannot conceal from himself the fact, that he is
every moment liable to lose all the objects which he values and
loves, and he knows, that at death, if not before, he must be
separated from them all. In fine, his treasure is laid up on
earth, his habitation is built upon the ice, his friends are like
himself, all frail, dying creatures; and he has nothing which he
can with propriety call his own; nothing on which he can lay
his hand and say, this object at least is safe. How then can he
be free from anxiety and apprehension, and how while subject
to these can he be happy? But from this cause of unhappiness
the man who early obtains satisfactory evidence that he is interested in God's pardoning mercy is free. His treasure, his portion,
his chief good, is laid up, not on earth but in heaven, and he
knows that it is safe, that it cannot be lost. Nor has he any
reason to be anxious respecting his temporal concerns, or his lot
in life; for he knows that his portion is allotted, and all his
concerns managed by unerring wisdom and goodness; that all
things shall work together for his good, and that it is his privi-

lege and his duty to be careful for nothing, but to cast all his cares on that heavenly Father who careth for him. Hence he can say, The Lord is my light and my salvation, whom shall I fear? the Lord is the strength of my life, of whom shall I be afraid? Although the fig tree should not blossom, nor fruit be in the vine; the labor of the olive should fail and the fields should yield no meat; the flocks should be cut off from the fold, and there be no herd in the stall; yet I will joy in the Lord, I will rejoice in the God of my salvation. Nay, though the earth should be removed, and the mountains be carried into the midst of the sea, though the waves thereof should roar and be troubled, and the mountains shake with the swelling thereof, yet the Lord of hosts is with me, the God of Jacob is my refuge.

4. That a man may rejoice and be glad all his days, he must early learn, in whatsoever state he is, therewith to be content. A discontented man is, of course, an unhappy man. But it is impossible that an unconverted sinner should be otherwise than discontented. To exhort him to be contented is the most idle thing imaginable. As well might we exhort a thirsty man not to feel thirst, while nothing is given him to satisfy it. The reason is obvious. While the soul is empty it cannot but feel uneasy, dissatisfied, discontented. But so long as it is without God, the only fountain of living waters, the only being who can fill the soul, it must be empty. It will crave something, and pine after something, which it cannot find. The situation of a man without God, as it respects happiness, is like that of a man without the sun, as it respects light. The latter may surround himself with lamps, and thus provide a supply of artificial light; but his lamps will often burn dimly, and will sometimes be extinguished; and even while they burn most brightly, their pale, sickly light will afford but a poor substitute for the pure, reviving, all-disclosing radiance of the sun; a substitute with which the eye could not long be satisfied. Just so a man, who is without God in the world, may surround himself with friends and earthly possessions, and make the comfort which they afford a substitute for the consolation of God, and the enjoyment of his presence. But it is, at best, a miserable substitute, a substitute with which the soul cannot be contented. But far different is the situation of one who is satisfied early with God's mercy. What the sinner seeks in vain, he has found. The light which

sheds its radiance on his path, is furnished, not by lamps, but by the sun, a sun which never sets. The water which quenches his spirit flows, not from broken cisterns, but from the inexhaustible fountain of living waters. Of this water, our Saviour says, he that drinketh of it shall never thirst, but it shall be in him a well of water springing up to everlasting life. Such a man has then the sources of contentment in his own bosom. He carries them with him wherever he goes; and when we recollect that, in addition to this, he has been favored by the mercy of God with a submissive temper, we need not be surprised to hear that he soon learns in whatsover state he is, therewith to be content.

Finally. That a man may rejoice and be glad all his days, it is absolutely necessary that he should early obtain the mastery of his appetites and passions, and be secured against the evils into which they would lead him. What these evils are, it is scarcely necessary to say, since they prevail but too extensively among us. Look around, and you will see on every side young men, whom appetites and passions are plunging into intemperance, sensuality, and every species of vicious excess, and thus ruining them not only for the future, but for the present world. You see them forming habits, whose chains it will be exceedingly difficult for them to break, and which, unless broken, will drag them away to destruction. And no young man can have any security that he shall not be left to form such habits, unless he obtains that security which is afforded by God's sanctifying grace and pardoning mercy; unless he early commits himself to that great and good Shepherd, who has engaged to preserve all his sheep. Until this is done, he is at the mercy of every gust of temptation, every sudden sally of appetite and passion. It is in vain that, in his sober moments, he resolves not to yield to temptation. How little such resolutions, how little any human restraints avail to secure him, melancholy observation but too clearly shows. How many promising young men have we seen who, while they remained under the parental roof, were moral, correct, and apparently fortified against temptation; but when they were removed from it, fell an easy prey to temptation, and sunk into the arms of vicious indulgence! And how many have we seen who, after passing safely through the dangerous period of youth, became the wretched victims of intemperance in manhood. Presume not then, young man, upon thine own strength. Where so many others have fallen, thou mayest fall. Against such a fall thou canst have no security, until thou obtainest the protection of God. Let him hold thee up, and then, and then only, wilt thou be safe. This safety is enjoyed by all who are satisfied early with his mercy. They are taught and assisted by his grace to crucify their affections and lusts, to keep under appetite and passion and bring them into subjection. They have a powerful Saviour, a prevalent intercessor to pray for them, that their faith may not fail; they are within the protection of his encircling arm, and have often reason to say to him, When my foot slipped, thy mercy, O Lord, held me up. In a word, though they may possibly be left occasionally to fall into some particular sins, for their humiliation and chastisement, they are infallibly secured against the formation of any vicious habits, for the power and truth of God are pledged, that no sin shall have dominion over them. On their perseverance in a virtuous course, their friends may, therefore, safely rely; and it may be confidently expected that, in domestic and social life, they will be happy, and rejoice and be glad all their days.

Here we might conclude our remarks; but there is one more view, and to Christians a very interesting view, of the subject which it is necessary to take. It is necessary to inquire, how far the happiness of the Christian, after his conversion, may be affected by the period when his conversion took place. In other words, will a man, who is satisfied early with God's mercy, probably enjoy more uninterrupted religious happiness after his conversion, than a man who does not obtain mercy until a later period of life. It can scarcely, I conceive, be doubted that he will. A man who does not become religious, till the season of youth is passed away, must of course, spend all the early part of life in sin. And what will be the consequence? He will commit many sins, the recollection of which must be painful to him as long as he lives; he will lose much time and many precious opportunities of improvement, and of doing good, which he will afterwards regret; he will afford his sinful propensities an opportunity to become strong; and it will, of course, be more difficult to subdue them, and his future conflicts will be more severe. His imagination will be polluted, and the consequences will trouble him as long as he lives.

He will, probably, in some degree, at least, be a tempter of others, and the recollection of this will be bitter as wormwood and gall. He can never have the satisfaction of reflecting, that he gave God his first and earliest and best affections; that when the world was all fresh and gay and smiling around him, he cheerfully forsook all to follow Christ. On the contrary, it must pain him to reflect, that he did not forsake the world, till he had proved its emptiness; that he did not follow Christ, until experience taught him that there was nothing else worth following. We may add, that the man who is not converted until a late period, will more than probably, indulge in vices, or form habits, which will cause him much unhappiness through life. Nay more, it will not be at all strange, should he injure his health and undermine his constitution, and have nothing left to offer to God, but a diseased body, and an enfeebled mind. We find Job exclaiming, Thou writest bitter things against me, and makest me to possess the sins of my youth, that is, to feel their bitter consequences. David also prays, that God would not remember against him the sins of his youth; an intimation that he either suffered, or feared, some evil on account of them. But all the evils which have now been enumerated are avoided by the man who commences a religious life in early youth. He is guilty of no vicious indulgences, he forms no bad habits, his affections are less entangled, and his imagination less polluted, and his future life will not be embittered by the recollection that he has tempted others to sin; that he has irrecoverably lost his best opportunities for improvement; or that he has injured his health or his reputation by the practice of vice. As he enters the narrow path early, he will probably make great progress in holiness, lay up much treasure in heaven, and be rich in good works. And he, and he alone, can say in his old age, O Lord, thou hast been my hope from my youth; now, when I am old and gray-headed, forsake me not. Is it not then, most evident, that he who enters on a religious course in early life, will enjoy more happiness than one who commences such a course at a later period? And is it not equally evident that, if a man would be glad and rejoice all his days, he should become religious in early youth? An application of the subject to several different classes in this assembly, will conclude the discourse.

1. Let me apply it to those among the young, who are de-

ferring the commencement of a religious life, because they suppose a late conversion to be more favorable to happiness. From the remarks which have been made, you may learn, my young friends, that you are laboring under a great mistake; that by delaying to seek and obtain mercy of the Lord, you are not only losing much present happiness, but exposing yourselves to many evils, and taking the most effectual way to render your whole future lives less happy. If you wish to rejoice and be glad all your days, you must, believe me, you must, commence a religious life without delay. If a man intended to cultivate a field, would it not be unwise to defer the commencement of his labors until the proper seed-time had passed away? If a man intended to become a scholar, would it not be unwise to spend his childhood and youth in idleness? Equally unwise is it for you to defer the commencement of a religious life till the season of youth is passed. It would be thus unwise, even could you be sure of being converted at any future period. But you cannot be sure of this. On the contrary, experience and observation combine with the Scriptures to teach us, that those who do not become religious in early life, will very probably never become religious at all. O, then, if you mean ever to hear God's voice, hear it to-day, and do not by delay harden your hearts.

2. Are there any in this assembly who were converted and satisfied with God's mercy in early life? If so, they may learn from this subject what cause they have for gratitude and joy. They who obtain mercy at any period of life have unspeakable cause for thankfulness. But none have so much reason for thankfulness as they who obtain it early. They can scarcely conceive how many evils and dangers and sufferings they have escaped by an early conversion. Let them then show their gratitude by improving diligently the long space which is afforded them to become rich in good works and make more than ordinary advances in religion. And let them consider how disgraceful it will be, if after spending a long life in the school of Christ, they should at last be found babes in knowledge and happiness.

3. From this subject those Christians who did not seek and obtain mercy in early life, may learn that they will have no reason to wonder or complain if they should continue to feel,

as long as they live, some of the evil consequences of their
early neglect of religion, and of their youthful follies and sins.
There are some evils of this kind which religion does not remove, and which it cannot be expected she should remove.
Should a young man, while engaged in some vicious pursuit,
lose a limb or an eye, and afterwards become religious, could
it be expected that religion would restore the limb or the eye
which he had lost? or would it be reasonable for him to complain on this account? And if a man wastes his childhood and
youth in sin, and afterwards becomes a Christian, can he justly
complain, though he should still suffer for his folly, though his
sinful propensities and habits should give him more than ordinary trouble; or though he should make less progress and
enjoy less happiness than he otherwise would? Certainly not.
Let him ascribe all his sufferings to their true cause, let him
trace them up to his early sins, and let him submissively say,
The Lord exacts of me less than my iniquities deserve. I will
bear the indignation of the Lord, because I have sinned against
him.

SERMON XI

How can I — sin against God? — GENESIS XXXIX. 9.

'This, my hearers, is the genuine language of a pious heart. It ought to be the language of every heart. To every tempter, to every temptation, our invariable reply should be, How can I sin against God! To persuade you to make this reply, whenever you are tempted to sin, is my present design. And perhaps I cannot prosecute this design more effectually, than by attempting to show you what is implied in the language which we wish you to adopt. This therefore I propose to do.

The meaning, the force of this language lies almost entirely in the word GOD. And O how many reasons, why we should not sin against him, are wrapped up in this one word! Could we, my hearers, make you see the full import of this word; could we pour upon your minds the overwhelming flood of meaning which it contains, you would feel, that no additional motives were necessary, to deter you from sinning against him whose name it is. But this we cannot do. Could we take this one word for our theme, and expatiate upon it through eternity, we should be able to tell you but a part, a small part, of its meaning. All we can do is, to tell you something of what it means, in the mind, in the mouth of a pious man. Suppose such a man placed before you. Suppose you see him assailed

and urged to sin, by every temptation to which human nature
can be exposed. Suppose that on the one hand, the world holds
up all her pleasures, riches and honors, and says to him, All
these things will I give thee, if thou wilt consent to sin. And
suppose that, on the other hand, she places before him poverty,
imprisonment, contempt, torture, and death, and says, To all
these evils I doom thee, if thou refuse to sin. Then hear him
reply, How can I sin against God? and listen while he tells you
what he means by this language. Notice his expressions; weigh
well the reasons which he assigns, and see whether he does not
act wisely, whether he does not constrain you to justify his
conduct in refusing to yield to temptation and sin against God.
And if you feel, as we proceed, that he completely justifies himself in the eye of reason, that he speaks and acts wisely, then
make his language and his conduct your own.

1. God, you may understand the good man as saying, is a
being of perfect, of infinite excellence. His works, as well as
his word, assure me that he is so. They assure me that from him
comes every good and perfect gift; that he is the Father of lights,
the source of all the intellectual and moral excellence, which is
possessed by creatures, whether in heaven, or on earth. Now
there must be more in the fountain, than there is in all the streams
which proceed from it. There must be more excellence in the
Creator, than in all the creatures which he has formed. How
then can I sin against him? There are many of my fellow
creatures, who possess much intellectual and moral excellence,
and whom I should therefore be unwilling to offend. And ought
I not, then, I appeal to you whether I ought not, to be far more
unwilling to offend him, who is the source of all excellence?
who is excellence itself? Do you ask me to be more particular?
I reply, God is holy. He is the thrice Holy One; he cannot look
on sin, but with the deepest abhorrence. How then can I sin
against him? How can I insult his spotless purity, by polluting
myself with sin, when the light of his holiness shines around
me? God is good, infinitely good, he is goodness itself. And
O, how can I sin against goodness, infinite goodness? God is
just, and his justice binds him to punish sin. He is Almighty,
and his power enables him to punish it. I am unable to resist
him, if I wished to do it. How can I, how dare I, then, offend
him, and provoke his justice to employ his power in destroying

me'? God is every where present, and knows all things. How then can I sin against him? How can I pollute by my sins a place which is made sacred, which is rendered holy ground, by his presence? God is infinitely wise. In his wisdom he counsels me not to sin; and how can I disregard the counsels of infinite wisdom? God is true; he is truth itself; he has told me that misery is the consequence of sin, and how can I disbelieve eternal truth? God is merciful and gracious. He has mercifully offered to forgive all my transgressions, great and numberless as they are. How can I then, if there is one spark of gratitude or ingenuousness in my heart, ever consent to offend him again? God is condescending. He has graciously condescended to feel and express an interest in my welfare, and in that of my fellow worms. And how can I then abuse his condescension? In fine, when I see that every thing glorious, excellent, and lovely is summed up in the character of one Being, how can I sin against that Being?

2. God is my Creator. He is the former of my body, the Father of my spirit. As such he is my nearest relative. How then can I sin against him? Look at this body. He contrived it. He formed every particle of it. He gave me these limbs, these senses. How then can I employ them in offending him? Consider my soul. He breathed it into me. He endowed it with all the faculties which it possesses. And can I suffer them to sin against him who gave them? Shall the thing formed rise up against him who formed it? I am not my own, I am the property of him who made me. Every thing which I possess is his. And how can I disregard his rights? How can I be so foolish, so ungrateful, so impious, as to sin against a Father; against such a Father, against him but for whom I had never existed? You would not justify me in offending an earthly parent. You would justly censure me, you would consider me as an unnatural wretch, should I plant thorns in the breast of a kind father, an affectionate mother. And ought you not much more to condemn me,—ought I not to abhor myself, should I offend and grieve my Father in heaven?

3. God is my Preserver and Benefactor. He has watched over me and preserved me, every moment since my existence commenced. He has shielded me from ten thousand evils and dangers. He has preserved me, while multitudes of my coevals

have perished. He is preserving me at this moment. How can
I then, while in the very act of experiencing his preserving goodness, requite him with disobedience? And while he has been
my constant preserver, he has in numberless other ways acted
as my benefactor. All the happiness which I ever tasted, he
imparted. All the blessings which I ever enjoyed, he gave.
Each of them bore this inscription, The gift of God. The food
which has nourished me, the garments which have clothed me,
the habitation which has sheltered me, the relatives and friends
whose kindness has cheered my existence; all come from him.
And even now, it is his light which shines around me; it is his
air which I breathe; the earth on which I stand is his; even
now my hands are filled with blessings which he has bestowed.
How then can I raise them against him? How can I requite
with ingratitude this kind, constant, unwearied benefactor!

4. God is my rightful Sovereign. As my Creator and Proprietor, he has the best of all possible titles to control me. He,
who gave and who preserves my existence, has surely a right
to prescribe the manner in which I shall spend it. He who gave
me my limbs and faculties has surely a right to say what I shall
do with them. And he has exercised this right. He has enacted laws for the regulation of my conduct. These laws he
has made known to me. And they forbid me to sin. They
forbid this particular sin, which I am now urged to commit.
And I see not how I can escape from the obligations which I
am under to obey them. I see not how I can escape from the
government of God, or cease to be his rightful subject. And
while I am one of his subjects, I see not how I can disobey him,
without becoming a rebel and a traitor, and thus exposing myself to his just displeasure. And how can I do this? How can
I consent to become a rebel against the King of kings, the Sovereign of the universe? How can I dare brave the displeasure
of Omnipotence, of one who governs all things by the word of
his power? And why should I wish to do it? All his commands are holy and just and good. They require nothing of
me which does not tend to secure my best interests, my everlasting happiness. They forbid nothing which would not debase
and injure me. Why, then, should I transgress, how can I transgress such a law as this, when in doing it I sinned against the
greatest and best of sovereigns?

5. God is the providential, as well as moral Governor of the universe, and the sole Dispenser of all blessings, natural and spiritual. As such I am constantly dependent on him for every thing which I need. I am in his hands; as he has given, so he can take away, all that I possess. He has only to speak the word, and all blessings forsake me, all evils come upon me; nor can all creatures united continue to me one blessing, which he sees fit to take away, or avert one evil which he commissions to assail me. How can I, then, unless I become a madman, consent to forfeit his favor and incur his displeasure, by sinning against him? Especially how can I do this, when I know that he is the Judge, as well as the Governor of the universe, and that, as such, he will summon me to his bar, and pronounce upon me a sentence, which will render me happy or miserable forever! I know he has power to execute this sentence. I know that he has power to destroy both soul and body in hell. And dare I, can I, then, offend him? Can I barter heaven for the temptation which now urges me to sin? Can I take the price of sin in my arms, and for the sake of it plunge into hell? Can all the rewards which you offer compensate me for the heaven, which I shall lose by sin? Are all the tortures, with which you threaten me, to be compared with those miseries, into which I shall sink myself by sin? You will not assert this. I cannot then,—O, no, no,—I cannot consent to sin against God. Ask me to do any thing else, however difficult or painful, and I will, if possible, comply; but ask me not to sin against God; ask me not to destroy body and soul forever, for this I cannot, cannot do.

6. God is the Father of our Lord Jesus Christ. As such so he loved our ruined race, that he gave his only begotten Son to die for its salvation. He gave him to die for me, for my relatives, for my fellow creatures. He gave him to die for us, when we were sinners, rebels, enemies; gave him, that we might be saved from the consequences of our own follies and vices. Through his crucified Son, he has offered me pardon and peace and everlasting life, on the easy terms of renouncing my sins, and believing in him. Nay more, he has besought me to accept of salvation on these terms, and to be reconciled to himself. He has shown himself willing to receive and welcome me no less kindly, than the father in the parable received and welcomed his returning prodigal son. And the Saviour, by

consenting to die for us, has evinced love and condescension
equally wonderful. He has done and suffered more for us than
any earthly friend would or could have done. Now if I consent to sin, I shall crucify afresh this Saviour; I shall dishonor
and offend and grieve the Father who gave him to die for me.
And how can I do this? How can I requite him evil for good?
Tell me, ye who urge me to sin, how can I so far divest myself
of gratitude, of ingenuousness, of all sensibility to kindness as
to be guilty of such conduct? Tell how I can ever justify myself, how I can ever prove that I am not a base ungrateful
wretch, if I should consent to sin against my God and Redeemer, after they have done all this. But you cannot tell me. You
can furnish me with no apology, with no shadow of an excuse
for such ingratitude. Tempt me not then to be guilty of it, for
I cannot, no, I cannot sin against the God and Father of my
Lord Jesus Christ, the God of all grace and mercy. I cannot
grieve and crucify afresh that Saviour who has voluntarily ex-
pired for me on the cross.

Thus, my hearers, have I endeavored to show you something
of what a good man means when he says, How can I sin
against God; and stated some of the considerations which he
may urge as reasons why he cannot consent to sin against him.
And now let me ask, Are not these reasons more than sufficient
to justify him in refusing to sin, however strongly he may be
urged to it? Is there any thing in this language which indicates
weakness, or superstition, or enthusiasm? Rather, does it not
approve itself to the understanding and conscience of every person present, as being perfectly reasonable? Would you not
censure and condemn him, should he consent to sin against God,
when considerations so numerous and so powerful forbid it? If
so, you must, would you be consistent, condemn yourselves
whenever you sin; for, my hearers, every consideration which
the good man has now been represented as urging to prove that
he ought not to sin against God, may be urged with equal force
to prove, that you ought not to sin against him. If the good
man ought to adopt such language, then each of you ought to
adopt it. If it is wise and proper that he should form such a
determination; then, for the same reason, it is wise and proper
that you should form it. And now to come to the great object
of this discourse, let me ask, will you not adopt it? We set

before you God, the infinite, everlasting God; a being absolutely perfect, in whom all possible excellence is concentrated and condensed; a being who is your Creator, your Preserver, your Benefactor, your rightful Sovereign, your Judge; a being who has so loved you, that he spared not his own Son; but delivered him up for us all, and whose offers of grace and mercy are continually sounding in your ears. This Being we set before you and say, How can you sin against him? And what we wish of you is, that each of your hearts should echo, How can I sin against God?

Let me then repeat the question, Is this, shall it henceforth be, the language of your hearts? Perhaps some may reply, It is, it shall be their language. We will no more sin against God. If we ever sin, it shall only be against our fellow creatures, or against ourselves, not against him. But, my friends, all sin is against God. Though in some forms it may be more immediately against ourselves, or our fellow creatures, yet in every form it is ultimately against him. It is against his law, his authority, his government, his glory. It strikes at him directly in all these respects. To say that we will no more consent to sin against God is equivalent to saying, We will no more consent to sin at all. And saying this implies repentance; for the same views which lead a man to say, How can I sin against God? will lead him to repent of having already sinned against him. Besides, God's first command is, Repent. To disobey this command is, therefore a sin. Of course, he who says, How can I sin against God? will say, How can I defer repentance a single hour? All the considerations which ought to have prevented him from sinning against God, will now operate to make him repent of his sins. He will say, Against this infinitely perfect Being, against infinite wisdom and power and holiness and justice and goodness and mercy and truth, I have sinned. Against my Creator, and Preserver and Benefactor, I have sinned. Against my Sovereign and Judge, against the mighty Monarch of the universe, against the God and Father of my Lord Jesus Christ, against my adorable crucified Saviour, I have sinned. And O, how could I do this? What cruel ingratitude, what impious folly and madness, possessed me! I abhor myself and repent in dust and ashes. And he who says this, will also believe in the Lord Jesus Christ. He will see

that unbelief is one of the greatest sins which can be committed against God; that it calls in question all his perfections, and
represents him as wholly unworthy of confidence. How then,
he will ask, can I any longer persist in it? Besides, he will
see that he needs such a Saviour as Jesus Christ, to save him
from the consequences of sins which he has already committed
against God, and from those sinful propensities which urge him
to sin afresh. This will operate as an additional reason why
he should believe without delay. Having exercised repentance
and faith in Christ, he will proceed to exhibit the effects of both,
by denying himself, crucifying his sinful propensities, and replying to every temptation; How can I sin against God?

And now, my hearers, if any of you mean to adopt the language of our text, you will soon have occasion to make use of
it. As soon as you leave this house, and through the remain-
der of the week, you will be assailed by temptations from
within and without, to sin against God. Those of you, who
have hitherto neglected religion, will be tempted to neglect it a
little longer. And those of you, who have professedly embraced
it, will be tempted to act in a manner inconsistent with your
profession. The situation of both classes will be this. On one
side, a thousand little tempters of various kinds will be whispering, Do consent to sin against God. Sin against him at least
in this one thing. It will be a trifling offence, and you can repent of it afterwards, and be forgiven. On the other side, God
will stand in all his infinite perfections, in all his endearing relations, and with the tenderness of a father, with the authority
of a master, with the majesty of a universal monarch, will say,
Yield not to these temptations; sin not against me. Then you
will be called to weigh the rights, the claims of Jehovah
against the pleadings of temptation. Then you must either
adopt, or reject, the language of our text. Now then, while
temptation is at a distance, while the voice of passion is silent,
while reason and conscience can speak and be heard, determine
which you will do. To assist in forming a right determination,
consider how frequently, how greatly you have already sinned
against God. How often, when temptation urged you, and God
forbade you to sin, have you yielded to the former, and disobeyed the latter. Are not those instances already sufficiently
numerous? Are they not too numerous? Are you not ready

to wish that, when tempted to sin, you had always replied, How can I sin against God? Do you feel nothing like sorrow, nothing like relenting, when you reflect how often you have sinned against all that is endearing in relation, against all that is sacred in authority, against all that is touching in kindness? Can you contemplate God impartially and say, I think I have treated him as well as he deserves to be treated. He has no reason to complain of the manner in which I have treated him. I have paid him all that I owe him. I have loved him and feared him, and obeyed and thanked him, as much as he has any right to expect? If you cannot say this; if you feel that you have not treated your God, your Creator, your Benefactor, your Redeemer, as he deserves, can you refrain from lamenting it? Is there nothing in your breast which makes you wish to fall at his feet and say, Lord, I have not treated thee as thou art worthy to be treated. I have sinned, I have committed iniquity. I have done foolishly. O, forgive me, for thy Son's sake forgive me, and let me offend thee no more. If any thing within urges you to do this, O yield to it; for it is the Spirit of God urging you to repentance. If you feel any disposition to do it, indulge that disposition; for it may prove the commencement of repentance. And if you repent of past sins, you will feel disposed and enabled to say with new resolution, How can I any more sin against God? for you will then come under the influence of new motives, and will see new reasons why you should guard against sin; for as soon as you become a penitent sinner, you will be a pardoned sinner; you will taste and see that the Lord is good; you will know something of the love of Christ which passeth knowledge; and that love will constrain you to live, not unto yourselves, but to him who died for you and rose again. Then you will say, How can I, a redeemed sinner, a pardoned sinner, whom Christ has bought with his own blood, who have by a most wonderful display of divine grace and mercy, been saved from the lowest hell, — how can I any more sin against my deliverer? I am become a member of Christ. How can I crucify my head? God has adopted me as a child: How can I sin against my Father in heaven? The Spirit of God has taken up his residence in my heart: How can I grieve him and provoke him to forsake me?

Such are some of the new motives under whose influence you

will come, if you now yield to him who urges you to repent.
O then yield to the gentle inward monitor which, I would fain
hope, is now whispering repentance.   Give way to those better
feelings which are beginning to rise within you; and under
their influence fall at the feet of your much injured and long
offended, but still gracious God.   Let me, I beseech you, let me
see peace restored between you and him before you leave this
house.   Come with me to his mercy seat and say, Other lords,
O God, have had dominion over us; but they shall rule us no
more.   We have sinned, greatly sinned against thee; but we
would sin no more.   O hold us back from sin; turn us from all
our iniquities; help us to say from the heart, we will be thy
people; and say thou to us, I will be your God.

SERMON XII

SOLOMON'S CHOICE.

And the speech pleased the Lord, that Solomon had asked this thing.
1 Kings iii. 10.

In the context we are informed that, soon after Solomon's coronation, the Lord appeared to him by night, and said, Ask what I shall give thee. And Solomon said, O Lord my God, thou hast made thy servant king instead of David my father, and I am but a little child; I know not how to go out or come in; and thy servant is in the midst of a great people that cannot be numbered for multitude. Give thy servant, therefore, a wise and understanding heart, to judge thy people, that I may discern between good and bad; for who is able to judge so great a people? And the speech pleased the Lord, that Solomon had asked this thing. And God said unto him, because thou hast asked this thing, and hast not asked for thyself long life, nor riches, nor the lives of thine enemies, but hast asked for thyself understanding to discern judgment; behold I have done according to thy word; I have given thee a wise and understanding heart, so that there shall be none like unto thee. And I have also given thee that which thou hast not asked, both riches and honor; so that there shall not be any among the kings like unto thee all thy days.

My friends, though our situation differs in many respects from that of Solomon, yet from this passage we may learn many interesting and important truths. We may learn from it, indeed, almost everything that is necessary to render us prosperous and happy, both with respect to this world and to that which is to come. To illustrate and enforce some of the principal truths which it teaches, is our present design.

(I.) The address which God made to Solomon when he said, Ask what I shall give thee, he does in effect make to each of us, especially to the young. It is true, the age of visions and revelations is past; God does not now speak to us with an audible voice, nor is it necessary that he should. The revelation which he has given us in his word, renders it needless. But the language in which he addresses us in his word is precisely similar to that in which he spoke to Solomon. By erecting a throne of grace in heaven, opening the way to it, inviting us to come to him with our requests, and promising to grant our petitions when they are agreeable to his will, he does in effect say to each of us, Ask what I shall give thee. I have set before thee the blessing and the curse, the way of life and the way of death. On the one hand, I set before thee Christ and holiness and everlasting life; on the other, sin and the world and eternal death. Choose then which thou wilt have. Wilt thou have the pleasures of sin, or the pleasures of religion? Wilt thou have treasures on earth, or treasures in heaven. Wilt thou have the praise of men or the praise of God? Wilt thou have Christ, or wilt thou have the world? To these questions of his Creator every man by his conduct returns a direct, unequivocal answer. If he pursues religion as the one thing needful, he practically replies, Lord, I choose religion; I choose thee for my portion, and Christ for my Saviour, and heaven for my rest. Give me but these, and I am satisfied. If, on the contrary, he devotes himself supremely to sinful or worldly pursuits, he no less directly replies, Lord I choose the world. I choose its pleasures as my happiness, its riches as my portion, its applause as my honor. Give me them and I ask nothing more. I shall not trouble myself as to the consequences of this choice hereafter. Let me but be happy in this world. Others, if they please, may have the other world to themselves.

(II.) Though we are not, like Solomon, kings; and therefore need not, as he did, qualifications requisite for that office; yet we all need spiritual wisdom and understanding, and may therefore all imitate his example in making our choice. For instance, the young may do this. Every one may say, Lord thou hast given me an immortal soul, a soul which thou hast made, and for the loss of which thou hast taught me, that the gain of the whole world would be no compensation. But I know not what to do with it. I know not how to keep it, nor where it will be safe, but am in danger of losing it continually. I find myself in the midst of a sinful, seducing world, exposed to innumerable snares and temptations, surrounded by artful and insidious enemies who often assume the garb of friends, with many paths opening before me, each of which appears to be the path to happiness. I am told that in this world scarcely any object appears in its true colors; but that good is often put for evil, and evil for good, darkness for light, and light for darkness. I am also told, and I begin already to find with truth, that I have a most deceitful heart, ever watching to betray me; that my understanding is blinded by sin, that I am inclined to evil, not to good; that my appetites and passions will unceasingly strive to lead me astray. Already have they begun to do it; already have I been guilty of many errors and mistakes. I fear that I shall be guilty of more. O then, thou Father of spirits, thou Father of lights, give me, I beseech thee, a wise and understanding heart, that I may discern between good and evil, and have strength to avoid the one and pursue the other. O condescend to be my shepherd, the guide of my youth; lead me in the way that is everlasting.

Every parent, also, has reason to adopt the prayer of Solomon. Every one, who sustains this relation, may say, Lord, in addition to my own soul, thou hast confided to my care the souls of my children, with an injunction to educate them for thee, and teach them the good and the right way. But we have no wisdom nor skill, nor strength to do this. Our children have derived from us a corrupt nature which we know not how to subdue. They are exposed to the influence of bad examples, and many other evils, against which we know not how to guard them. Even we ourselves shall set before them a bad example, unless thy grace prevent. We are in danger of ruining them by too much indulgence, on the one hand, or too much strictness and severity on the other. When we look around us we find but few, even among the wise and good, who succeed in educating their children aright; how then can we hope to succeed, we who are like little children ourselves, and need every moment to be taught, and guided, and upheld by thee. Give us then, O our heavenly Father, give us a wise and understanding heart, that we may know how to perform this great duty, and be preserved from the guilt of ruining the immortal souls committed to our care, and compelling thee to require their blood at our hands. Again,

Professors of religion have reason to imitate the example of Solomon. By admitting us into thy church, O Lord, they may say, thou hast in a measure committed to our care the honor of thy religion, the success of thy cause. If we display a wrong spirit, or conduct in a sinful or imprudent manner, thy religion will be despised, and thy great name blasphemed by many around us; we shall be as stumbling blocks in the path of life to occasion the destruction of our fellow creatures, perhaps of our nearest friends. This, O Lord, we are in continual danger of doing. We are exposed to dangers from within and from without, on the right hand and on the left. While we avoid one extreme, we are in danger of running into another. When we aim to recommend religion by cheerfulness, we are in danger of falling into levity and vain conversation, and when we endeavor to avoid levity, we are liable to prejudice our friends against religion by gloominess and melancholy. Against these and innumerable other dangers, to which we are exposed, we have no skill or wisdom to guard. We know neither how to go out nor how to come in. Give thy servants therefore, O Lord, a wise and understanding heart, that we may adorn thy religion, and honor thy great name. Give us that wisdom which is from above, which is pure, peaceable, full of good fruits, without partiality and without hypocrisy. Make us what thou requirest us to be, wise as serpents and harmless as doves. I might proceed to show that ministers, magistrates, and indeed persons in every situation and relation of life, have abundant cause to pray frequently for a wise and understanding heart, that they may know how to perform the duties of their respective stations. As an encouragement for all to do this, I observe,

III. That God is pleased with those who make the choice and sincerely offer up the prayer of Solomon. Our text informs us that God was pleased with his conduct on this occasion, and

since he is, yesterday, to-day, and forever, the same, he is pleased
with all who imitate his example. He is pleased with their
conduct,

1. Because it is the effect of his grace. We are told that the
Lord rejoices in his works, and with reason does he rejoice in
them; for they are all very good. If he rejoices in them he
must, of course, be pleased with them. But to induce persons
to make the choice and offer up the prayer of Solomon, is always
his work, the effect of his grace. It is one of those good and
perfect gifts which come down from the Father of lights; for
no man, who is not taught and influenced by the Spirit of God,
will ever make this choice or sincerely utter this prayer. Men
naturally choose and ask very different objects. Should God
say to an impenitent sinner, Ask what I shall give thee, he
would reply, — Lord, give me temporal prosperity, give me
pleasures or riches or honor; for these are the great objects
which every sinner loves and desires, and in the acquisition of
which his happiness consists. When the Lord looketh down
from heaven upon the children of men, he seeth that there are
none that understand, none that even seek after God. Before a
man can sincerely choose God for his portion, and prefer spiritual wisdom to all earthly objects, his natural views must therefore be changed; he must be taught to love and value the objects
which he naturally despised, and to despise the objects which
he supremely loved and pursued. In a word, he must become
a new creature, and to create him anew is the work of God.
Since then God is pleased with all his works, and since this is
his work, he must be pleased with the choice and with the
prayer mentioned in our text.

2. He is pleased with it, because it indicates opinions and
feelings similar to his own. In the opinion of Jehovah, spiritual
wisdom, that wisdom of which the fear of God is the beginning,
is the principal thing, the one thing needful to creatures situated
as we are. In comparison with this he considers all temporal
objects as worthless. His language to us is, above all things
get wisdom and with all thy gettings get understanding. Now
those, who make the choice which Solomon made, estimate objects according to their real value; that is, according to their
value in the estimation of God. Their opinions and feelings in
this respect correspond with his; and since all beings are neces-

sarily pleased with those who resemble them; God cannot but be pleased with those who resemble him in this respect. These opinions and feelings are a part of his own image, and he must love his own image and be pleased with it wherever it is seen.

3. God is pleased with those who thus pray for a wise and understanding heart, because such prayers are indicative of humility. When Solomon said, I am as a little child, I know not how to go out, or how to come in, give thy servant therefore a wise and understanding heart, it evidently indicated a low or humble opinion of his own qualifications, and a deep conviction of his need of divine illumination. Similar language indicates similar feelings in all who adopt it. It indicates that they are not too proud to be taught, that they possess what our Saviour calls the temper of a little child. Now no temper so well becomes such creatures as we are; no temper is so pleasing to God to no temper does he make so many precious promises as this. God resisteth the proud, but giveth grace to the humble. He that humbleth himself shall be exalted. To this man will I look, even to him that is poor and of a contrite spirit, and trembleth at my word. Thus saith the high and lofty one that inhabiteth eternity, whose name is Holy; I dwell in the high and holy place, with him also that is of a contrite and humble spirit, to revive the spirit of the humble, and to revive the heart of the contrite ones. These promises are sufficient proofs that God is pleased with humility, and since the language of our text indicates humility, God cannot but be pleased with all who sincerely adopt it.

4. God is pleased with such characters, because their conduct evinces that they are actuated by a benevolent concern for his glory and for the happiness of their fellow creatures. It is evident that Solomon in our text was actuated by such a temper, and not by a selfish regard to his own interests. He does not say, give me wisdom and understanding that I may have the praise of it, that my fame may be extended, but that I may discern between good and evil, and know how to rule this thy great people. He knew, as he observes in the context, that God had placed him on the throne. He therefore feared that if he should prove incompetent to the duties of this station, God who called him to it would be dishonored. He feared that the mistakes and faults of the servant would reflect disgrace upon the master

who employed him. He also knew that the happiness of his people depended much upon his own qualifications for government. It was a regard for the honor of God, and for the happiness of his people, therefore, rather than for his own sake, that he wished for wisdom and understanding. A similar disposition actuates those who sincerely imitate the conduct of Solomon at the present day. When the young pray for wisdom to guide them in the journey of life, the parent for assistance in educating his children, the professor for grace to adorn his profession, and the magistrate or minister for necessary qualifications, it is not so much for their own sakes as for the sake of others. It is that they may be enabled to honor God and do good to their fellow creatures by a faithful performance of their respective duties. It is true that many selfish, unhallowed desires may, and often do, intrude on such occasions; but still the prevailing governing disposition is such as has been described. Now this is a disposition exceedingly pleasing to God, whose name and whose nature is love, and who requires us to exercise that charity which seeketh not her own.

Once more; God is pleased with those who imitate the example of Solomon, because it actually and greatly tends to promote his glory. This it does in two ways. In the first place, by praying to him for wisdom, we do in effect profess a belief that he exists, that he is a prayer hearing God; and, especially, that he is the only wise God, the Father of lights, the author and giver of every good and perfect gift. As we honor a man, when we apply to him for counsel and advice in difficult cases, so we honor God, when we apply to him for wisdom and grace. In the second place, by confessing that we are as little children, — ignorant, blind, and helpless, and praying for a wise and understanding heart, we do in effect give God the glory of all that we are enabled to do in his service, or for the happiness of our fellow creatures. Our language is, not unto us, O Lord, not unto us, who are foolish and ignorant, but unto thee, who art the author of all wisdom and goodness, be the glory of every thing which we are enabled to perform. When we read of the wisdom of Solomon in connection with our text, we are led to admire not Solomon, but him who first taught him to pray for wisdom, and then gave him all that he possessed. When St. Paul says, by the grace of God I am what I am, he evidently turns away the attention of his admirers from himself to God, and refers to his grace the glory of all he did and suffered in the cause of Christ. So when persons at the present day confess that they have no wisdom or goodness of their own, and pray that God would give them a wise and understanding heart, they give him the whole glory of all the wisdom and understanding which they afterwards exhibit through life. Now since God's glory is exceedingly dear to him, and since this conduct thus tends to promote his glory, he must evidently be pleased with those who imitate it. As a farther inducement to imitate the example of Solomon, I observe,

IV. That all who make his choice, and adopt his prayer, shall certainly be favored with a wise and understanding heart. That Solomon received this gift you need not be told. Equally certain is it that all who imitate him shall receive it in such a degree, as their situation and circumstances require. This is evident, in the first place, from the fact already adverted to, that it is God who by his grace inclines them to make this choice. It is he alone who convinces us of our natural blindness and ignorance, and of our need of divine illumination. It is he who teaches us to estimate objects according to their real worth, and to choose spiritual wisdom in preference to all earthly objects. It is he who opens the way to the throne of grace, and gives us all the graces which are necessary to enable us to pray acceptably. Surely, then, he will not after all this refuse to hear the prayers which he has himself taught us to make. He cannot but gratify the desires which he has himself inspired. We know not, says the apostle, what to pray for as we ought, but the Spirit itself helpeth our infirmities, and maketh intercession for us with groanings which cannot be uttered. And he that searcheth the heart knoweth what is the mind of the Spirit, because he maketh intercession for the saints, according to the will of God.

That God will gratify the desires of those who thus pray for wisdom, is farther evident from his express promises. If any of you lack wisdom, let him ask of God, that giveth liberally to all men and upbraideth not; and it shall be given him. If thou cry after knowledge and lift up thy voice for understanding; if thou seek her as silver and search for her as for hid treasures; then shalt thou understand the fear of the Lord, which is the beginning of wisdom, and find the knowledge of God. In a word, If ye, being evil, know how to give good gifts to your children; how much more shall your heavenly Father give the Holy Spirit to them that ask him?

Once more; as a farther inducement to make the choice of Solomon, I observe, that this is the surest way of obtaining a competent share of the good things of the present life. Because thou hast asked this thing, said God to Solomon, and hast not asked for thyself long life, nor riches, nor the life of thine enemies, behold I have done according to thy words; and have also given thee what thou hast not asked, both riches and honor, so that there shall not be any among the kings like unto thee, all thy days. In a similar manner Christ promises to reward similar conduct in his disciples. Seek ye first the kingdom of God, and all these things shall be added unto you. In this, as in other respects, it is true that he who loseth his life for Christ's sake shall save it; that is, he who from a principle of supreme love to Christ and his religion neither desires nor seeks for riches and honor, shall receive as large a portion of them, as an infinitely wise Father sees it best for him to possess.

IMPROVEMENT. Is it true, as we have asserted, that God does in effect say to every person present, or at least to every young person, Ask what I shall give thee? It becomes us all then to inquire what reply we are making to this address. Say then, my hearers, what are you asking God to give you? Some of you, I fear, do not ask any thing of him. Prayer is a duty to which you are almost or altogether strangers. But still your conduct has a language, and what does it say? What is the object of your prevailing desire and pursuit? What would you ask for, if you should pray and ask for that which you uniformly love and desire? If we may judge from the conduct of a large proportion of this assembly, they would be far from adopting the language of Solomon. Many of the young would say, Lord, let us be admired and beloved for wit, beauty, dress, accomplishments. Let our days be filled up with a round of diversions and amusements. Let us live a long life of ease, gaiety and worldly pleasure, and when old age comes, if there be any such thing as conversion, let us be converted, and taken to heaven. Others would say,—Lord, give us wealth with all the blessings it bestows. Let us outstrip all our rivals in the acquisition of property, and excel them in the elegance of our habitations, our dress, our equipage; while the prayer of a third class would be,—Lord, grant us honor and distinction. Raise us to an elevated rank in society, and let those, who are now our equals, bow down to us. In short, if we may judge from the conduct of many of you, long life, pleasure, riches and honor, the very things which Solomon did not ask, would be the favors for which you would petition, and for the sake of which you would be willing to renounce the gift of a wise and understanding heart. Now if this be the case, you can surely have no reason to wonder or complain, if God should take you at your word. He has put a price into your hands to get wisdom; but like the fool you have no heart to it. He has told you that godliness is profitable for all things, having the promise of the life which now is, as well as of that which is to come; but you will not believe him. You have, therefore, no promise for this life or the next; and if, in the other world, you should find yourselves in the wretched situation of the rich man who fared sumptuously every day, and, like him, beg for a drop of water to mitigate your anguish, God may justly say to you, as Abraham did to him, Son, remember that thou in thy life time receivedst thy good things. Thou didst choose the world for thy portion, and thou hast had it. Christians, on the contrary, had all their evil things in the other world; but now they are comforted and ye are tormented. But if any of you are conscious that you have made the choice, and that you are daily uttering the prayer of Solomon, this subject is to you full of consolation and encouragement. God is pleased with your choice. He is pleased with those who have made it, he is pleased whenever you approach him in prayer with the language of Solomon on your lips. You have not perhaps been aware how many graces you were exercising, how much you were honoring and pleasing God; while, lying in the dust, ashamed and broken hearted before him, you have said,—Lord, I am ignorant, weak and helpless, as a little child, entirely unfit for the situation in which thou hast placed me, and ignorant how to go out or come in as I ought. Give me therefore, O God, a wise and understanding heart, that I may know my duty and practise it by glorifying thee, and promoting the happiness of my fellow creatures. You did not realize, perhaps, while saying this, as you have often done, to God, you were exercising faith, humility and benevolence, and promoting the glory of God. Yet all this you were doing; all this you will do, whenever you sincerely repeat this language. It will please the Lord whenever you ask this thing, and the more frequently and fervently you ask it, the more will he be pleased. Nor shall you ask in vain. Your prayer shall be answered by the bestowal of increasing measures of knowledge and grace; and the less you think of and desire temporal blessings, the more certainly will God bestow them upon you in such a degree as your present and future happiness requires. Pray then without ceasing, and be steadfast, unmoveable, always abounding in the work of the Lord, forasmuch as ye know that your labor is not in vain in the Lord.

1 Thess 5:17 & 1 Cor. 15:58

SERMON XIII

CHARACTER AFFECTED BY INTERCOURSE.

He that walketh with wise men shall be wise; but a companion of fools shall be destroyed.—PROVERBS XIII. 20.

WE have often reminded you that the terms wisdom and folly, wise and foolish, have a very different signification in the writings of Solomon, from that which they bear in the works of uninspired men. By wisdom, he means something of which the fear of the Lord is the prime constituent; for he says, the fear of the Lord is the beginning of wisdom: a good understanding have all they that do his commandments. By wisdom, then, he means religion; for religion begins with the fear of God. Of course, by the wise, he intends those who are religious; those who, to use the language of an apostle, are wise unto salvation. By folly, on the contrary, he means sin; and, by the foolish, those who love and practise it; or, in other words, impenitent sinners, who are destitute of the fear of God with which wisdom begins. The import of our text then is this, He that walks with religious men will become religious; but a companion of sinners shall be destroyed. These two assertions I now propose to consider separately, with a view to illustrate their meaning, and convince you of their truth.

I. He that walks with religious men will become religious. The term walk, as used, by the inspired writers, always signifies a continued course of conduct, or a manner of living, in which men persevere till it becomes habitual. Thus the phrase, Enoch walked with God, evidently signifies that he lived in a religious manner. He did not repair to God occasionally, when want or affliction or fear of death impelled; he did not merely take a few steps in that path in which God condescends to walk with men, and then forsake it; but he pursued that path habitually and perseveringly; he lived with God, in contradistinction from those who live without him in the world. So the phrase, to walk in the way of God's commandments, evidently signifies, to pursue a course of holy obedience, without turning aside to the right hand or to the left. To walk with religious men, then, is not merely to mingle occasionally in their society, or to unite with them in performing some of the more public duties of religion; but it is to make them habitually our chosen companions and friends, and, in subordination to God, our guides. It is not, for instance, walking with religious men to go with them to places of public worship; for David says of Ahithophel, who died as a fool dieth, We walked to the house of God in company. Nor is it walking with religious men to converse with them occasionally on religious subjects; for David says of the same Ahithophel, We took sweet counsel together: that is, we had conversation pleasant to me, and, as I then thought, to him, respecting subjects of a religious nature. It is not walking with religious men to reside with them, to live in a pious family, and to attend with its members at the family altar; for a person may do this reluctantly, and his chosen associates, the companions of his pleasure, may be of a very different character. Nor does uniting with religious men in promoting some of the great objects which the Christian world is now pursuing, necessarily prove that we walk with them; for we may be led to do this by wrong motives, as well as by those which are right. But to walk with religious men is to choose them for our associates, our fellow travellers in the journey of life; and this implies an agreement with them in our views and objects of pursuit. Can two walk together, says the prophet, except they be agreed? A question which plainly implies that they cannot. In order that two persons may walk together, they must be agreed, first, respecting the place to which they will go; for if one wishes to go to one place, and the other to a different place, they cannot be companions. In the second place, they must agree in opinion respecting the way which leads to that place; for if they disagree in this they will soon separate. In these two particulars, then, all who would walk with religious characters must agree.

Now the place to which every religious person, is travelling is heaven. Every such person, the Scriptures inform us, is a pilgrim and stranger on earth, seeking another and better country, that is a heavenly. Of course, all who would walk with them must make heaven the object of their pursuit, the place which they aim to reach.

Again; in the opinion of every truly religious person, the only way to heaven is Jesus Christ; for I, says he, am the way, the truth and the life; no man cometh to the Father but by me. All those who walk with religious persons must agree with them in assenting to this truth. I do not mean that they must immediately and cordially embrace it, for they would then themselves be religious; but they must have such a conviction that there is a heaven, and that an interest in Jesus Christ is necessary to obtain it, as will draw them away from sinful society and sinful pleasure, and induce them to associate with Christians, to unite with them in attending diligently all the means of grace, and to listen with interest to religious conversation; they must, in short, have such a conviction of the truth and reality and importance of religion as to adopt the resolution and the language of Ruth: Entreat us not to leave you, nor to return from following after you, for where you go, we will go, where you dwell we will dwell; your people shall be our people, and your God our God, nor shall any thing part us. Nor is it sufficient to adhere to this resolution for a short time only, for every person, who becomes the subject of serious impressions, forms such a resolution, and adheres to it so long as these impressions remain. During this period he loses all relish for worldly pleasures, and for conversation of a worldly nature, and can enjoy no society but that of Christians. But in too many cases this state of mind is of short duration. Their serious impressions are effaced, their desire for earthly and sinful objects revives, they forsake religious pursuits, and religious society, and return more eagerly perhaps than ever, to their former courses, their former associates. Such persons cannot be said to walk with religious characters, in the sense of our text; they do at most but take a few steps with them, and, instead of adhering to the resolution of Ruth, imitate the conduct of Orpah, who after a short struggle between her convictions and her inclinations, went back to her country and to her idols. But those, who instead of thus drawing back to perdition persevere to the end of life in the course which has been described, really walk with religious persons, and will themselves become religious. There are several circumstances and considerations which, taken collectively, prove the truth of this assertion, though no one of them taken separately would be sufficient to prove it.

In the first place, the simple fact, that a person chooses to associate with religious characters, in religious pursuits, proves that he is already the subject of serious impressions; that his understanding is convinced of the reality and importance of religion: that his conscience is awakened, and that, to use the language of inspiration, the Spirit of God is striving with him; for it is most certain that, unless this is the case, no person will ever forsake his sinful pleasures and pursuits, and his sinful companions for the society of Christians. All his natural feelings and inclinations render him averse to their society, and prevent his finding pleasure in religious pursuits; while, at the same time, they urge him to pursue worldly objects, and give him a relish for the company of worldly associates. He is also aware that, should he forsake his worldly companions for the society of Christians, he will expose himself to their contempt and become the subject of their ridicule. What then is to induce him to act contrary to his natural feelings and inclinations, and to exchange society which he loves, and in which he finds pleasure, for that which is disagreeable, and to expose himself to ridicule and contempt? It is most evident that nothing can do this but the power of an awakened conscience, of strong conviction produced by the Spirit of God. He then, who begins to walk with religious persons, is already the subject of religious impressions, the Spirit of God is operating upon his mind, and this affords some reason to hope that he will become really religious. At least his situation is much more hopeful than that of a person who feels no religious concern.

In the second place, he who walks with religious persons, will see and hear many things which powerfully tend to increase and perpetuate those serious impressions of which he is already the subject; while, at the same time, he will be withdrawn from the operation of many of those causes by which such impressions are effaced. There is nothing which tends more powerfully to obliterate these impressions, than the society, the conversation, and example of the world. These causes have destroyed more, who once were not far from the kingdom of God, than perhaps all other causes united. Indeed it is, humanly speaking, impossible that any serious impressions should remain long upon a mind, which is exposed to the full malignant influence of these causes. But he who walks with religious persons, is very much withdrawn from this fatal influence. Not only so, but he is brought under a different and salutary influence. He moves in a circle where God and the Redeemer, and the soul, and salvation, and heaven, are regarded as objects of supreme importance; and where the world, with all which it contains, is considered as comparatively worthless. He moves in a circle where he sees religion exemplified, where it is presented to him not as a cold abstraction, or as a lifeless form, but living, breathing, and acting, in the person of its disciples. He sees the salutary and happy effects which it produces; he sees that it does not, as he once thought, render its votaries gloomy or morose or misanthropic, but that its fruits are love and joy and peace. In addition, he hears much conversation on religious subjects, much that is calculated to instruct him, to warn him, and to increase his conviction of sin, and his desire to become truly religious. Besides he is almost daily brought under the operation of some of the means which God employs to produce and increase conviction, and to effect conversion. It is therefore, to say the least, highly probable that he will become truly religious.

In the third place, as the term walk signifies a continued course of conduct, it is evident that one, who walks with religious men, must be the subject of serious impressions for many years successively. We have already seen that no one will begin to walk with religious persons, till he becomes the subject of serious impressions. Equally evident is it, that no one will continue to walk with them after his serious impressions are effaced. He then who does continue to walk with them through life, must be the subject of serious impressions through life.

But no one, it is presumed, ever heard of an instance in which a person, who was the subject of serious impressions through life, did not become religious. It is true persons may be seriously affected, occasionally, and perhaps for years together, and at different seasons, may associate much with religious characters, without becoming religious; but such persons cannot be said to walk with good men in the sense of the text; for their religious impressions are often effaced for a considerable time, and long intervals of carelessness succeed, during which they forsake in a great measure religious pursuits, and religious society. But it is believed that no instance can be found, of a person who continued through life to walk with religious characters, and yet never become religious. We readily allow, indeed, that such a thing is possible; there is nothing in the nature of things to prevent it. God could, if he pleased, produce convictions of sin, and apprehension of future punishment which should last through life, and yet never be followed by conversion. But this is not his method. His method is, to give up those who obstinately resist his grace, to hardness of heart and to blindness of mind, and thus leave them to walk in their own ways, and to be filled with the fruit of their own devices. Hence the serious impressions of those who finally perish are usually of short continuance; or if they continue long, it is with many interruptions. Nothing but real grace, but genuine religion, will enable a man to endure to the end. He then who continues to walk with religious men to the end of his life will become religious. Indeed he must have become so before many years, perhaps before many months had been spent in such a course.

II. Let us now consider the second assertion contained in our text, A companion of sinners shall be destroyed. By a companion of sinners is evidently meant, one who chooses for his associates persons regardless of religion. It does not render us companions of sinners to reside with them, to transact business with them, or to visit and converse with them for the purpose of performing kind offices, or of promoting their eternal interests. But if we select them as our intimate associates; if we choose to spend our leisure hours in their company; if we find pleasure in their society, and prefer it to that of religious persons; then we are certainly their companions in the sense of the text, and shall perish with them. The truth of this assertion will appear evident from the following considerations viewed collectively.

In the first place, it is certain that he, who is in this sense a companion of sinners, is the subject of no religious impressions, that he has few if any serious thoughts. The very fact, that he chooses such persons for his associates and companions, proves that he resembles them; that his views and feelings respecting religion correspond with theirs, and that their conversation is agreeable to his taste. Referring to such characters, our Saviour says, They are of the world, therefore speak they of the world, and the world heareth or listeneth to them. Hence it appears that they whose conversation is of a worldly nature, and they, who listen with pleasure to such conversation, are alike of the world. Besides, we have already seen that as soon as any person becomes the subject of serious impressions, he wishes to associate with serious characters. Such persons only will converse with him on that subject which lies nearest his heart, and which therefore is most interesting; from such persons alone can he obtain that information which he desires; and they alone can understand and sympathize in his feelings. To speak on worldly subjects to such a person, will be like singing songs to a heavy heart. How can he, who is burdened with a load of guilt, and feels that his soul is in danger; that his eternal interests are at stake — find pleasure in conversing on subjects comparatively worthless and trifling? It is impossible. Nothing then can be more certain than the fact, that he, who selects irreligious persons for his companions, and finds pleasure in their society, is not the subject of any serious impressions. He exactly resembles those with whom he associates, and is like them pursuing the broad and crowded road which leads to destruction.

In the second place, he who chooses for his companions, persons regardless of religion, takes the most effectual way to prevent any serious impressions from being ever made on his mind. Experience and observation unite to prove, that the human mind, as is said of the chameleon, takes the complexion of those with whom it associates, and that the force of example, especially of bad example, is almost irresistible. There is in human nature a principle of association, in consequence of which we can scarcely avoid becoming, in some degree at least, conformed to those with whom we associate on intimate and friendly terms. The operation of this principle is powerfully assisted, and its effects increased, by that desire to please which is natural to man. Hence he, who selects persons regardless of religion as his companions, will become more and more like them; he will imitate their example; he will become thoroughly imbued with their spirit; and receive their principles and maxims as the perfection of wisdom. He will see them treat religion with indifference and neglect; he will hear them speak of it, if they speak of it at all, with levity, if not with contempt; he will find that they consider attention to it as quite unnecessary, and regard those who are the subjects of serious impressions as weak and deluded. Now it is evident that nothing can tend more powerfully than this to prevent him from ever becoming the subject of such impressions. It is evident that, by mingling in such society, he will become hardened against the truth, and fortified against every argument, motive, and consideration of a religious nature which can be presented to his mind. He will come to the house of God, not with any desire to receive instruction, but merely to spend an idle hour in vain thoughts, or in unprofitable gazing, or in listening for something to which he may plausibly object, or turn into ridicule; and while divine truth drops around him like the rain, and distils as the dew, there will be, if I may so express it, an umbrella spread over his head which will suffer no salutary drop to fall upon him; or in the language of Scripture, there will be a veil upon his heart, through which the light of divine truth cannot penetrate. It is therefore evident, not only that such a person has no serious impressions, but that there is very little reason to hope he will ever be the subject of them.

In the third place, he who selects persons regardless of religion for his associates, takes the most effectual way to banish those serious thoughts which will occasionally rise in the minds even of the most careless. God employs various means to excite such thoughts. An attack of disease, the death of a companion, or an awakening sermon, often occasions them. Now if a person in whose mind such thoughts arise, would entertain them willingly, cherish them, commune with his own heart and seek the society of religious persons, the consequences might be

most happy and lasting. But if he associates with persons regardless of religion, his serious thoughts will almost infallibly
be banished. Suppose, for instance, that a person, who comes
careless and thoughtless to the house of God, finds his attention
arrested, his understanding convinced, his conscience awakened
by the truths which he hears. While listening to these truths,
he probably forms a kind of vague, undefined resolution, that
he will pay more attention to religious subjects than he has done.
But he leaves the house of God, and almost unavoidably falls
in with some of his irreligious companions. He soon finds that
the truths, to which he has been listening with interest, have
not affected them in the same manner. If he ventures to hint,
that the sermon was convincing, or the subject of it important,
his remarks are received with the most frigid indifference, or
with a look of surprise mingled with contempt. He is therefore obliged to repress his serious thoughts, and such thoughts
when repressed soon leave us. Besides, he must make an effort to enter into conversation, or his companions will suspect
him of being serious,—a suspicion which he cannot bear to have
them entertain. The subject of conversation will, of course,
be of a worldly nature; it will excite worldly thoughts, and
thus his serious thoughts will be banished, so that, before he
quits his companions and returns home, the effect of the truth
which he has heard is entirely obliterated. I dare appeal to
many of you, my hearers, for the truth of these remarks. Many
of you cannot deny that you have been religiously affected by
the truth which you have heard in this house; nor can you deny
that, when you were thus affected, the society, conversation and
example of your irreligious companions, banished your serious
thoughts and lulled you to sleep again in the lap of sinful security. Thus it will always be, while you choose such companions.
You may be a thousand times roused, and a thousand times
may resolve that you will be more attentive to religion ; but so
long as you are a companion of sinners, your serious thoughts
will be banished and all your resolutions broken.

Finally, he, who associates with persons regardless of religion,
will inevitably form confirmed habits of feeling, thinking and
acting, which will operate most powerfully to prevent him from
ever becoming religious, and thus effect his destruction. The
language of inspiration is, Can the Ethiopian change his skin

or the leopard his spots? then may those, who are accustomed to do evil, learn to do well. But by associating with irreligious companions, men soon become accustomed to do evil. They acquire confirmed habits of neglecting religion, of delaying preparation for death, and of banishing serious thoughts. They also become more blindly devoted to the world, more fond of the society, conversation, and pursuits of those with whom they associate, and of course more enslaved by their influence and example. Thus, to use the language of Scripture, their bands are made strong, so strong that they will probably never break them. Nor is this all, there are among us few men, at least few young men, totally regardless of religion, whose morals are perfectly pure; few, who are not addicted to some species of vice. One is profane, another is intemperate, a third is debauched, and a fourth is not strictly honest. These sins may, at first, disgust a young man, whose morals are as yet uncontaminated; but if he continues to associate with those who are guilty of them, his disgust will infallibly, though gradually, subside. He will first tolerate these vices, for the sake of those who practise them; then he will learn to give them soft, extenuating names; next he will be taught that it is a proof of spirit and genius in a young man, to plunge into some excesses; finally he will take the plunge, and be entangled in a whirlpool, from which there is little reason to hope he will ever escape. What thousands and what millions of once promising youth have been ruined in this manner! Multitudes of our race have died in consequence of taking the plague, the yellow fever, the small pox, from the diseased; but far greater multitudes have been ruined, both for this world and for the next, by taking the infection of vice from vicious companions.

From the preceding remarks, it appears that he, who associates with persons regardless of religion, has no present religious impressions; that he takes the most effectual way to prevent such impressions from being made on his mind, and to efface them when they are made; and that he is continually forming habits most unfavorable to religion, and thus bringing himself into a state in which he can no more learn to do well, than an Ethiopean can change his skin, or a leopard his spots; of course, he will die without religion, and the doom of all who die without religion, is destruction. The companion of sinners then will be destroyed.   It remains to make some improvement of the subject.

1. From this subject we may learn what course we are pursuing, and what will be our fate if we continue in our present course till the end of life.   We cannot but know who are our chosen companions and associates; with whom we love to converse, and in whose society we find most pleasure.   We cannot but know whether they consist of persons apparently religious, or of those who pay no regard to religion.   Say then, my hearers, who are your associates?   Are you walking with religious characters, or are you companions of sinners?   I ask this question, not only of those out of the church, but of those who are in it; for, strange as it may appear, there are many in the church of Christ, who are companions of sinners.   They are united to the church only by the external tie of a profession; they do not walk with it; their hearts are not with it, but with the world. They feel most at home in worldly society; in such society they find most pleasure.   In worldly conversation they engage with most interest; worldly objects they pursue with most ardor. Now such persons, notwithstanding their profession, are companions of sinners in the sense of our text.   Say then, my hearers, what are you?   Are you with Christ or against him?   Can you truly say to God, in the language of the psalmist, I am a companion of them that fear thee, and that keep thy precepts? Are such characters your chosen associates, in whose company you find most pleasure, with whom you love to spend your leissure hours?   Then you either are religious, or if you continue to pursue this course through life, will become so.   But if you are a companion of those who pay no regard to religion, you are certainly irreligious, and if you pursue this course, destruction, everlasting destruction, will be your portion.

2. Let me beseech all present, and especially the young, to be guided by this subject in making choice of their associates. Remember that you are immortal beings, choosing companions for eternity.   Remember, that if you choose to associate with persons regardless of religion now, you must associate with them forever.   You must be partners with them in their destruction.   Remember too, that when you meet them in the other world, you will find them stripped of every quality which now renders their society pleasing.   For from him which hath not,

shall be taken away even that which he seemeth to have. Then those who are now your tempters shall be your tormentors, and feel a diabolical gratification in adding to your wretchedness. On the other hand, if you walk with good men, you shall have them for your companions through eternity; and not as they are now, stained by many imperfections, but perfect in every intellectual and moral excellence. Nor is this all. You shall also enjoy the society of angels, of your Redeemer, of your God. O then, be companions of them that fear God. Shun the society of every one who is addicted to any vice, as you would shun a man infected with the plague; for if you associate with such a person, there is almost a moral certainty that his vices will become yours. Still more earnestly would I press an attention to this subject on those who are the subjects of serious impressions, or who have any serious thoughts. Do you wish to have such thoughts forever banished, such impressions effaced from your mind? do you wish to live without religion, to die without hope, and to perish forever? Then choose for your companions persons who are regardless of religion. On the other hand, do you wish that your serious thoughts should continue, that your serious impressions should become deep and lasting, and that they should end in conversion? do you wish to live religiously, to die triumphantly, to be happy eternally? Then shun irreligious society and walk with good men. Choose them for your companions, listen to their instructions, request their prayers, imitate their example, attend with them on all the means of grace, converse with them freely respecting your religious concerns. Pursue this course without interruption, and the issue will be happy.

Finally; permit me, in the name of all God's people, to address to each of you the invitation which Moses gave to Hobab; We are journeying to the place of which the Lord said, I will give it you; come thou with us, and we will do thee good; for the Lord hath spoken good concerning Israel.

We are on probation on Earth
We Inherit the promises after this life

SERMON XIV

CHARACTER OF DANIEL.

O Daniel, a man greatly beloved.—DANIEL X. 11.

ONE of the great excellences of Scripture is, that it points out to us the path of duty, not only by precept, but by example. Not to mention the perfect pattern of a holy life, which it sets before us in the character and conduct of Christ, it presents to our view men of like passions with ourselves, in almost every possible variety of situation; and while it urges us, by the most powerful motives, to become followers of those who, by faith and patience, now inherit the promises, it clearly describes the way which led them to glory; and teaches us, by their example, in what manner to discharge the duties, support the trials, and overcome the temptations, of our probationary state.

Of those whose characters are thus recorded for our imitation, few, if any, will be found superior to Daniel. His life as described in Scripture, appears to be without blemish. He is almost the only eminent saint there mentioned, of whom no fault is recorded. *Job Noah Enoch* Nor was his character for goodness merely of the negative kind. Even during his life, he was placed by Jehovah himself, in the same rank with Job and Noah; men eminent in their day for faith and piety. In addition to this infallible testimony in his favor, we find him, once and again, addressed by an angel, as a man peculiarly dear to God. O man greatly beloved, says he, fear not; peace be unto thee; be strong, yea, be strong: for I am come to give thee skill and understanding, for thou art greatly beloved. The same title is given him in our text, by one who appears to have been the Son of God. I looked, says the prophet, and behold a man clothed in linen, whose loins were girded with fine gold. His body also was like the beryl; and his face as the appearance of lightning, and his eyes as lamps of fire, and his arms and his feet like in color to polished brass, and the voice of his words like the voice of a multitude. And he said unto me, O Daniel, a man greatly beloved, understand the words that I speak unto thee, and stand upright; for to thee am I sent.

My friends, nothing is more indispensably necessary to the welfare of all creatures, than the favor of their Creator. To be greatly beloved of God is the highest honor and happiness, to which we can possibly attain, either in this world or the next. Hence it becomes a matter of infinite importance for us to know how this privilege is to be obtained. This knowledge we may easily acquire, from an attentive consideration of the life and conduct of Daniel. We know from infallible testimony that he was greatly beloved; and have therefore every reason to conclude that all who resemble him will enjoy the love and favor of God. Let us then carefully examine his character, and ascertain, if possible, why he was so greatly beloved by his Creator.

The first thing in his character which deserves our attention, is his early piety. Like Josiah, though he was very young when carried captive to Babylon, yet even then he appears from his conduct to have been eminently pious. He must therefore, like Josiah, have begun at a very tender age, to seek after the Lord God of his fathers. At a period of life, when most young persons are wholly engrossed by follies and trifles, and know nothing of spiritual and divine things, he was well acquainted with the law of God; and, though a child in years, was a man in knowledge and understanding. This remembrance of his Creator in the days of his youth, when mankind generally forget him, was doubtless one among other things, which gave him so distinguished a place in the divine favor; for God's language to his creatures is, I love them that love me.

Another trait in the character of Daniel, deserving our atten-

Youth is No excuse

tion, is the caution, zeal and resolution which he displayed, in keeping himself unspotted from the world. This, the apostle James informs us, is an essential part of pure and undefiled religion; and for this, Daniel was highly distinguished. When carried to Babylon, he, with a few companions, children in whom was no blemish, but who were well-favored, and skilful in all wisdom, and cunning in knowledge, and understanding science, and possessing ability to stand in the king's presence, was selected from the other captives, and taken into the royal palace; that they might acquire the learning and language of the Chaldeans. In this situation, the king appointed them a daily provision of his own meat, and of the wine which he drank; so nourishing them for three years, that, at the end thereof, they might stand before the king. But Daniel purposed in his heart, that he would not defile himself with the king's meat. Various reasons might induce him to adopt this resolution. He might do it from love of country, and his fellow captives, with a view to show his sorrow for their calamities. He could say with Nehemiah, why should not my countenance be sad; why should I indulge my appetite in feasting when the city and place of my father's sepulchres lieth waste, and the gates thereof are burned with fire? If I forget thee, O Jerusalem, let my right hand forget her cunning: if I do not remember thee, let my tongue cleave to the roof of my mouth; if I prefer not Jerusalem above my chief joy. For a Jew to be joyful when his nation was thus smarting under the judgments of heaven, was not only unsuitable and improper, but highly displeasing to God: for we find in the prophet Amos, a wo denounced against those who eat the lambs out of the flock, and the calves out of the stall, and drink wine in bowls, in a time of public calamity, but are not grieved for the afflictions of Joseph. A regard to his country, and to this threatening, might possibly have some influence in producing Daniel's resolution not to defile himself with the king's meat. But it was, more probably, from a principle of obedience to the divine law. You need not be told, that, by the law, the Jews were strictly forbidden to eat certain animals, which were used for food among the heathen; and that all kinds of food which had been previously offered in sacrifice to idols, were considered by them as unclean. Had Daniel shared in the king's provision, he would have been under the necessity of eating, not only meats which had been offered to idols, but meats which were absolutely forbidden by the law of Moses. He, therefore, resolved not to defile himself by partaking of it; but to live only on herbs and water. If we consider the circumstances of his situation, my friends, we shall find reason to admire the firmness, zeal, and tenderness of conscience, displayed in this resolution. In age, he was but a child. The royal delicacies which he was invited, and even commanded to partake of, would doubtless have been highly gratifying to his appetite; and he might easily have invented many plausible excuses for enjoying them. He might have pleaded that he was a captive, and under obligation to obey those into whose power Providence had thrown him. He might have pleaded that by refusing to partake of the king's meat, he should bring upon himself much ridicule and reproach, and perhaps expose himself to severe punishments. He might have pleaded that the Jewish ceremonial law was not intended to be binding in a foreign country; and that since he was among the Chaldeans, he was under the necessity of complying with their manners and customs. With much less plausible excuses than these, do young persons, in general, satisfy themselves for complying with the sinful customs and manners of the world. But Daniel, notwithstanding his tender age, had sufficient firmness of mind to reject them. Be the consequence what it might, he was determined to maintain his integrity, and to preserve himself unspotted in the midst of a luxurious court, and ensnaring examples. Thus he early began to deny ungodliness, and every worldly lust, and to live soberly and temperately, presenting his body as a living sacrifice, holy and acceptable to God. This conduct doubtless had a tendency to secure the divine favor, and to render him a man greatly beloved by his Creator. It proved that he was not ashamed of his religion, his country, or his God; and that like Moses, he chose rather to suffer affliction with the people of God, than to enjoy the pleasures of sin for a season.

A third remarkable trait in the character of Daniel, is the holy indifference and contempt with which he looked down on worldly honor, wealth and applause. We have already seen how little he valued, even in his youth, those worldly, sensual pleasures, by which the young are so often fascinated and ensnared. As little did he value wealth and honor. Though he was of royal descent, and though he had, from his infancy, been educated in courts where religion was neglected, God dishonored, and the world idolized as the one thing needful; and though he possessed, in the court of Babylon, every possible opportunity and advantage, for acquiring riches and honors, yet he seems to have overcome all these temptations, and to have considered all these ensnaring objects, for which millions barter their souls, as trifles unworthy of his pursuit. It is true, he obtained both riches and honors; but it is no less true that he never sought them. They came to him unasked and undesired. He evidently appears to have preferred a calm, retired, humble station, to all that kings and courts could give. Witness the manner in which he treated the monarchs under whose government he lived. Instead of flattering them, as did others, and as he would have done, had he desired to secure their favor, he never failed to reprove them for their sins, when a favorable opportunity was offered him. Hear with what holy boldness he reproved the proud Nebuchadnezzar, the most powerful monarch on earth. Break off thy sins, says he, by righteousness; and thine iniquities by showing mercy to the poor. This was strange language to the ears of a prince, who was accustomed to hear nothing but the most extravagant praises and flatteries; and who was never addressed by his subjects without their prostrating themselves before him. With the same holy zeal and fortitude did he reprove the impious Belshazzar. When he offered to clothe Daniel in scarlet robes, adorn his neck with a chain of gold, and make him the third ruler in the kingdom, he replied with a holy contempt for these glittering trifles, let thy gifts be to thyself, and give thy rewards to another. Thou, O Belshazzar, hast not humbled thine heart, though thou knewest all that befel thy father, for his pride; but thou hast lifted up thyself against the Lord of heaven, and the God in whose hands thy breath is, thou hast not glorified. This, my friends, is not the language of a man of the world, who wished for the riches and honors which kings bestow on their favorites? No; it is the independent language of a man crucified to the world, and regardless of what that world could bestow. This trait in his character was indispensably necessary to render him beloved by his Maker; for we are expressly assured that the love and friendship of the world are enmity with God.

Another part of Daniel's character which we are called to notice, is his exemplary piety and devotion. He was emphatically a man of prayer. Though he lived in the midst of the tumult, noise, and confusion of a court, and during a great part of his life, had almost the sole direction of the counsels and offices of a powerful nation, which must necessarily involve him in an ocean of business, cares, and perplexities; yet he daily found much more time for secret prayer, than many Christians can find at the present day, who have nothing but their own private concerns to engage their attention. He never pleaded, as an excuse for neglecting this duty, that his body was too much wearied, and his mind too much perplexed by constant care and fatigue, to perform it. No; whatever obstacles might oppose it, or however loudly necessary business might demand his attention, he prayed to God regularly three times in a day; and he would much sooner have thought of neglecting his daily food, and sleep, than of omitting these accustomed devotional exercises. He lived, in this respect, like a man who knew that his soul needed daily refreshment, as well as his body; and who felt that, without God, he could do nothing. Praying was not with him, an idle form, a heartless ceremony, or a duty performed merely to quiet his conscience. No; it was his joy and delight; it was the very life of his soul; and with almost as much ease, might the sun be turned from his course, as he from his daily approaches to the throne of grace. Even the commands of the king, and the certainty of being cast into the den of lions, could not, for one moment, deter him from the performance of this duty. My friends, do you love prayer thus fervently and sincerely? How often, think you, should you approach the throne of grace, if your way to it lay through a den of lions?

But to return. In addition to the prayers which Daniel offered up, three times in a day, he frequently set apart seasons for more especial attention to this duty. He set his face, as he expresses it, to seek the Lord God by prayer and supplication, with fasting, and sackcloth, and ashes; and in the performance of these duties, he sometimes spent the greater part of every day for weeks together. Since God loves those who love him, we cannot wonder that a man whose fervent love for his Maker led him so frequently and constantly to the mercy seat, should be greatly beloved in return.

(7) Another trait in the character of this eminent saint, was his strong faith, and confidence in God. That he possessed such a faith is evident from the frequency and fervency of his prayers; since none truly pray, but those whose faith is strong and lively. That his faith was of this character is further evident, from his conduct, and from the testimony of Scripture. It was this which enabled him, without shrinking, to enter the lion's den, and which preserved him there unhurt. He was taken up out of the den, we are told, and no manner of hurt was found upon him; why?—because, says the inspired penman, he believed in his God. This, this alone preserved him. Like Moses, he endured as seeing him who is invisible. By faith, he could realize God's presence, and his ability to shut the lions' mouths. It was in consequence of possessing such a faith as this, that Abraham was called the friend of God. My friends, is your faith of this kind? Does it produce effects similar to these? Does it support and comfort you in dangers, trials, and temptations? It will do so, if it be genuine. But if it is not, if it is mere natural, speculative belief, it will have little effect. It will not overcome the world, it will not lead you to encounter perils and difficulties, for the sake of Christ; it will not enable you to see him who is invisible. It is without fruits; it is dead.

Again; profound humility, and a consequent disposition to give the glory to God, is another remarkable trait in the character of Daniel. This appears in his confessions and praises. Notwithstanding his eminent piety, we find him saying, O Lord, we have sinned, and have committed iniquity, and have done wickedly, and have rebelled by departing from thy precepts, and thy judgments. He seems to be at a loss for expressions sufficiently strong to describe the greatness of his sins, and heaps words together, in order, if possible, to show the deep sense which he entertained of his guilt and unworthiness. In the exercise of the same humble temper, we find him renouncing all pretensions to any worthiness or righteousness of his own; and depending entirely on the sovereign mercy of God. He might have trusted to his own prayers and merits, with as much propriety as any man that ever existed; but instead of this, we find him saying, O Lord, unto thee belongeth righteousness, but unto us confusion of face: we do not present our supplications before thee for our righteousness, but for thy great mercies. The same humble temper is strikingly expressed in his languuge to Nebuchadnezzar, when he revealed to him his dream with its interpretation. Instead of taking to himself the glory of this interpretation, he says, There is a God in heaven, who revealeth secrets; but as for me, this secret is not revealed to me for the sake of any wisdom that I have more than others. Here, my friends, you see the genuine language of humility. He was afraid that the king would suppose, either that he had discovered this secret by his own wisdom, or that it was revealed to him for the sake of his own superior goodness; and that thus, God would lose the glory of his own work. With a view to prevent this, and to lead the king to give the glory to God, he modestly disclaims all praise, and refers it to him to whom it was due. He who thus humbles himself shall be exalted.

(10) The last trait in the character of Daniel, which I shall mention, is, that his religion was habitual, uniform, consistent, and lasting. He was always the same. In childhood, in youth, in manhood, and in age; he inflexibly followed the path of duty, and steadfastly adhered to the God of his fathers. Nothing could seduce, nothing could drive him from his course, or induce him to deviate from it, for one moment, in the smallest possible degree. Of this, his conduct, when his enemies conspired to ruin him, affords a striking and satisfactory proof. When he knew that the decree, condemning any one who should pray to God for thirty days, to be cast into the den of lions, was irrevocably passed, he went into his house and prayed to God, as usual, three times a day; his windows being open towards Jerusalem. Yet how many plausible excuses might he have made, for conducting differently; and how many would he have made, had he resembled some professing Christians of the present day. He might have pleaded that his life was of great consequence to his countrymen; that it was in his power to do much good, in his then elevated station; that he was bound to obey the king his master; that it was his duty to preserve his own life; and that it would do no harm to any one, on such an occasion, to abstain from prayer for thirty days. At least, he might have urged that it would be justifiable, in such circumstances, to shut his windows, and pray in private; and thus disappoint the wicked designs of his enemies. These excuses, — any one but a real Christian would have made, and considered himself jus-

tified in omitting prayer entirely, or at least performing it ir secret. But Daniel was really religious, and therefore could not be deceived by these plausible excuses. He knew that he was watched. He knew that if he neglected to pray with his windows open, as usual, his enemies would assert that he had omitted that duty. He knew that, in this case, it would be said, See, Daniel, notwithstanding his pretended firmness and piety, can, like others, make his religion bend to his interest. He prefers his life to his duty. He cannot trust in his God to save him. His God, therefore, can be no better than the gods of the nations; and his religion is no better than ours. Thus God would be dishonored, the Chaldeans would be prejudiced against the true religion, and a glorious opportunity of suffering for Jehovah, would be lost forever. These reasons did not allow Daniel to hesitate a moment respecting what he ought to do; and for him to know what he ought to do, and to do it, were the same. He never troubled himself about consequences. He only asked, what is duty? When he once saw the path of duty, he would follow it though hell should open her mouth in his way. This, the whole tenor of his conduct proves; and a similar course must be pursued by all who wish to be, like him, beloved by their Maker.

IMPROVEMENT.—1. From this subject we may learn, my friends, how religion dignifies, and ennobles our nature, when it is entertained in its power and purity. How noble, how dignified, how sublime, does the character of Daniel appear! That you may see this in its true light, bring him forward; and compare him with the nobles, princes, and great ones of Babylon. See them indulging in sensual pleasures, proud of their wealth and birth, panting for riches, honor, and applause, seeking these transitory trifles by every possible means, neglecting immortal honors and glories; and meanly envying and hating that excellence, which they could not reach. See Daniel, on the contrary, calm, firm, and self-collected; with an eye fixed on God and heaven, despising the trifles which they pursued, aiming at the glory of his Maker, and the happiness of his fellow creatures, and following with unconquerable, undeviating resolution, the path of duty. While they grovelled on the earth, his head, and his heart were in heaven;—while their minds were darkened by the clouds of ignorance and prejudice, and their breasts con-

O my how beautiful

vulsed by the storms of ambition, avarice, envy, and revenge; his exalted soul dwelt in regions of eternal day, far above the clouds of mental ignorance, and the storms of contending passions. That you may, still more clearly, discern the superiority of his character, compare him with the kings whom he served. See Belshazzar, making a great feast, to a thousand of his lords; and surrounded by every thing, which could dazzle or delight the senses. See Nebuchadnezzar, walking in the midst of his palace, reflecting with self-complacency, on the nations he had subdued; and proudly exclaiming, Is not this great Babylon that I have built, for the house of the kingdom, by the might of my power, and for the honor of my majesty? Then turn your eyes to the prophet. See him, with that heroic boldness, which nothing but true piety can give, reproving the pride of one of these kings, and the impious extravagance of the other; see him, in defiance of threats, and impending danger, bending his knees to the only being whom he feared; see him, with unshaken calmness and serenity, sitting in the midst of ravenous lions, who, like lambs, crouch at his feet; — and then say which was the more dignified character, he, or the proud kings of Babylon. Nay more, say which possessed the more enviable titles and honors; he or they? They were styled princes, on earth. But he, as a prince, had power with God and prevailed. They were honored, admired, and applauded by their fellow-worms; but he was greatly beloved by his God. Who would not be Daniel in the lion's den, rather than Belshazzar, at his feast, or Nebuchadnezzar on his golden throne? O how evidently does it, in this instance, appear, that the righteous is more excellent than his neighbor. Such being the superior excellence of Daniel's character, permit us farther to improve the subject, by inquiring,

2. Do you, my friends, possess a similar character? This, all must allow to be an important question; since if we do not resemble Daniel, we are not, like him, beloved of God. Say then, does your temper, your conduct resemble his? Did piety like his distinguish your early years? Have you kept yourselves unspotted from the world, when temptations to sensual indulgence were peculiarly plausible and urgent? Have riches as little attraction for you as they had for him? Is your piety habitual, the same in all circumstances; and are you equally

fervent and persevering in prayer? Have you the same strong
faith, and equally triumphant in the darkest times; and do you
manifest the same deep humility, and unmoved firmness and
resolution?

Lastly, permit me to improve this subject, by urging all present
to imitate the conduct of Daniel. To induce you to this, consider what an unspeakable honor and privilege it is, to be greatly
beloved of God. It is the highest honor and happiness to which
a creature can arrive. It includes every thing, which creatures
can possibly desire; for, if God love us, then all things are ours,
all things must work together for our good, and nothing can do
us any real injury; for, says the Apostle, if God be for us, who
can be against us? O then, if you love life, if you love happiness, if you love yourselves, be persuaded to copy the example
of Daniel. Let those of you who are young, begin early, like
him, to seek after the Lord God of your fathers, and remember
your Creator in the days of your youth. Begin from this day
to cry unto him, My father, thou art the guide of my youth.
Let those who have lost this precious season, remember that it
is not yet too late, and strive to redeem the time which they
have wasted, by double watchfulness, zeal and diligence. Above
all, let those who profess to be the people of God, consider their
peculiar obligations, to imitate this ancient worthy. Would to
God, my professing friends, you could be prevailed upon to feel
the force of these obligations. Would to God, that every member of this church were a Daniel, in weanedness from the world,
in humility, in resolution, in faith, and in prayer. How would
religion then revive and flourish among us. How would gain-
sayers be confounded. How would our hearts be encouraged,
and God be glorified. How would your own souls rejoice.
My Christian friends, why will not each of you be a Daniel?
Are there no motives, no considerations, which will rouse you to
exertion? Is there nothing in your natures, on which we can
operate; no spark of holy ambition, of sacred zeal, which can
be blown up into a flame? O that we could breathe a divine,
celestial ardor, into your souls, and fire you with inextinguish-
able, insatiable desires after growth in grace. O that we could
persuade you to pursue religion, with that patient, zealous,
habitual, unwearied diligence, and resolution, with which you
pursue the things of this world. Then should we see our wishes

realized; then would this church be as a crown of glory, in the hand of the Lord, and as a royal diadem, in the hands of our God: then would there not only be some, but many, among us, to whom angels might say, Fear not, but be strong, O ye, who are greatly beloved of your God.

Amen.

SERMON XV

OUR OBLIGATIONS TO GOD AND MEN.

Render unto Cæsar the things that are Cæsar's; and to God, the things that are God's.— MARK xii. 17.

At the period of our Saviour's residence on earth, the Jews were greatly divided in opinion, respecting the lawfulness of paying tribute to the Roman emperors, under whose government they were. The Pharisees, prompted by ambition, and a wish to obtain popularity, earnestly contended that, as the Jewish nation were the peculiar people of God, they ought not to submit or pay tribute to a heathen power. The Herodians, as is generally supposed, maintained that, in their present circumstances, it was not only necessary but lawful. In this dispute, the common people sided with the Pharisees, while all who wished to secure the favor of the Roman government, took part with the Herodians. In these circumstances, the enemies of our Lord flattered themselves that by proposing to him this much disputed question, they should infallibly draw him into a snare. Should he decide in favor of the lawfulness of paying tribute, they could represent him to the people as an enemy to their liberties, and thus excite against him their indignation. Should he on the other hand, assert that to pay tribute was unlawful, they could accuse him to the Roman Governor, as a mover of sedition. The plot was artfully laid, and its execution artfully conducted; but in vain did human craftiness attempt to circumvent divine wisdom. Instead of directly replying to their question, our Saviour called for a piece of money, and asked, whose image and superscription it bore. They said Cæsar's. Render then, said he, to Cæsar the things that are Cæsar's, and to God, the things that are God's.

The spirit of this passage requires us to regard the rights of all beings as sacred, and to give them all what is theirs; or, as it is elsewhere expressed, to render to all their dues; tribute to whom tribute is due, custom to whom custom, fear to whom fear, and honor to whom honor is due. This important practical truth, we now propose to consider. I do not conceive that it requires any proof. You will, I doubt not, readily acknowledge, that we are bound to render to every being, what is his just due. All that is necessary, then, is to show what is due to the several beings with whom we are connected. In attempting to do this, I shall show.

I. What is due to God, and

II. What is due to men from each of us.

I. What is due to God; or, what are the things, the property of God, which our Saviour here requires us to render him.

The question may be answered very briefly; in one word; and that word is, all; for it is very easy to show that all things are in the most perfect sense the property of God. No right of property can be more perfect than that which results from creation, and surely no one present will deny that all things were created by him. Agreeably he claims them all. The earth is the Lord's and the fulness thereof; the world and all that dwell therein, for he founded and established it. The silver, he says, is mine; and the gold is mine; mine is every beast of the forest, and the cattle upon a thousand hills. Of course, we, and all that we possess are God's property, more strictly so than any thing which we call our own is our property, and he claims it all. But general remarks do not affect us. It is therefore necessary to descend to particulars, and mention separately the things that are God's and which he requires us to render to him.

1. Our souls with all their faculties, are the property of God. He is the Father of our spirits. Glorify God, says the voice of inspiration, in your spirits which are his. If any of you hesitate to acknowledge the justice of his claim to your souls, look at them for a moment. Contemplate their immortality, their

wonderful faculties, the understanding, the will, the imagination, the memory, and then say, whose image and superscription do they bear? Who gave you these faculties? Who
endowed them with immortality? Must it not be the king
immortal, the only wise God, to whom it is owing that there is a
spirit in man; who has given us more understanding than the
beasts of the field, and made us wiser than the fowls of heaven?
Our souls then, with all their faculties, are his, and to him they
ought to be given. Is it asked, what is implied in giving our
souls to God? I answer, we give them to him when we employ
all their faculties in his service; in performing the work which
he has assigned us. We give them to him when our under-
standings are diligently employed in discovering his will; when
our memories retain it, our hearts love it, our wills submit to it,
and the whole inner man obeys it. This is what is implied in
the first and great command, thou shalt love the Lord thy God
with all thy heart, and with all thy mind, and with all thy soul,
and with all thy strength.

2. Our bodies are the property of God. As he is the Father
of our spirits, so also is he the former of our bodies. Thine
eyes, says the psalmist, did see my substance, yet being imperfect; and in thy book all my members were written, when as
yet there were none of them. Thy hands, says Job, have made
me and fashioned me round about; thou hast clothed me with
skin and flesh and fenced me with bones and sinews. The
same work God has performed for each of us. Hence the Apostle exhorts us to glorify God with our bodies which are his, and to
present them as living sacrifice to God, holy and acceptable
in his sight, which is our reasonable service. Rendering to God
his own, implies then the giving of our bodies to him. This is
done when we employ our members as instruments of righteousness unto holiness. It is neglected when we use them as instruments of unrighteousness unto sin.

3. Our time is God's property. This is indeed implied in the
remarks which have already been made. Our time is that part
of duration which is measured by our existence. But during
every moment of our existence, we are the property of God.
To his service, therefore, every moment of our time ought to be
consecrated. If, at any moment, we are not serving him, we,
during that moment, withhold from him ourselves.

4. All our knowledge and literary acquisitions are God's property. They were acquired by us in the use of that time, and of those faculties which are his; and, of course, he may justly claim them as his own. And we find, that he does claim them. He compares our faculties and his other gifts to a sum of money, entrusted by a master to his servants, to be employed and increased for his benefit. And by the punishment which that master inflicted on a slothful, unfaithful servant, who neglected to improve his talents, he shows us what will be the doom of those who do not cultivate their faculties, or who do not consecrate to him, the fruits of that cultivation. Indeed, it is difficult to conceive how we can justify ourselves in acquiring knowledge, unless with a view to serve him more effectually. If it be not sought with this view, it must be sought merely for the purpose of gratifying, enriching, or aggrandizing ourselves; a motive to action, of which God does not approve, and which is in direct opposition to the letter and spirit of our text.

5. Our temporal possessions are God's property. They are all, either the gifts of his providence, or, as was remarked respecting our literary acquisitions, were obtained by the use of time and faculties which belong to him. They are his also by the right of creation, a right, as has been observed, of all rights the most perfect. Agreeably, we find that men are frequently represented in the Scriptures, not as the owners of their possessions, but merely as stewards, to whose care the Lord of all things has entrusted a portion of his property, to be employed agreeably to his directions. These directions allow us to employ such a portion of the property thus entrusted to us, in supplying our own wants, as is really necessary to our support and happiness, or as is consistent with the rules of temperance and the demands of benevolence. But, if any part of it be spent in gratifying what St. John calls the lust of the flesh, the lust of the eye, or the pride of life, it is devoted to a purpose for which our master never designed it, and he will consider and treat us as unfaithful stewards.

Lastly; our influence is God's property. This follows as a necessary consequence from the preceding remarks. All our influence over others results either from our natural faculties, our knowledge, or our wealth; all of which have been shown to be the property of God. Of course, the influence which we derive from any of these circumstances, is his also, and ought ever to be exerted in promoting his honor and interest in the world. It appears, then, that rendering to God the things that are God's, implies consecrating to his service, our souls, our bodies, our time, our knowledge, our possessions and our influence. He who withholds from God any of these things, or any part of them, does not comply with the precept in our text.

II. I proceed, as was proposed, to show what things are due from us to men. At first view it may seem as if nothing were due; or, at least, that we have nothing which we can render to them; for if, as has been shown, we, and all that we possess are the property of God, what remains for men? I answer, if God had not required us to render something to men, nothing would be due to them, nor should we have the smallest right to bestow any thing upon them. But as God is the sole and sovereign proprietor of everything that exists, he has a perfect right to say how it shall be disposed of. He has a right to appoint such receivers as he pleases, and he has in part appointed our fellow-creatures to be receivers of a large portion of what we owe him. To this portion, they have, therefore, a just claim. And when we regard this claim, when we give any thing to men, in compliance with the will of God, he considers it as given to him. The question, what is due from us to our fellow creatures, is then equivalent to the inquiry, what are those things which God requires us to give to men, and to which they have therefore a right; a right, founded in his revealed will. This question I now propose to answer.

1. All men, without exception, have a right to our love; a right to expect that we should love them as we love ourselves; and that as we have opportunity, we should do to them, as we should wish them, in a change of situation, to do to us. This, as I need not inform you, God expressly requires. Love thy neighbor as thyself. Whatsoever things ye would that men should do to you, do ye even so to them. Nor are our enemies to be excepted; for, says our Saviour, Love your enemies, bless them that curse you; do good to them that hate you, and pray for them that despitefully use you and persecute you. All men then, so far as they are known by us, have a right to our love, and to all the kind offices which love would prompt us to perform. Every man, who dies without having done all the world,

all the good which it was in his power to do, dies in debt to the world, or to the world's Creator. Withhold not good, says the voice of inspiration, from him to whom it is due, when it is in the power of thy hand to do it. Do good to all men, as ye have opportunity. To him that knoweth to do good, and doeth it not, to him it is sin. Much more then have our fellow creatures a right to expect that we should do them no injury. They have a right to our good opinion, till they forfeit it by misconduct. They have a right to expect that we refrain from speaking evil of them, except when duty requires it; to expect that persons, reputation and property, should be in our hands as safe as in their own. It is scarcely necessary to add, that all with whom we transact any business, have a right to be treated with the most perfect fairness and honesty. Love will, of course, lead to this. Justice requires it. God commands it. Let no man, he says, overreach or defraud his brother in any matter; for the Lord is the avenger of all such. Now the man who knowingly takes or retains the smallest portion of another's property, is dishonest, unjust, and exposes himself to this threatening.

Nor will it avail anything for him to plead that he takes no more than the law gives him; for human laws are necessarily imperfect; and their application must, in many cases, be still more so. They often allow men to take, or to retain that, to which, by the law of God, they have no right. And remember, that we are to be tried, not by the laws of men, but by the law of God. He then, who, in any case, takes more than the law of God, the law of love allows, or retains what that law forbids him to retain, is condemned by it. The rust of his unlawful gain, says an apostle, shall witness against him, and eat his flesh, as it were fire. Among such unlawful gains, must be included all that is acquired by defrauding the public revenues. The only difference between defrauding the public and defrauding an individual, is, that in the former case, we cheat many, and in the latter, only one. The sum which each man pays the public, is paid for a valuable consideration. It is paid for the secure enjoyment of life, reputation, liberty and property. If one man pays less than he ought for this purpose, others must pay more, and then they are defrauded.

2. To all whom God has made our superiors, we owe obedi-

ence, submission and respect. As subjects, we are bound to
obey, honor and pray for our rulers. Let every soul of you be
subject to the higher powers. Submit to every ordinance of
man for the Lord's sake. Thou shalt not speak evil of the ruler
of thy people. Pray for all that are in authority. As children
we are required to honor and obey our parents. But as this
duty has been recently under consideration, it is needless to
enlarge. Servants are required to be obedient to their masters
with all reverence, not answering again, and to account their
masters worthy of all honor; and they, adds the apostle, who
have believing masters, let them not despise them, because they
are brethren, but rather do them service because they are faithful.
We may add that the aged, considered merely as such, have a
claim to respect. Thou shalt rise up, says Jehovah, before the
hoary head and honor the face of the old man.

3. To our inferiors we owe kindness, gentleness and condescension. They have a right to expect that their feelings should
not be needlessly wounded, and that regard should be paid to
their comfort and convenience. Parents provoke not your
children to wrath. Masters forbear threatening. Let all condescend to men of low estate. The poor and afflicted have special
claims. The afflicted have a right to our sympathy; the industrious poor to pecuniary relief. With respect to this duty, many
indulge erroneous opinions. They allow that we ought to be
just and honest, to pay our debts, but with respect to liberality
to the poor, they seem to imagine that we are left at liberty to
do as we please. But if the law of God be adopted as our rule
we shall find that it requires charity no less than justice. We
shall find that we owe a debt to the industrious poor, which,
though they cannot, strictly speaking, demand, God requires us
to pay. In his sight, the man who is not charitable to the poor,
is dishonest and unjust. But with respect to the indolent poor,
the decision of Scripture is, that if any man will not work,
neither shall he eat.

4. Those of us who are members of Christ's visible church,
owe to each other the performance of all the duties, which result
from our connexion. We are bound to watch over our professing brethren, to admonish them when needful, and to seek in all
things the peace and welfare of the church. We are also under

special obligations to promote their temporal interest; for while the Scriptures command us to do good to all men, they add, specially to those who are of the household of faith.

Lastly; there are some things which we owe our families and connexions. As husbands and wives, we owe each other the strict and faithful performance of the promises which we made, when we were united. As parents, we owe our children the best education for this world and the next, which it is in our power to give them. As heads of families, we are bound to provide for their wants, to the utmost of our power, for he who neglects to do this, has denied the faith and is worse than an infidel.

Thus, my hearers, have I stated the principal things which we owe to God, and to men, and the payment of which is implied in rendering to both the things which are theirs. The justice of this statement, I think no one can deny, who does not deny the authority of the Scriptures. On this ground I am prepared to meet any man, and defend the truth of every position which has been advanced. It only remains to improve the subject.

1. In view of this subject, how great, how incalculable is the debt which we have contracted, both to God and to men. All the things which have been enumerated justly belong to them, and ought to have been paid them, from the first moment of our moral existence. But surely I need not attempt to prove that we have not paid them. We have not even rendered to men, the things that are men's; much less have we rendered to God the things that are his. Every day, every hour of our waking existence, we have withheld something both from God and from men, which was due to them. Every day and hour, therefore, our debt to him is increasing. Well then may our Saviour represent us as owing a debt of ten thousand talents. Well may God accuse us of robbing and defrauding him. Will a man, says he, rob God? Yet ye have robbed me. How vain, how false then, are the pretences of those who assert that they have injured no one, that they pay every one his own; and how presumptuous are the hopes which they build upon this assertion! They make all religion to consist in paying their pecuniary debts, and in avoiding any instance of dishonesty, which is for-

bidden by human laws. They deny or forget that God has any
rights; they think it neither unjust nor dishonest to withhold
from him his property. But, my hearers, though we forget
God's rights, he will not; nor will he suffer them to be disregarded with impunity. He knows how to claim and to receive
what is his. He has death ready to arrest us. He has an
eternal prison from which there is no escape, in which multitudes of unfaithful stewards are now confined, and in which he
will confine us, till the uttermost farthing be paid; unless we
can find a surety, able and willing to take our debts upon himself. Hence,

2. We may learn our need of an interest in the Saviour, and
the impossibility of being saved without him. We evidently
cannot discharge our past debts. Should we, from this moment
become perfect, and render both to God and men all that is
theirs, it would not prevent our debt from increasing. It could
make no satisfaction for the past. It could cancel no part of the
debt which we have already contracted, and for that we should
still be answerable, and must still be condemned. In this view
the situation of every sinner is desperate. He is loaded with a
debt which he is unable to pay, which is constantly increasing,
and which he must discharge or perish. But though we have
thus destroyed ourselves, in Christ there is help. He becomes
surety for all that believe in him; takes upon himself the debt,
which they can never discharge, and thus sets their souls at
liberty. By the assistance of his grace, and through him as
their mediator, they are enabled to present themselves to God,
living, holy and acceptable sacrifices. This is the way and the
only way of salvation.

And now, my hearers, what shall we say to these things? I
make no appeal to your passions. I appeal to your understand-
ings and consciences, and ask, is it not just that God should
require us to render to him and to men, what is due to each
respectively? Is it not just that he should punish those who
neglect to do this? Have we not all, even the best of us, neglected to do this? Was it not infinitely good and merciful in
God to provide a surety to discharge debts, which we might
most justly have been called on to pay! Are we not under
infinite obligations to him, who consented to become our surety,

and who to save our forfeited lives, laid down his own? And do not reason, conscience, and a regard to our own happiness, combine with Scripture in urging us, to accept the offers of this divine Benefactor; and constrained by his love, to live henceforth to him and not to ourselves! To these questions, my friends, there can be but one true, reasonable, scriptural answer. Practically give them that answer, and your souls shall live.

SERMON XVI

PARTICIPATION IN OTHER MEN'S SINS.

Neither be partaker of other men's sins. — 1 TIMOTHY v. 22.

IN this chapter the apostle gives Timothy particular directions
respecting the duties of his pastoral office; and solemnly charges
him before God and the elect angels, to observe these directions;
not preferring one man above another, and doing nothing by
partiality.   One of the most important of his official duties con-
sisted in ordaining other men to the work of the ministry by
prayer and the imposition of hands.   As it was of the greatest
importance that none should be introduced into the ministry
who were not suitably qualified, the apostle particularly enjoined it upon him to use great care and circumspection in
examining and setting apart persons for this sacred office; and
enforced a compliance with this injunction by intimating to him,
that, should he neglect it, he would participate in the guilt of
every unworthy character, on whom he should carelessly lay
hands.   Lay hands, says he, suddenly on no man, neither be
partaker of other men's sins, but keep thyself pure.

My hearers, though this caution was originally addressed to
an individual with reference to the duties of a particular office,
it is of universal application.   In many other parts of Scripture
we are all indirectly, if not directly, cautioned to beware of
partaking in the guilt of others; and introducing improper

characters into the ministry, is by no means the only way in which a disregard of this caution may be shown. In every state of society, and especially in such a state as exists in a civilized country, under a form of government like ours, we are connected with our fellow creatures so intimately, and by such numerous ties, that there are very many ways in which we may become accomplices, or at least partakers, in their sins; and indeed, without great care and watchfulness, it is impossible to avoid being so. In consequence of these connexions, the sins of an individual become the sins of many, and there is no doubt that, in the sight of God, a large proportion of every man's guilt is contracted by sharing in the guilt of others. This being the case, the subject which we have chosen is, I conceive, peculiarly suitable for a day of public humiliation, fasting and prayer. On such a day, we are called upon to humble ourselves before God, not only for our personal sins, but for all the sins of others in which we have made ourselves partakers. In discoursing on this subject, I shall endeavor to show, when we make ourselves partakers in other men's sins; and to state some of the reasons which should induce us to guard against partaking in them.

I. When do we make ourselves partakers in other men's sins? I answer, generally speaking we partake in the guilt of all those sins which we tempt or assist others to commit; of all the sins which we voluntarily or carelessly occasion by our influence or example; of all the sins which we might but do not prevent; and of all the sins against which we do not bear testimony when we have opportunity to do it. On each of these particulars it would be easy to enlarge and to confirm our observations by appropriate quotations from the Scriptures, but these quotations will be more properly introduced in succeeding parts of our discourse. Now from these observations it follows,

1. That ministers make themselves partakers in the sins of their people, when those sins are occasioned by their own negligence, by their example, or by unfaithfulness in the discharge of their official duties. But why do I mention this to you? Not because you are in danger of partaking in this way of other men's sins, but because my subject naturally leads to this remark; because I am willing to preach to myself as well as to

you, and because this remark suggests a sufficient excuse, if excuse be necessary, for the pointed observations which I may be
called upon to make in the progress of my discourse; for from
this remark it follows that, if you are in danger of sharing in
the guilt of other men's sins, it is my duty, as a minister of
Christ, to warn you plainly of that danger, and to point out the
way in which you may avoid it; and should I neglect thus to
warn you, I should myself share in the guilt of all your sins,
and of all the sins of which you make yourselves partakers.
Now this I can by no means consent to do. I am willing to
participate in all your sorrows and afflictions, but I am not willing to share in your sins. I have enough and more than
enough of my own to answer for, without participating in
yours. Let this be my apology, if in this, as well as in my
other discourses, I use great plainness of speech.

2. Parents participate in the sins of their children, when they
occasion, and when they might have prevented them. That
this remark is perfectly just, when applied to such parents as
set before their children a vicious example, I presume none will
deny. Should a parent voluntarily pain the bodies of his children, or communicate to them a dangerous and infectious
disorder, all would unite in reprobating his unnatural conduct.
But is it not as abominable for a parent to pain the minds, as
the bodies of his children? And can any poison operate upon
their bodies more fatally or more certainly, than the vicious example of a parent will operate upon their minds? If he be
intemperate, or indolent, or profane, will not his children, unless
a gracious providence prevent, most probably resemble him?
And may he not be most justly considered and punished as a
partaker of their sins; sins, which come, if I may so express
it, recommended, and, as it were, sanctified to them by the example of those, whom God and nature had constituted the*
guides of their youthful steps?

But while almost all unite in justly execrating the wretch,
who thus poisons the souls of his unsuspecting offspring, there
is another class of parents, who, though perhaps equally guilty
in the judgment of God, meet with scarcely a censure from the
lips of man. I mean those who set their children an irreligious
example. This class includes every parent who is not himself
truly and exemplarily pious. And why should this class be

thought less guilty, than that already mentioned? Is not irreligion as surely destructive to the soul as immorality? Are not impenitence, and unbelief, and insensibility to religion, as positively forbidden, and as severely censured in the word of God, as are intemperance or profanity or theft? Will not every impenitent or irreligious character be as certainly doomed, as a robber or murderer? Why then is an irreligious, less guilty than an immoral parent? But many, who belong to this class, will reply, we teach our children to treat religion and its institutions with respect. We speak of the Scriptures to them with reverence, and bring them with us to the house of God on the sabbath. True, you do so, but they can perceive but too clearly that you do not cordially love the Bible, or honor its Author, or comply with the instructions of the sanctuary. They there hear many duties inculcated which they do not see you practice. They see, they hear nothing of religion in your families, they see you turn your backs upon the Lord's table; they see you live without God in the world; they see you anxious for their success in this life, but perceive no concern for their happiness in the next. Now what shall prevent them from following your example? And what shall save them from endless perdition if they do? And by what mode of reasoning will you prove, should they perish, that you were not partakers of their sins, and accessaries to their eternal ruin? My friends, it will be terrible to hear a ruined child exclaim at the last day, Lord, I lived as my parents taught me to do, I trod in their steps, I omitted nothing which they prescribed; but they led me along, they were the cause of my sins, and of my destruction. My hearers, if it be true that he who provides not for the temporal wants of his own house, hath denied the faith and is worse than an infidel, what shall be said of those parents, who, instead of providing for the spiritual necessities of their children, voluntarily occasion their eternal ruin?

But further, parents partake in the guilt of their children's sins when they might and do not prevent them. If it be true, as the Scriptures assert, that a child, trained up in the way he should go, will not depart from it when he is old, then it follows that, whenever children do forsake the right way, it must be ascribed, either wholly or in part, to the negligence of their parents. Either their parents did not warn, and teach, and re-

strain them as they ought, or they did not pray for a blessing
on their endeavors with sufficient earnestness, or they did not
seek for wisdom from above to enable themselves to perform parental duties in the most wise and prudent manner.   It is probably in this last respect that Christian parents are most deficient.
They do not properly realize how much heavenly wisdom is
necessary to the right education of children; and, therefore,
though they warn and pray for their children, yet they do not
pray sufficiently for wisdom for themselves.   This omission
renders many parents, whose conduct is otherwise unexception-
able, partakers in the sins of their children, and their children's
children.   They will, probably, unless divine grace prevent,
educate their children as we educated them ; and their children,
when they become parents, will follow their example, and where
the spreading mischief will end, God only knows.   How careful, how diligent, how prayerful, then, should parents be.   Every
parent should consider himself as a fountain, from which proceed streams, that will grow broader and deeper as they run,
and should recollect, that it depends on himself, under God,
whether these streams shall prove poisonous or salutary, convey
virtue and happiness, or vice and misery, wherever they flow.
Remember the story of Eli.   His sons made themselves vile,
and he restrained them not, and his negligence not only made
him a partaker in their guilt and punishment, but entailed the
judgments of God on his descendants, to the latest generation.
    3. The remarks, which have been made respecting parents,
will apply, though perhaps somewhat less forcibly, to masters
and guardians, and all who are concerned in the government
and education of youth.   Human laws, you are sensible, make
masters answerable, in many instances, for the conduct of their
apprentices and servants, and the law of God does the same.
It is a maxim in both, that what a man does by another, he
does by himself.   If a master allows his servants or dependants
to use profane language, to neglect the institutions of religion,
to profane the Sabbath, to spend his leisure hours with vicious
companions, or to indulge in any other wicked practices, when
he might prevent it, it is nearly the same in the sight of God, as
if he were guilty of the same things himself; and he will be
considered as partaking in their sins.   You might almost as
well spend this day in the streets or in places of amusement, in

idleness and sin, as suffer your children, servants or dependants to do it. Hear the character and blessing of Abraham, ye parents, masters, and guardians. And the Lord said, shall I hide from Abraham the thing that I do? seeing that Abraham shall become a great and mighty nation, and all the nations of the earth shall be blessed in him? For I know him that he will command his children and his household after him, and they shall keep the way of the Lord, to do justice and judgment; that the Lord may bring upon Abraham that which he hath spoken of him.

4. Churches become partakers of the sins of an individual member, when these sins are occasioned by a general neglect of brotherly watchfulness and reproof, and when they are tolerated by the church in consequence of a neglect of church discipline. When this is the case the sins of an individual become the sins of a whole church. This is evident from Christ's epistles to the seven churches of Asia. He commends the Ephesian church because they could not bear them that were evil, while he severely reproves and threatens other churches for tolerating among them those things which he abhorred. In a similar manner St. Paul rebuked the Corinthian church for neglecting to excommunicate one of their members who was guilty of a notorious offence; and charges them to put away that wicked person. To these remarks we may add, that every member of a church makes himself a partaker of the known sins of his fellow members, when he neglects to bear testimony against their sins, and to use proper means for bringing them to repentance.

5. We all make ourselves partakers in other men's sins, when we either imitate or in any other way countenance and encourage them. In this way the whole human race make themselves partakers of the sin of our first parents. They imitate them in desiring forbidden fruit, in disobeying God's commands, in endeavoring to hide themselves from his presence, and in attempting to excuse their sinful conduct when called to an account for it. By this conduct all men tacitly justify our first parents, and do in effect say, had we been in their place we would have acted as they did. Thus, to use a law term, they become accessaries after the fact. In a similar way do persons often make themselves partakers of the sin of their wicked an-

cestors. They imitate and then justify their conduct. An attention to this truth will show us why God threatens to visit the iniquities of the fathers upon the children, and why he often executes this threatening by punishing one generation for the sins of those who have gone before them. He does so because those, whom he thus punishes, imitate and thus participate in the sin of their ancestors. This is evident from the case of the Jews in our Saviour's time. Behold, says he, I send you prophets and wise men and scribes; and some of them ye will kill and crucify, and some of them shall ye scourge in your synagogues; and persecute from city to city; that upon you may come all the righteous blood shed upon the earth, from the blood of righteous Abel to the blood of Zacharias, son of Barachias, whom ye slew between the temple and the altar. Verily, I say unto you, it shall all be required of this generation. Now the reason assigned for requiring of that generation all the righteous blood shed by their ancestors, is, that they imitated and thus justified their conduct. Their fathers murdered the prophets, and they did the same to Christ and his apostles; thus making the sin of every preceding generation their own.

In the same way we may make ourselves partakers of the sins of our contemporaries. When a province rises up in rebellion against its sovereign, every rebel partakes in the guilt of his fellow rebels, since by his example he encourages and justifies them. So in this rebellious world, every impenitent, unbelieving sinner, partakes in the guilt of all other sinners. In justifying himself he justifies them, by persisting in sin he encourages them to do the same, and thus in effect makes their sins his own.

6. Members of civil communities partake of all the sins which they might, but do not prevent. When a person has power to prevent any sin, he is left to choose whether that sin shall, or shall not be committed. If he neglects to prevent it, it is evident that he chooses it should be committed, and by thus choosing it he does in effect make it his own. He shows that he does not hate sin, that he has no concern for the glory of God, but is willing that God should be dishonored and offended. If he is deterred from attempting to prevent sin by fears that he shall draw hatred or trouble or expense upon himself, it proves that he loves himself more than God; and that he is more con-

cerned for his own interests, than for the welfare of society. Besides, all allow that men ought, if possible, to prevent gross crimes and public calamities, and even human laws would condemn as an accomplice the man who should witness a murder or robbery without preventing it or giving an alarm, when he had power to do it. And why then may not God justly condemn us as partakers of all the sins which we might have prevented! My friends, whether you think it just or not, he will do it; and you will hereafter be called to an account for all the violations of the Sabbath, all the profanity, all the intemperance, all the vice of every kind of which you have made yourselves partakers by neglecting to employ those means for their prevention, which God and the laws of your country have put into your hands.

7. If private citizens partake of all the sins which they might have prevented, much more do rulers and magistrates. To prevent and punish vice is the very object for which they are appointed, the great duty of their office; their office is ordained of God, and they are required by him not to bear the sword in vain, but to be a terror to evil doers, and a praise and encouragement to such as do well. To the faithful and impartial performance of this duty, their oath of office also binds them; and when they thus perform it, they are indeed what they are called and designed to be, ministers of God to us for good. But if they neglect their duty, violate their oaths, and prove false to God, they must answer to him for the incalculable mischief which they will occasion; and all the sins, which they might have prevented, will be set down to their account. Next to the doom of unfaithful ministers, that of unfaithful rulers and magistrates will probably be most intolerable.

Lastly: Subjects who have the privilege of choosing their own rulers and magistrates, make themselves partakers of all their sins, when they give their votes for vicious or irreligious characters. I hope, my hearers, it is not necessary to assure you that this remark has no party political bearing. In making it I certainly do not mean to censure one party more than another, nor do I intend the most distant allusion to any of our rulers or magistrates; for I am taught not to speak evil of dignities. I merely state it as an abstract principle, which cannot be denied, without denying the truth of Scripture, that when we vote for vicious or irreligious men, knowing them, or having good reason to suspect them to be such, we make ourselves partakers of all their sins. It is evident that the case bears a great resemblance to that referred to in our text. If Timothy made himself a partaker of the sins of every unworthy character whom he carelessly admitted into the ministerial office, then we certainly make ourselves partakers of the sins of every improper character whom we voluntarily assist in appointing to any public office. But as many, even among good men, do not appear to think sufficiently of this truth, it may not be improper to insist upon it more particularly.

In the first place, God has plainly described the characters whom we ought to choose for rulers and magistrates. Thou shalt provide out of all the people able men, such as fear God, men of truth, and hating covetousness, and place such to be rulers. And again, he that ruleth over men must be just, ruling in the fear of God. He has also told us, that when the righteous are in authority the people rejoice, but that when the wicked bear rule the people mourn. If then we choose different men for our rulers, we slight God's counsels and disobey his commands.

Again: We are taught in the Scriptures, that we must give an account to God of the manner in which we employ the talents and improve the privileges with which he favors us. Now the right of choosing our own rulers is undoubtedly a most precious privilege. This, I presume, you will readily acknowledge; for we frequently hear of the precious right of suffrage. Now what account of this privilege can they give to God, who have abused it by assisting to place in authority such characters as were enemies to himself and his government, such characters as he has forbidden us to appoint?

Once more; rulers and magistrates are servants to the public. Now we have already reminded you, that what a man does by his servant, he does by himself. If then we voluntarily assist in appointing vicious or irreligious rulers, we make ourselves partakers of all their sins, and must account for all the good which might have been done, had we chosen different characters.

Thus have I attempted to show when we become partakers of other men's sins. If any think I have asserted more than I nave proved, I reply, we meet with instances in the inspired writings, in which God punished ministers for the sins of their people, parents for the sins of their children, children for the sins of their parents, churches for the sins of individual members, rulers for the sins of their subjects, and subjects for the sins of their rulers. But surely he would punish none for the sins of other men, who had not made themselves partakers of those sins. These facts attended to are, therefore, a sufficient proof of all that we have advanced.

I proceed, as was proposed,

II. To state some of the reasons which should induce us to guard against partaking of other men's sins. The first reason which I shall mention is, that if we partake of their sins, we shall share in their punishment. Hence when God was denouncing vengeance upon the mystical Babylon, he says, come out of her, my people, that ye be not partakers of her sins, and that ye receive not of her plagues. Hence, too, the many woes denounced against the companions of sinners of different classes.

Another reason that should induce us to guard against this is, that we shall have sin enough of our own to answer for, without participating in the guilt of others. He who realizes what sin is, what it is to answer for it, and how numerous and great are his own personal sins, will surely wish to avoid sharing in the transgressions of his fellow sinners. But on this part of our subject, time forbids us to enlarge, and requires us to hasten to the improvement.

In the former part of the day, my friends, I endeavored to make yon acquainted with your own personal transgressions. I have now attempted to give you a knowledge of the additional guilt you may have contracted by partaking of the sins of others. And is there an individual present, who does not, in some of the ways which have been mentioned, partake of the sins of those around him? Look first, my friends, into your houses; reflect on the conduct of your children, servants, and apprentices, and see if there be no sins there which you might prevent. In the next place, look through the town; that it is full of sin you need not be told. The cry of it ascends not only into the ear of God, but into those of man. Among all the vices which provoke God, ruin men, demoralize society, and bring down the judgments of heaven, there is scarcely one which is not prac-

tised among us. If a man wishes to indulge in profanity, sab-
bath-breaking, intemperance, gaming, or debauchery, he knows
where to find companions to countenance and assist him, and
where to find places set apart on purpose for such abominations.
Many of these vices stalk abroad among us, in open day. There
is not virtue enough in the community to drive them back into
their dens, or to make them hide their heads. The inhabitants
of our moral pest houses are suffered to range at large, and
spread the contagion of their vices. No wonder, then, that our
children inhale the infection; and that many of the rising generation promise to outstrip in wickedness every generation that
has gone before them. If it should, God have mercy on our
country; for surely nothing but infinite mercy can save it from
destruction! Now, my friends, it becomes us to inquire to whom
is the prevalence of these vices to be ascribed? If we have no
laws to restrain them, then the blame must rest upon our legislators; and those who choose them are partakers in their guilt.
But if we have laws to restrain these abominations, then the
blame must rest on those whose business it is to execute the
laws; and all who prevent, all who do not assist in the execution of these laws, must share in the blame. For my own part,
I am determined that, if loud and repeated testimonies against
these things can prevent it, none of this blood shall rest with
me; and I advise every one, who has any concern for his own
soul, or for his eternal happiness, to adopt the same resolution;
for it will be no light thing to be found partakers, at the judgment day, of the enormous sins which are committed in this
town. Happy will it then be for him who can truly say, I am
clear from the blood and from the guilt of all men.

2. It is impossible not to perceive how completely our subject justifies the conduct of those much insulted individuals,
who have voluntarily associated for the purpose of assisting in
executing the laws, and suppressing vice and immorality among
us. Their God, the God whom our fathers worshipped, and
whom we, their degenerate sons profess to worship, commands
them not to be partakers in other men's sins. They have obeyed
the command, and what has been their reward? The same
which all the faithful servants of God in all ages have received
from those whose welfare they labored to promote, by separat-
ing them from their beloved sins. They have been ridiculed,

insulted, turned out of those seats of office, which they honorably and faithfully filled; and are indebted wholly to a good Providence, and to the laws which he has given, for their preservation from worse evils. Many of you, my hearers, have calmly sat by and seen this done, if you have not assisted in doing it. And, my friends, those who thus revile and oppose the friends of virtue and religion, would treat Christ and his apostles in a similar manner, were they now on earth.

* * * *

SERMON XVII

PRAYER FOR RULERS.

I exhort, therefore, that, first of all, supplications, prayers, intercessions, and giving of thanks be made for all men; for kings, and all that are in authority, that we may lead a quiet and peaceable life, in all godliness and honesty.—1 TIMOTHY II. 1,2.

It appears from the preceding chapter, that Timothy had been left, by St. Paul, at Ephesus; to watch over the church in that city, and to guard against the introduction of error, by false teachers. In this chapter, the apostle gives him particular directions respecting some of the social and relative duties which were to be enjoined upon all, who professed to be the disciples of Christ. Among these duties, he mentions first in place, as first in importance, that of intercession; or praying for others. I exhort, says he, that, first of all, supplications, prayers, intercessions, and giving of thanks, be made for all men; for kings, and all that are in authority. It is evident that persons in authority are included in the direction to pray for all men. It appears, however, that the apostle did not think it sufficient, to inculcate the duty of praying for them, in this general way only. He felt that it was necessary to make a particular mention of this duty, in a clause by itself. He does, in effect say, While I exhort you to pray for all men, I urge you, especially to pray for those who possess the supreme power, and for all that are in authority. He thus evidently intimates, that, in addition to the general reasons, which should induce us to pray for all men, there are particular reasons why we should pray for those who rule. I propose, in the present discourse, to state the reasons why we should pray, with peculiar frequency and importunity, for all who are invested with authority.

I. We ought to pray for those who are in authority, more frequently and earnestly than for other men, because they, more than other men, need our prayers. In other words, they need a more than ordinary share of that wisdom and grace which God alone can bestow; and which he seldom or never bestows, except in answer to prayer. This is evident in the first place, from the fact, that they have a more than ordinary share of duties to perform. All the duties which God requires of other men, considered as sinful, immortal, and accountable creatures, he requires of rulers. It is incumbent on them, as it is on other men, to possess personal religion; to exercise repentance toward God, and faith in the Lord Jesus Christ; to love and fear, and serve their Creator; and to prepare for death and judgment; for Jehovah's language to them is, Though ye be as gods, ye shall die like men, and have your portion like one of the people. In addition to the various personal duties, of a moral and religious nature, which are required of them, as men, they have many official duties, which are peculiar to themselves; duties which it is, by no means, easy to perform in a manner acceptable to God, and approved of men. They are appointed, and they are required to be ministers of God for good to those over whom they are placed. They are, in a certain sense, his representatives, and vicegerents on earth; for by him they are appointed, and to him they are accountable for the manner in which they discharge their duties. By me, says he, kings reign and princes decree justice; by me princes rule, and nobles, yea, all the judges of the earth. Promotion cometh not from the north, or from the south; but it is God that setteth up one, and putteth down another. There is no power but of God, the powers that be are ordained of God. Since then, legislators, rulers and magistrates are the ministers and vicegerents of God for good, they are sacredly bound to imitate him, whom they represent; to be such on earth, as he is in heaven; to take care of his rights, and see that they are not trampled upon with impunity; to be a terror to evil-doers, and a praise and encouragement to such as do well. They are also bound, by obligations, which ought ever to be regarded as sacred, and inviolable, to seek the welfare of those over whom they are placed, to prefer it, on all occasions, to their own private interests; to live for others, rather than for themselves; and to consider themselves, their time, and their faculties, as the property of the State. As the influence of their example must be great, it is their indispensable duty to take care that this influence be ever exerted in favor of truth and goodness; and to remember that they are like a city set upon a hill, which cannot be hid. Now, consider a moment, my hearers, how exceedingly difficult it must be for a weak, short-sighted, imperfect creature like man, to perform these various duties in a proper manner, and how large a share of prudence, and wisdom, and firmness, and goodness, is necessary to enable him to do it. Surely, then, they who are called to perform such duties, in a peculiar manner need our prayers.

2. Those who are invested with authority, need, more than other men, our prayers; because they are exposed, more than other men, to temptation and danger. While they have a more than ordinary share of duties to perform, they are urged by temptations, more than ordinarily numerous and powerful, to neglect their duty. They have, for instance, peculiarly strong temptations to neglect those personal, private duties which God requires of them as men, as immortal and accountable creatures; and a performance of which is indispensably necessary to their salvation. They are exposed to the innumerable temptations and dangers which ever attend prosperity. The world presents itself to them in its most fascinating, alluring form; they are honored, followed, and flattered; they enjoy peculiar means and opportunities for gratifying their passions; they seldom hear the voice of admonition or reproof; and they are usually surrounded by persons who would consider every expression of religious feeling as an indication of weakness. How powerfully, then, must they be tempted to irreligion, to pride, to ambition, to every form of what the Scriptures call worldly-mindedness? How difficult must it be for them to acquire and maintain an habitual, operative recollection of their sinfulness, their frailty, their accountability to God, their dependence on his grace, and their need of a Saviour. How difficult, in the midst of such scenes and associates, as usually surround them;

to keep death in view; to be in a constant state of preparation for its approach; to practise the duties of watchfulness, self-denial, meditation and prayer; and to preserve, in lively exercise, those feelings and dispositions which God requires, and which become a candidate for eternity. How strongly, too, must they be tempted to make the performance of their official duties, an excuse for neglecting those personal duties, which God requires of all men, in whatever station or circumstance they may be placed. I will only add, with reference to this part of our subject, that the Scriptures intimate with sufficient clearness that those temptations are, in most instances, but too fatally successful. They inform us, that not many mighty men, not many noble, are saved. Our Saviour farther declares, that it is hard for a rich man to enter into the kingdom of God; and it would be easy to shew that the causes which render it difficult for a rich man, operate with equal force to make it difficult for men clothed with authority, to enter this kingdom. We may remark farther, that they have many powerful temptations to neglect, not only their personal, but their official duties. They are tempted to indolence and self-indulgence; tempted to prefer their own private interest, to the public good; tempted to pay an undue regard to the selfish wishes and entreaties of their real, or pretended friends; tempted to adopt such measures as will be most popular, rather than those which will be most beneficial to the community; tempted to forget the honor and the rights of Jehovah, and suffer them to be trampled on with impunity. It can scarcely be necessary to add, that persons who are exposed to temptations so numerous and powerful, peculiarly need our prayers.

3. This will appear still more evident if we consider, in the third place, that, should those who are clothed with authority, yield to these temptations, and neglect either their personal or official duties, the consequences will, to them, be peculiarly dreadful. Their responsibility is greater than that of other men. They have greater opportunities of doing both good and evil, than other men. If they do good, they will do much good. If the influence of their example, and their exertions, be thrown on the side of truth and goodness; no one can compute how great, or how lasting, may be the salutary effects which they will produce. On the contrary, if they do evil, they will do

much evil. They will, like Jeroboam, make their people to sin. We are informed, by an inspired writer, that one sinner destroyeth much good. This remark is true of every sinner; but it is most emphatically true, of sinners who are placed in authority. One such sinner may destroy more good, and prove the cause of more evil, than a whole generation of sinners who are placed in a lower sphere. And even if they do not actually do evil, they may occasion great evil, and incur great guilt, by neglecting to do good. Says the voice of inspiration, To him that knoweth to do good, and doeth it not, to him it is sin. In another place, we are taught that men partake in the guilt of all those sins which they might have prevented. Legislators, rulers, and magistrates, then, are answerable to God for all the possible good which they neglect to do; and they share in the guilt of all the sins which they might, but do not, prevent. So far as those who are invested with authority, neglect to prevent, to the utmost of their power, open impiety, irreligion, disregard of the Sabbath, and of divine institutions, profanation of God's name, intemperance, and other similar evils; they share in the sinfulness and guilt of every Sabbath-breaker, profane swearer, and drunkard, among those over whom they are placed.

How great, then, is the responsibility of all who are invested either with legislative, judicial or executive authority! How aggravated will be their guilt, how terrible their punishment, should they prove unfaithful to their country and their God! Surely then, they, above all other men, need our prayers; since they have peculiarly difficult duties to perform, are under peculiar temptations to neglect those duties; and, if they neglect them, will receive a punishment peculiarly severe. And remember, my hearers, that we assist to place them in this difficult and dangerous situation. Are we not then sacredly bound to afford them all the assistance in our power, to obtain for them all that wisdom and grace from heaven, which it is in the power of fervent and persevering prayer, to draw down? Shall we place them, as watchmen, upon a steep and slippery precipice, where it is exceedingly difficult to stand, and infinitely dangerous to fall; and neglect the only means which can render their standing secure? God forbid. It is unreasonable, it is ungenerous, it is cruel and unjust,—cruel and unjust, not only to them, but to ourselves, and to the community. This leads me to observe,

4. We ought to pray with peculiar earnestness for all who are in authority, because our own interest, and the great interests of the community require it. This motive, the apostle urges in our text. Pray, says he, for all in authority, that we may lead quiet and peaceable lives, in all godliness and honesty. These expressions plainly intimate, that, if we wish to enjoy peace and quiet; if we wish godliness and honesty, or, in other words, religion and morality, to prevail among us, we must pray for our rulers. That we depend on them, under God, for the enjoyment of these blessings, is too obvious to require proof. How much, for instance, do the morals, the peace and prosperity of a State, depend upon the enactment of wise and equitable laws. And how much integrity, wisdom, and prudence, how much knowledge of human nature, of political principles, and of the science of legislation, is necessary to enable men to frame such laws. And from whom shall legislators obtain these qualities, if not from the Father of lights, from whom cometh down every good and perfect gift; to whom it is owing that there is a spirit in man, and whose inspiration gives us understanding. Again; if the morals, peace and prosperity of a State depend much on the formation of good laws, no less do they depend on the proper execution of those laws. Indeed, the best laws, unless strictly and impartially executed, are perhaps worse than none; since they only serve to show the vicious and abandoned that legal restraints may be disregarded with impunity. But it evidently depends much on rulers and magistrates whether the laws shall be executed with strictness and impartiality; and perhaps it requires more firmness, integrity, and wisdom to execute them in this manner, than it does to enact them. Permit me to add, that it is exceedingly important that those by whom the laws are enacted and executed, should themselves exemplify obedience to the laws; for if they disregard their own enactments, it can scarcely be expected that others should obey them.

Farther; the peace and prosperity of a nation, evidently depend much upon the measures which its rulers adopt, in their intercourse with other nations. A mistake or error in this respect, apparently trifling, may not only involve a nation in great embarrassment, but can plunge it into all the evils of war, and it is too much to expect of fallible, short-sighted creatures, that they should never fall into error, unless they are guided by him who sees the end from the beginning, and who can never err.

Once more; the peace and prosperity of a nation depends entirely on its securing the favor of God. This, I presume, no one will deny. But his favor cannot be secured by any nation, unless its rulers are just men, ruling in his fear. We have already observed, that rulers share in the guilt of those national sins which they might, but do not, prevent. We may add, that nations share in the guilt contracted by their rulers, and in the punishment of their sins. Of this remark, many striking verifications are recorded in the Scriptures. Indeed, if those who are placed in authority, become impious, irreligious, or immoral, they will soon, by the force of their influence and example, impart much of their own character to the people over whom they preside; and thus render them fit objects of the divine displeasure. Permit me to add, that we cannot rationally expect to be favored with wise and good rulers; we cannot expect that God will bestow on them those intellectual and moral endowments which are necessary to render them ministers for good, unless we fervently ask of him these blessings; for favors which we neglect to ask, he may refuse to bestow. Nay more, he will probably punish our negligence and impiety, by turning our national counsels into foolishness. We are informed, that when he pleases, he can take the wise in their own craftiness, and carry headlong the counsel of the froward; that he leadeth counsellors away spoiled, and maketh judges to become fools; that he removeth the speech of the trusty, and taketh away the understanding of the aged; that he taketh away the heart of the chief of the people, so that they grope, as in the dark; and that he can, on the other hand, counsel our counsellors, and teach our senators wisdom. If, then, we wish to enjoy the protection of wise and equitable laws; if we wish our rulers to be endowed with wisdom, prudence and integrity; if we wish to see our country prosperous and happy; to see learning and liberty, morality and religion flourish; let us never forget to pray with earnestness and perseverance, for all who are invested with authority.

There are some things, in our present situation, which render this exhortation peculiarly seasonable. In the first place, is there not reason to believe, that the duty here enjoined, is a duty which we, and our countrymen generally, have too much neglected? Have we not all been much more ready to complain of our rulers, than to pray for them? Some have complained of our national government, and some of our State government; but where is the man who has prayed for either, as he ought? Have we not reason to believe that, if one half the breath which has been spent in complaining of our rulers, had been employed in praying for them, we should have been much more prosperous and happy, as a nation, than we now are? If any feel convinced that we have erred in this respect, let me remind them that now is the time to correct our error. We are now commencing a new mode of political existence. Now, then, is the time to correct past errors, and to establish right principles.

In the second place, it is now peculiarly important and necessary that we should pray for our legislators and rulers, because the duties which they are now called to perform, are peculiarly arduous; and because much, very much depends upon the manner in which these duties shall be performed. Not only our own temporal interests, but the future prosperity of the State, the welfare of our children, and of our children's children, will be seriously affected by the official conduct of our present chief magistrate, counsellors, and legislators. To them is committed the difficult and responsible work of shaping the commencement of our course; and such as is its commencement, will probably be its progress and its termination. Surely, then, every one who has a tongue to pray, ought to employ it in earnestly supplicating the Father of lights, to impart to our present rulers, a double portion of his own Spirit; and to give them, as he did Solomon, a wise and understanding heart, that they may know how to rule and guide this people. Let every one who calls himself a disciple of Christ, remember that one of his Master's commands is, Pray, supplicate. intercede for all who are in authority. View them, my friends, in the light of this subject, and methinks you cannot deny them your prayers. See them placed in an awfully responsible station, where they have numerous and difficult duties to perform, where they are exposed to peculiarly powerful temptations, where they are in imminent danger of losing everlasting life, and incurring aggravated guilt and condemnation. Remember that they are men, and of course. weak. fallible. and mortal. Look forward to the other world, and see them there reduced to a level with other men, and standing before the tribunal of God, where nothing remains of all the honor and influence which they once possessed, except the consequences of the manner in which they employed it. View them in this light, and you cannot but feel for them, and pray for them, that they may obtain mercy of the Lord to be faithful, and receive a crown of righteousness in the great day.

To conclude; how desirable is it both to rulers and people, that such a disposition should exist; that the religion which enjoins and produces it, should universally prevail among us. What an encouragement would it be to rulers, to unite their own morning supplications with those of the people over whom they were placed, and with what confidence might they engage in the duties assigned them, believing that he whom they and their subjects had addressed, would direct all their paths. Then religion, and morality and peace and harmony would prevail. Rulers would love their subjects, and seek their good; and subjects would love the rulers, in whose behalf they were daily addressing the throne of grace; while the God whom they both worshipped, would command the blessing upon them, out of Zion; and the world would see how good and pleasant it is for rulers and subjects to dwell together in unity. It is, however, necessary to remark, that all these blessings can scarcely be expected from the prayers of the people alone. They must be attended with the prayers of their rulers. All the considerations which have been urged, as reasons why we should pray for those who are in authority, may be urged with still greater force, as reasons why they should pray for themselves. In this way alone, can they obtain that wisdom and grace which are indispensably necessary to render them faithful in this world, and happy in the world to come. Never, perhaps, since the foundation of the world, has a state been so prosperous, so happy, as was the Jewish nation, while under the government of one who began his reign by saying, Lord, thou hast set thy servant over this great people, and thy servant is as a little child, and knows not how to go out, or come in before them. Give thy servant, therefore, a wise and understanding heart, that I may know how to rule this thy people. God grant that this may be the sincere prayer of all our rulers, and that all the people may say, Amen !

SERMON XVIII

LOVE TO CHRIST INDISPENSABLE.

Jesus saith to Simon Peter, Simon son of Jonas, lovest thou me more than these? He saith unto him, Yea, Lord; thou knowest that I love thee. He saith unto him, Feed my lambs. — JOHN XXI. 15.

WE have in this chapter a particular account of an interview between our Saviour, and some of his disciples after his resurrection. Of the disciples, present at this interview, Peter was one. The shameful manner in which he had denied his master, you, doubtless, recollect. Though he had unfeignedly repented of his sin, and, in consequence, obtained pardon, his master thought proper on this occasion to remind him of it again. With this view he addressed to him the question in our text; and as Peter had thrice denied that he knew him, he thrice repeated the question, and thrice drew from him the declaration, Lord thou knowest that I love thee. And you will observe, my hearers, that, while thus examining this backsliding disciple, he asked him no other question. He did not inquire what Peter believed, or whether he had repented; for he well knew that, where love is present, faith and repentance cannot be absent. The question before us is then, evidently, in our Saviour's view, a most important question. And were he now present, it would probably be the only question, or at least, the first question, which he would ask of each of us. If any one present wished for admission to his church, his table, nothing more would be indispensably necessary to his admission, than an ability to answer this question with truth in the affirmative. Nay more, this is, in effect, the only question which Christ will ask us at the judgment day, the question on our answer to which our destiny will depend; for the language of inspiration, the word by which we shall be judged is, Grace be with all them that love the Lord Jesus in sincerity; but if any man love not the Lord Jesus, let him be accursed when the Lord comes; and the Judge himself has expressly declared that no man, who does not love him more than he loves any other object, can be his disciple. My design in the present discourse is, to show why the exercise of supreme love to Christ is thus indispensably necessary to our salvation.

1. The exercise of love to Christ is indispensably necessary, because the want of it proves that we do not, in the smallest degree, resemble him; proves that we are destitute of goodness, and, of course, entirely sinful. It may with truth be asserted, that no man acquainted with the New Testament, who does not love the Lord Jesus Christ, can be a good man, or possess the smallest degree of love or desire for goodness. It will be readily allowed that Christ was perfectly good. Every good man will, in some degree, resemble Christ. Now those who resemble each other, will, if they are acquainted, love each other. Place good men in the same town, and as soon as they know each other, they will be friends. Or place them at a distance, and let them become acquainted with each other's character by report, without any personal intercourse; and they will feel a mutual affection and wish to meet. But if all who resemble each other, love each other, then every good man loves good men; much more, will every good man love Christ, who is goodness itself, goodness personified, goodness in its most attractive form. If he loves goodness in the stream, much more will he love it in the fountain. He then who does not love Christ, does not, in any degree, resemble him; does not possess the smallest share of goodness; and, as no one can really desire what he does not love, does not even desire to be good. Agreeably, we find that all good beings in heaven, and on earth, have ever loved Christ, so far as they have had opportunity to become acquainted with his character.

2. Love to Christ is indispensably necessary, because without it we cannot perform those duties which he requires of his disciples and which are necessary to salvation. For instance, we are required to repent of the sin we have committed against him; but to do this without love is evidently impossible. Can you, my hearers, mourn, can you feel truly grieved, in consequence of having offended a person whom you do not love? You may, indeed, feel a selfish sorrow, if you fear that punishment will follow the offence; but this is not that godly sorrow which works repentance, and which Christ requires. No; when a child mourns that he has grieved his parents, it is because he loves them. When you feel grieved in consequence of having offended a friend, it is because he is your friend. Love then, love to Christ, is an essential part of those emotions which the inspired writers call a broken heart and contrite spirit. Again, we are required to believe, to confide, to trust in Christ. But can we confide in a being, can we trust our all for time and eternity in the hands of a being, whom we do not love? Can a dying man commit his immortal soul with pleasure to the care of one whom he does not love? Can we even firmly believe the promises, and rest with implicit confidence on the assurances, of one whom we do not love? Evidently not. Where there is no love, there will be want of confidence, there will be suspicion. Indeed, the only reason why sinners find it so difficult to believe in Christ is, they do not love him.

Farther; we are required to obey the commands of Christ, to be his servants, his subjects. Now obedience to many of his commands, involves the performance of duties which seem disagreeable, and submission to sacrifices, which we are naturally unwilling to make. He commands us, for instance, to deny ourselves, to take up the cross, to crucify our sinful affections and desires, to part with every thing cheerfully at his call, to make sacrifices, which he compares to cutting off a right hand and plucking out a right eye. Now we may be willing to do all this for the sake of one whom we supremely love; for love makes hard things easy, and bitter things sweet. But can any man feel willing to submit to all this for the sake of one whom he does not love? Can any man prefer the interest of Christ to his own, and the honor of Christ to his own reputation, unless he loves Christ more than he loves himself? Yet this Christ

So if you do not know & understand the love of Jesus you don't know love at all.

206   L O V E   T O   C H R I S T

expressly requires of all who would be his disciples. In addition to this, we are required to imitate Christ. We are told that he has set us an example that we should follow his steps. But can any one strive to imitate a person whom he does not love? In other words, can he sincerely endeavor to acquire a character with which he is not pleased, in which he sees nothing beautiful or lovely?

Again; we are commanded to rejoice in Christ. Rejoice in the Lord always, says the Apostle, and again I say, rejoice. But how is it possible to rejoice in a being for whom we feel no affection? We can easily rejoice in a friend; but by what unheard of process shall we bring ourselves to rejoice in one whom we do not love? Farther, we are commanded to remember Christ, to commemorate at his table his dying love. But how hard it is to retain in our memories, an object which has no place in our affections. How little pleasure can we find in coming to the table of one whom we regard with indifference? We may indeed, bring our bodies; but our hearts will be absent, and the whole service will be uninteresting to ourselves, and no better than solemn mockery in the estimation of Christ.

Finally, we are commanded to love the friends, the disciples of Christ, and to love them for his sake. But to obey this command without love to Christ is evidently impossible. We cannot love children for the sake of their parents, unless we first love the parents; nor can we love the disciples of Christ for his sake, unless we love Christ himself. It appears, then, that to obey any of Christ's commands without love, is impossible. We may add, that, even if it were possible to obey him without love, our obedience would be unacceptable and worthless; for he searches the heart, he knows what is in man, he cannot be deceived by mere external services and professions, nor is it possible that he should be pleased with them, since he sees them to be insincere.

3. The exercise of supreme love to Christ is indispensably necessary, because without it we cannot relish the society of his disciples, or enjoy communion with them, or consistently unite with them in religious duties. The Apostle John informs those to whom he wrote, that his design in writing his epistle was, to bring others to the enjoyment of fellowship with himself and his fellow disciples. These things declare we unto you that ye also may have fellowship with us; and truly our fellowship is

with the Father, and with his Son Jesus Christ. Now communion consists in a joint participation of the same views and feelings. That we may enjoy communion with Christians, then, it is necessary that our views and feelings should resemble theirs. But they have exalted views of Christ, and feel supreme love for him. He himself informs us that he has not a disciple in the world, who does not love him more than he loves any other object. (How then can one who does not love Christ, relish the society of his disciples, or enjoy communion with them, or unite in their religious services?) How unpleasant must be the situation of such a man when surrounded by a circle of lively Christians. Their hearts glow with love to an object in which he sees no beauty. They speak to him of the amiableness and excellence of the Saviour, but he knows not what they mean. Yet he must endeavor to say something, though he has nothing to say; or else maintain a sullen silence, and thus excite doubts of his sincerity. (In short, he must feel like a deaf man at a concert of music, or like a blind man in a gallery of pictures, surrounded by others whose senses are gratified and whose admiration is excited.) It is the same, when he attempts to unite with Christians in the performance of religious duties. They thank the Saviour, but he feels no gratitude. They praise the Saviour, but he sees nothing to admire; their hearts ascend to heaven on the wings of devotion, but his remains behind. He may indeed find himself able to converse with them on some religious subjects, to contend eagerly for some truths, and to declaim fluently respecting doctrines; but when the beauties and glories of Immanuel are the theme of conversation; when any affection for him is expressed, he must either be silent, or say what his heart does not feel, what it never felt.

Once more; supreme love to Christ is indispensably necessary, because without it we could not possibly be happy in heaven. This, my friends, is capable of strict demonstration. You will allow that no man can be happy who is where he does not wish to be. No man can wish to be in a place where he is separated from all that he loves. But the man who does not love Christ, would find nothing in heaven to love; would find himself separated from all that he loves. All the objects which he ever loved, all the pursuits, employments, and society in which he ever found pleasure, he leaves behind him when he leaves this world. He would, therefore, feel like a stranger in heaven; he would look back to this world as his home; he would wish to return here, for where our treasure is, there will our hearts be also; and as that wish could not be gratified, he would not be happy. (But this is not all.) To a man who does not love Christ, the society and employments of heaven would appear exceedingly disagreeable. We have already seen that such a man cannot enjoy the society or cordially unite in the devotions of Christians on earth. For similar reasons, he would find it still more difficult to enjoy the society, or join in the praises of heaven. All who reside there love the Saviour perfectly. They feel and express for him the most ardent and intense affection. Their happiness very much consists in seeing, serving, and praising him. Now what happiness could be found in such society and employments, by a man who does not love the Lord Jesus? You well know that nothing can be more irksome, than to praise what we do not admire; to express ardent affection, when we feel the most perfect indifference. Yet this would be the situation of one in heaven, who does not love his Redeemer. He must, through endless ages, praise what he does not admire, and profess love which he does not feel; and what is still worse, he must utter these praises and professions to one who knows their insincerity. It would be sufficiently painful to flatter one whom we do not love, even if we could deceive him by our flatteries, and induce him to believe we were sincere. But to flatter one whom we cannot deceive; to stand and utter lies to him, while we are conscious that he knows them to be lies, this would be misery indeed. But it is needless to enlarge. Nothing can be more evident than the fact, that a man who does not love Christ supremely would be unhappy in heaven. Indeed every such person, who is at all acquainted with his own heart, must be conscious of the fact. You doubtless recollect the unhappy man who was executed in this town for murder, about ten years since. While in his dungeon, after listening to the description which inspired writers give of heaven, he told me that he should rather remain in that dungeon through eternity, than go to such a heaven as he had heard described. Now I appeal to those of you who do not love the Lord Jesus, whether your feelings are not in some degree at least similar to his? If you hesitate to admit this, permit me to make the following supposition. Suppose some town in our country should be made, as nearly as possible, to resemble heaven. Suppose all the inhabitants without exception, to be, not only pious, but eminently so. Suppose all worldly amusements, all political discussions, all commercial transactions, all secular conversation, to be banished from among them; while the presence of Christ should be enjoyed in a peculiar manner, and all the employment should be to love and praise and serve him? Would you joyfully choose that town, in preference to all other places, for your earthly residence? Could you, while retaining your present character, while destitute of the love of Christ, cheerfully leave every thing behind, and live happily in such a place? If you reply, No, then is it much more evident that you could not be happy in heaven. If you reply, Yes, we could be happy in such a situation, — I ask, why then do you not, so far as is possible, live such a life of religion here? Why are not those who appear to love Christ most sincerely, and to praise him most ardently, your chosen companions? In a word, if you could be happy in heaven, why do you not seek happiness by living a heavenly life on earth?

From what has been said you may learn, my hearers, why the inspired writers lay so much stress on the exercise of love to Christ; why he requires it of all his disciples. It is not for his own sake. It is not because our love can add any thing to his happiness. But it is because that, unless we love him, we are destitute of goodness, and of all love and desire for goodness; and are unable to obey his commands, to enjoy communion with his people, or to be happy with him in heaven. The commands which require us to love Christ are not then mere arbitrary commands; but are founded in the nature of things, and obedience to them is necessary.

From this subject we may learn,

1. In what respects many characters highly esteemed among men are deficient, essentially deficient, in the sight of God. I allude to persons whose dispositions appear to be amiable, whose morals are correct, whose religious opinions are perhaps agreeable to truth, and who pay a decent respect to religious institutions. Can you not easily conceive, my friends, that a man may possess all these qualities and yet be destitute of love to Christ? Do you not know among your acquaintances many

persons who have pleasing manners, amiable dispositions, and who live moral lives, and yet do not appear to feel any love to Christ? Are there not some such persons among your acquaintances, whom you would be surprised to hear speaking of the Saviour with affectionate warmth, or expressing grief for having neglected him, or urging others to love him? Do you not perceive that a great alteration must take place even in these moral, amiable persons, before they can sincerely adopt the language, in which Paul and other primitive Christians express their affection for the Saviour; and still more, before they can cordially unite with the redeemed in crying, Worthy is the Lamb to receive glory, and honor, and power, and blessing? If so, you surely cannot blame us for asserting that something more than morality is necessary; that a man may be what is called a good moral man, and yet be no Christian; and that a radical change of heart is necessary to moral men, as well as to immoral and profane. Nor will you complain if, adopting the language of the poet, we exclaim,

> "Talk they of morals? O thou bleeding Lamb!
> Thou Maker of new morals for mankind;—
> The grand morality is love of thee."

The young ruler mentioned in the gospel appears to have possessed all the qualities mentioned above; but yet he lacked one thing, essential to his Maker's approbation, and his own happiness.

2. Is the question in our text the great important question which Christ addresses to all, and on our ability to answer which satisfactorily every thing depends? Permit me, then, to address this question to every one who wishes to ascertain the reality of his title to an admission into Christ's visible church, to an approach to his table, to the heavenly inheritance. Does any one present wish to know whether he is prepared for admission to the visible church? Christ, who keeps the door, says to him, Lovest thou me? If thou dost, enter freely. Does any one already in the church, who has lost his first love, or practically denied his master, wish to know whether he is forgiven, whether, notwithstanding this conduct, Christ will make him welcome to his table? The only question to be answered is, Lovest thou me? And if any one wishes to know whether he

is prepared for heaven, the question is still the same. Will you say, it is impossible for any one to answer this question decisively? It appears from our text, that this is a mistake. Peter could say to his heart-searching Lord, when his penetrating eye was fixed full upon him, Lord, thou knowest that I love thee. If Peter could thus certainly know, and confidently assert, that he loved Immanuel; all who sincerely love him may say the same, unless their love is so faint that they cannot perceive it. And O how happy is the man who can truly say this! With what delight must he approach Christ's table! With what confidence can he meet death! with what triumphant joy may he join with the Apostle in exclaiming, — I know whom I have believed, and am persuaded that he is able to keep that which I have committed to him against that day.

My soul + my Heart + My Mind

SERMON XIX

THE CHARACTERS WHOM CHRIST LOVES.

I love them that love me. — PROVERBS VIII. 17.

THESE are the words of Christ. He who is styled the WORD
OF GOD in the New Testament, calls himself the WISDOM OF GOD
in the Old. Under this character he is represented as standing
in the public places of resort, and soliciting the attention of all
who pass by : Unto you, O men, I call; and my voice is to the
sons of men. The motives which he sets before them to induce
a compliance with his call are numerous and powerful. In the
first place, he claims their attention on account of the endless
duration of his existence. I was set up, says he, from everlasting, from the beginning, or ever the earth was. When God
prepared the heavens, I was there; when he set a compass upon
the face of the deep; when he gave to the sea his decree, when
he appointed the foundations of the earth; then was I by him,
as one brought up with him; and I was daily his delight, rejoicing always before him. In the next place, he claims attention
on account of the dignity and excellence of his character:
Counsel is mine, and sound wisdom; I am understanding; I
have strength. By me kings reign and princes decree justice;
even all the judges of the earth. In the third place, he urges
them to listen to his instructions because of their excellence,
plainness, truth and utility : Hear, for I will speak of excellent

things; my mouth shall speak truth. All the words of my mouth are in righteousnes; they are all plain to him that understandeth. Receive my instruction, and not silver, and knowledge rather than choice gold; for wisdom is better than rubies; and all the things that may be desired are not to be compared to it. In the fourth place, he urges them to love and obey his voice by promises on the one hand, and threatenings on the other: Blessed are they that keep my ways; for riches and honor are with me, yea durable riches and righteousness. I cause those that love me to inherit substance, and I will fill their treasures. Blessed is the man that heareth me, watching daily at my gates, waiting at the posts of my doors; for whoso findeth me, findeth life, and shall obtain favor of the Lord; but he that sinneth against me, wrongeth his own soul; all they that hate me love death. Lastly, he urges them to love him on account of his long attachment to mankind, and his readiness to reciprocate affection; I was ever rejoicing in the habitable parts of the earth, and my delights were with the sons of men. I love them that love me, and they that seek me early shall find me. The love which Christ here professes to entertain for those who love him, is an affection of a peculiar kind, entirely different from that general love which he feels for all his creatures; and infinitely more desirable. There is a sense in which he loves even his enemies. He loves them with a love of benevolence, a love which leads him to mourn over them when they obstinately refuse to comply with his invitations. Thus we are told that, while on earth, he was grieved with the hardness of their hearts; and wept over rebellious Jerusalem, when he contemplated the miseries that were coming upon her. He also loves the holy angels with a love of complacency and delight because they bear the image and obey the will of his Father. But the love which he entertains for his people, is an affection of a still more tender and peculiar kind; an affection, the nature and extent of which can be learned only from a consideration of the causes which produce it. To state these causes, or, in other words, to show why Christ loves those who love him, is the principal object of the present discourse.

1. The foundation of that love which Christ feels for all who love him, was laid in eternity. All who now love him, together with all who ever will love him to the end of time, were given

to him by his Father before the foundation of the world; to be his peculiar people. God promised him in the covenant of redemption, that if he would make his soul an offering for sin, he should have a seed and a people to serve him; and that his people should be made willing in the day of his power. No sooner were this people given to him, than he loved them with a peculiar love; for he who calls the things that are not, as though they already were, can love creatures who were not, as if they were already in existence. Suppose, my friends, that when God promised a son to Abraham and Sarah, twenty-five years before his birth, he had given them a picture containing an exact likeness of this son. Would they not have immediately begun to love this picture of their future offspring; and would not their affection and their desire to see and embrace him have increased with every succeeding year? Something like such a picture of his future spiritual offspring, Christ has possessed from the first moment in which they were promised him by his Father. Their names are all written in his book of life; and their image has been ever present to the eye of his mind from that period to the present time. Hence, long before they love him, nay long before they begin to exist, they are beloved by him with a strong and tender affection, or as the prophet expresses it, with an everlasting love. Their image has so long dwelt in his mind, and so long been the object of his affectionate contemplations, that they have become, as it were, a part of himself, and he can no more cease to love them than he can cease to exist. All who are thus loved by Christ, because they are given him of his Father, will sooner or later return his affection; for, says he, all that the Father giveth me shall come to me; and him that cometh to me I will in no wise cast out. For these he prays. I pray for them, says he, I pray not for the world but for them whom thou hast given me. These he will bring in. Other sheep, he said to his disciples, I have who are not of this fold. Them also I must bring, and they shall hear my voice. These he will keep. My sheep, says he, never perish. My Father who gave them to me, is greater than all, and no one is able to pluck them out of my Father's hand. Thus he knows his sheep, loves them, prays for them, and resolves to bring them home to his fold, before they love or know him.

2. Christ loves those who love him, because he has done and suffered so much for their salvation. You need not be told, my friends, that we naturally love and prize any object in proportion to the labor and expense which it costs us to obtain it. How highly then must Christ prize, how ineffably must he love his people. How dear did their salvation cost him. He purchased them with his blood. To win their love and effect their redemption, he exchanged the height of glory and felicity for the depths of wretchedness and degradation. At an infinitely less expense he could have created thousands of worlds. Nor is this all. From the birth to the death of his people, he watches over them with unremitting attention. Every hour and every moment, they need and experience his watchful care. He forgives their sins, alleviates their sorrows, sympathizes in their trials, heals their backslidings, wipes away their tears, listens to their prayers, intercedes for them with his Father, enables them to persevere, and accompanies them through the valley of the shadow of death. All this care and attention naturally tends to increase his love for them. If a shepherd becomes affectionately attached to a flock, which he has long fed, guided and protected; if a mother loves, with increasing tenderness, a sick child who, for a long period, needs her pity and care; with what an inconceivable strength of affection must our great Shepherd love his sheep for whom he has done and suffered so much, and whom he feeds, guides and protects with such unceasing vigilance in their journey through the wilderness of this world? If his love was originally sufficiently strong to bring him from heaven to earth, and carry him through such an unparalleled series of toils and sufferings, what must it be now, when he has so much more cause to love them? If it was stronger than death, even before he died for them, who can conceive of its strength since he has arisen and reascended to heaven?

For this, among other reasons, his love for them must be greater in degree, and of a different kind from that, which he entertains for the angels of light. He loves them, indeed, but he never died for them; he never sympathized with them in affliction; he never watched over them for years with unceasing attention, nor led them by the hand through such a world as this. He loves them, as a parent loves a child that enjoys vig-

orous and uninterrupted health; but he loves his people, as
parents love a child that has often been sick, and at the point
of death. He loves them, as the father in the parable loved his
elder son who had ever been with him; but he loves his people
as the same father loved the returning prodigal, who was dead
and alive again; who after being lost was found. And perhaps
we are warranted, from this parable and those which precede
it, to conclude that there is more joy in heaven over one of our
fallen race who repents, than over ninety and nine of these
blessed spirits who need no repentance.

3. Christ loves those who love him, because they are united
to him by strong and indissoluble ties. That a most intimate
and lasting union subsists between Christ and his people, is evident from numerous passages of Scripture. This union is
sometimes compared to that which subsists between the bride-
groom and the bride. Fear not, says he to his church, for thy
Maker is thy husband. Sometimes it is compared to the union
between the branches and the vine. I, says he to his disciples,
am the vine; ye are the branches. Sometimes it is shadowed
forth by the connection between the head and the members.
Christ, says the apostle, is the head of the church, and we are
members of his body, his flesh, and his bones. In other places
it is compared to the union between the soul and the body. Ye,
says St. Paul to believers, are the body of Christ. And again,
he that is joined to the Lord is one spirit. Lastly, this mysterious union is described in still stronger terms by our Saviour as
resembling that which subsists between himself and his Father.
He that eateth my flesh and drinketh my blood, says he, dwel-
leth in me and I in him. To the same purpose he prays, that
all his disciples may be one; as thou Father art in me, and I
in thee, that they also may be one in us; I in them, and thou
in me, that they may be made perfect in one, that the world
may know that thou hast loved them, as thou hast loved me.
The expressions here employed to describe this union are the
strongest which language can afford, and sufficiently show that
it must be a union of the strongest and most intimate kind.
The bond of this union, on our part, is faith; but the union itself is formed by the appointment of God, who has constituted
Christ and his people one great body, and by the Spirit of
Christ which dwells in the hearts of all believers. As the numer-

ous branches of the vine are one with the root, because the same vital principle is common to both; or as the different members of our bodies are one because they are actuated by the same soul, so Christ and his people are one, because the same infinite Spirit dwells in them all and binds them together. Hence the afflictions of the church are called the afflictions of Christ; and hence we are told, that in all their afflictions he is afflicted, and that whoever touches them touches the apple of his eye. How strong then must be the love of Christ for his people! They are not only his brethren, his sisters, his bride, but his members, his body; and he consequently loves them as we love our members, as our souls love our bodies. Nothing can be stronger than the language of St. Paul on this subject. No man, says he, ever hated his own flesh, but loveth and cherisheth it even as the Lord does the church; plainly implying that we may as soon cease to love and cherish our bodies, as Christ to love and provide for his people.

4. Christ loves those who love him, because they possess his spirit and bear his image; in one word, because they are holy. Similarity of character always tends to produce affection, and hence every being in the universe loves his own image whenever he discovers it. Even children become more dear to their parents, when they resemble them; and our nearest relations are beloved with increased affection, whose dispositions and opinions and pursuits correspond with our own. Especially does Christ love his own image in his creatures, because it essentially consists in holiness, which is of all things most pleasing both to his Father and himself. But all who love Christ bear his image. He has no children or friends who do not resemble him; for if any man have not the Spirit of Christ he is none of his. If any man be in Christ he is a new creature, created anew after his image in knowledge, righteousness and true holiness. And though the image of Christ in his people be at first imperfect, yet the love which they entertain for his person and character, constantly tends to increase the resemblance, since we naturally imitate those whom we highly love and revere. By contemplating his glory, as displayed in the gospel, they are gradually changed into the same image from glory to glory. They love what he loves; they hate what he hates; they pursue the same objects that he pursues. They are not of

the world, even as he is not of the world.   They learn of him
to be meek and lowly in heart, and to cultivate that charity
which seeketh not her own.   Like him their principal concern
is to glorify God and finish the work he has assigned them.
Like him they pity, forgive, and pray for their enemies; and
like him they are tenderly solicitous for the salvation of sinners.
In a word, Christ, as the apostle expresses it, is formed in them.
And as those who love Christ will obey his commands, and as
he commands his disciples to be perfect even as their Father in
heaven is perfect, so they are constantly aiming at a perfect
conformity with this perfect pattern.

That this conformity to his image and obedience to his commands, are pleasing to Christ and excite his affection, is evident
from his own language.   I have not called you servants, says
he, to his disciples; but I have called you friends; and then are
ye my friends, if ye do whatsoever I command you.   The fruits
of holiness thus produced by his people on earth, imperfect as
they are, are on some accounts more pleasing to him even than
those produced by the angels in heaven.   Holiness in heaven is
like flowers in spring or like fruit in autumn when they are expected; but holiness in a world so depraved as this is like fruit
and flowers in the depth of winter; or like the blossoms and
almonds of Aaron's rod, which proceed from a dead and sapless
branch.   When the delicious fruits of southern climes can be
made by the gardener's skill to flourish in our northern regions,
they are far more admired and prized, than while growing in
rich abundance in their native soil.   So when holiness, whose
native land is heaven, is found in the comparatively frozen and
barren soil of this world, which lieth in wickedness, it is viewed
by celestial beings with peculiar pleasure and agreeable surprise.

Lastly; Christ loves those who love him, because they rejoice
in and return his affection.   It is the natural tendency of love
to produce and increase love.   Even those whom we have long
loved on account either of their relation to us, or of their amiable qualities, become incomparably more dear to us when they
begin to prize our love and return it.   Hence it is easy to conceive that Christ loves his people because of their love to him.
And if he so loved them before they existed, and even while
they were his enemies, as to lay down his life for their redemp-

tion, how inexpressibly dear to him must they be, after they become his friends! To this, the apostle alludes when he says, if when we were enemies we were reconciled to God by the death of his Son, much more, being reconciled, we shall be saved by his life. It is indeed utterly impossible to conceive the immeasurable extent of his love to those who are thus reconciled to him. Well might the apostle say, it passeth knowledge. He feels none of those jealous fears respecting the sincerity of his friends, which men are prone to entertain, and which often interrupt their friendship for each other.

No; he knows that his people love him, and he knows how much they love him. He knows that he is precious to their souls, more precious than the air they breathe, than the light of heaven. He knows that they love him better than father or mother, husband or wife, brother or sister, son or daughter, yea far better than their own lives; and that for his sake they are ready to renounce and forsake them all. He knows that his love sweetly constrains them to live to his service, and that they rejoice when they are counted worthy to suffer pain and shame for his name. He knows that they look upon him as their Redeemer, their Friend, their Shepherd, their Physician, their Advocate, their Wisdom, their Strength, their Life, and their All; that the enjoyment of his presence and favor constitutes all their felicity; that they consider no earthly affliction comparable to his absence or displeasure, and that the weakness of their love to him is their constant grief and shame. He knows that they prefer him to themselves, that they wish for a heavenly crown only that they may throw it down at his feet; and that the principal reason why they desire heaven is, that they may see and serve and praise him, and ascribe all the glory of their salvation to him. And how then can he refrain from loving those who thus love him; whom he has himself taught to love him. With what unutterable emotion of mingled pity, sympathy, and love must he look down on those who are thus attached to him in the midst of a rebellious world, and who for his sake are denying themselves, taking up the cross and striving to follow him in defiance of all the inward and outward opposition which they are called to encounter? Hear what he says to such: I know thy works. I have set before thee an open door, and no man can shut it; for thou hast a little strength, and hast kept my word, and hast not denied my name. Because thou hast kept the word of my patience, I also will keep thee in the hour of temptation which shall come on all the earth, and I will cause thine adversaries to come and worship before thy feet, and to know that I have loved thee.

Thus have I attempted to state the principal reasons why Christ loves those who love him. He loves them because they are given him by his Father; because he has done and suffered much for their salvation; because they are united to him in the most intimate and indissoluble manner; because they possess his spirit and bear his image; and because they rejoice in and return his affection. Either of these causes alone would induce him to love them with a strength of affection, of which we can form no conception. What then must be the degree of love produced by all these causes united? He only can tell, who knows the Son even as the Son knows him. The love of Christ passeth knowledge. Its heights and depths, its length and breadth, are unsearchable by finite minds.

IMPROVEMENT. 1. This subject may enable every one to answer the important question, does Christ love me? This is a question which all true Christians will frequently, and anxiously ask, and which many of them feel unable to answer in a satisfactory manner. When they consider the spotless purity of Christ, and his hatred of sin, and their own exceeding sinfulness and unworthiness, they are ready to exclaim, how is it possible that he should love us? O that he were on earth, that we might ask him this question, or that some kind angel would favor us with a glimpse of his book of life, or assure us that we are the objects of his love. But these wishes are needless. Say not in your hearts, Who shall ascend up into heaven, to ask whether Christ loves us; for the answer to this question is near you even in your hearts. If you love Christ he loves you. If you are his friends, he is most certainly yours. Were he now on earth, and should you ask, Lord, canst thou condescend to love us? he would answer your question by another, and say as he did to Peter, Lovest thou me more than these worldly objects around you? Look into your hearts then, my friends, for an answer to this question. Can not some of you reply, Lord, thou knowest all things, thou knowest that I love thee. Thou knowest that, notwithstanding our coldness, our ingratitude, and numberless imperfections, the desire of our souls is still to thee, and to the remembrance of thy name? If you dare not say this, can you not venture to say, we know that Christ is just such a Saviour as we need; the way of salvation by him is exactly suited to our circumstances; we know that his yoke is easy, and his burden light; and that it appears to us above all things desirable to obey his commands, and imitate his example; we know that we love all who love him and bear his image; and that it gratifies us to hear him praised and extolled; we know that his presence alone renders us happy, and that in his absence nothing affords us consolation? My friends, if you can truly say this, you need not wish for Christ to come and assure you of his love. He has already done it; he has done it in the words of our text; and you may feel more assured of it than if you had heard it asserted by a voice from heaven. Unworthy as you are, he loves you infinitely more than you can conceive; and will continue to love you while eternity shall last. Away, then, with your doubts and anxieties. Dismiss every fearful anxious thought; listen not to the suggestions of unbelief, but believe the words of Christ, and open your hearts to admit the consoling enrapturing assurances of his love. Come to his table, as to the table of a friend, who will give you a cordial welcome, and not as to the table of a master of whom you are servilely afraid? Why should you hesitate or fear to do this? Do you not invariably find that, when you feel the fullest assurance of his love, you are most engaged in his service; and that, on the contrary, when you doubt it, your hands are weakened, and your hearts discouraged! If this be the case, it is at once your duty, your interest, and your happiness to believe, to be certain, that you love Christ, and that he loves you; and in proportion as you believe this, will be your progress in the Christian race. This St. Paul well knew, and therefore, when he wished Christians to be filled with the fulness of God, he prayed that they might know the love of Christ. If any of you still doubt, and wish for more satisfactory evidence, the preceding observations may teach you how to obtain it. In proportion as your love to Christ increases, so will your evidence of his love to you increase. All your doubts arise from the weakness and inconstancy of your love. Labor and pray, therefore, that your knowledge of Christ may be increased, and his love shed abroad in your hearts.

Thus will you soon be enabled to say with Peter, Lord, thou knowest that I love thee.

2. If Christ loves those who love him, then he will love those most who are most ready to return his affection, and to do all things, to suffer all things for his sake. My Christian friends, do you wish for a large share of Christ's love; for a distinguished place in his affections? Then instead of shrinking from the cross, press it to your hearts, and like the first disciples rejoice when you are counted worthy to suffer for him. Afflictions, reproaches, and persecutions, are the honors and preferments of Christ's earthly kingdom; for if we suffer with him, we shall also reign with him; and the greater our sufferings, the brighter will be our crown, the more exalted our thrones. Every one who forsakes father or mother, wife or children, houses or lands, for Christ's sake, shall receive a hundred fold, and in the world to come, everlasting life. Be not contented then with giving Christ few and small proofs of your affection; but labor to love him as he has loved you, and be as willing to suffer for him, as he was to suffer for you. Should you love him more than all the saints and angels, his love would still infinitely surpass yours. Be persuaded then to give him all your hearts. Are you not sometimes ready to wish that you had a thousand hearts to give him, a thousand tongues to speak his praise, a thousand hands to labor in his service? And will you then withhold any part of what you already possess? No; give him all, for all is infinitely less than he deserves; and the more you give him, the more will you receive.

3. How happy are they who love. It has been often and justly observed, that to love, and to be beloved by a deserving earthly friend affords the greatest happiness which the world can give. What happiness then must they enjoy, who love and are beloved by the infinite fountain of love,—God's eternal Son, the brightness of his glory, the possessor of all power in heaven and earth; source of every thing amiable and excellent in the universe. What pure, ineffable, exalted delight must they find in communion with such a friend; and what indescribable benefits must they receive from his love! What can created minds conceive of, what can the heart form a wish for, beyond the friendship of such a being? Nay, what creature could have dared to raise his wishes so high, had not God himself encour-

his love of Jesus you have to experience yourself.

aged us to do it? O, it is too, too much; not too much indeed for God to give, but far too much for man to deserve. But in vain do we attempt to give you adequate ideas of the happiness resulting from the love of Christ. It is one of those things, which it is impossible for man to utter; and the joy which it produces is a joy unspeakable. If any would know it, they must learn it, not from language, but from their own experience, for language sinks under the weight of a subject, which it was never intended to describe. We can only say that, to love and be beloved by Christ, is the very essence of heaven.

4. The truths we have been considering afford most powerful motives to induce sinners to love Christ. Benevolent, pitiful, and compassionate as he is; he cannot, at present, my impenitent hearers, but view your characters with abhorrence and disgust. Even now he looks round about upon you with anger, being grieved for the hardness of your hearts. He knows that you do not love him, He sees that you do not comply with his invitations, or obey his commands. He seldom if ever, hears a prayer from your lips. He sees that you refuse to comply with his dying request, that you are even now about to turn away from his table, where his people commemorate his dying love. How then can he love you. How can he but be displeased and grieved, to see himself and the blessings he offers thus slighted and despised. Still, however, he waits to be gracious. He once more sends you terms of reconciliation. And what are the terms? He requires your love. Be his friends, and he will be yours. And can you hesitate respecting a compliance? Shall infinite loveliness offer to love perfect deformity, and shall perfect deformity refuse to love infinite loveliness? My friends, think again of his offers. Are they reasonable? Are they not more than reasonable? Even your fellow worms will not love you unless you return their love. And can you then expect, that your offended Creator and Redeemer, the King of kings and Lord of lords, will love you on easier terms; will love you while you persist in grieving, neglecting and provoking him? My friends, you ought not to expect this. You cannot expect it. Will you not then comply with his terms? Look at him again. You will find his portrait, his likeness, the very picture of his heart in the gospel. Study it attentively. See what majesty and meekness, what dignity and

tenderness; what glory and condescension, what grace and sweetness, there is in every feature. See infinite power, unsearchable knowledge, unerring wisdom, boundless goodness,— see all the fulness of the Godhead, veiled in flesh and coming down from heaven to win your affections. This is he who says, I love them that love me. My friends, how can you forbear to love such a being. Methinks you could not but love him though hell should be the consequence. How then can you refuse, when heaven will be the reward.

SERMON XX

THE SAFETY OF RELIGION.

He that walketh uprightly, walketh surely. — PROVERBS X. 9.

THE term walk, as used by the inspired writers, signifies a course of conduct. To walk uprightly, then, is to pursue a course of uprightness, or integrity. Our text assures us, that he who pursues such a course walketh surely. He walks safely, for he is safe while pursuing such a course; and safety, or eternal salvation, will be the end of it. He may therefore walk confidently, or with an assurance of present safety, and of final salvation. If any proposition of a religious nature be demonstrably true, it is this. It is demonstrably true, that God is righteous. It is demonstrably true, that, possessing this character, he must regard the righteous with approbation and complacency; or, as an inspired writer expresses it, The righteous Lord loveth righteousness; for he cannot but approve of his own character; he cannot but love his own image in his creatures. And it is demonstrably true, that those whom he loves and approves must be safe here, and happy hereafter. We may, therefore, consider it as a most certain and well established truth, that he who walketh uprightly walketh safely.

But here a question arises, and a difficulty occurs. What is it to walk uprightly? It is well known, that various opinions are entertained respecting this question, and that different persons answer it in a very different manner. Now how shall we ascertain which of these various opinions is correct? And unless we can ascertain which of them is correct, of what service is our text? What does it avail us to know that he who walketh uprightly, walketh safely, unless we can ascertain what it is to walk uprightly? My hearers, if I am not greatly deceived, our text will assist us in surmounting this difficulty. If it is true that he who walketh uprightly walketh safely, then it must be true that he who walks safely, walks uprightly. If then we can ascertain which is the safe course, we shall ascertain which is the upright course. If we can ascertain who walk safely, we shall ascertain who walk uprightly. It will, therefore, be my object in the following remarks, to show which is the safe course, or who walk safely.

Every religious course, whether right or wrong, safe or unsafe, includes two things; first, the doctrines which are believed; and secondly, the precepts which are obeyed by those who follow it. In other words, it includes sentiments, and conduct or practice. It will be proper to consider these two things separately. Let us then inquire,

I. What sentiments are safe, or what we may safely believe. In answer to this inquiry we may remark,

1. It is safe to believe that the Scriptures are a revelation from God, and that those who wrote them were inspired. This, it is presumed, no infidel will deny. No infidel will pretend that we expose ourselves to any evil, or danger, in a future state, by believing the Scriptures to be the word of God, even though it should prove that they are not so; for believing them does not lead to the neglect of any duty, which infidels regard as necessary to the attainment of future happiness. Allowing then, for argument's sake, that they should prove not to be a revelation from God; those who believed that they were so, will still stand on as safe ground, as those who rejected them. It is then safe to believe the Scriptures. But it is not safe to disbelieve them; for if they are the word of God, all who do not receive them as such, will perish. And no one will deny that it is possible they may be the word of God. No one can, with the least shadow of reason, pretend, that it is not probable they are so. A book which thousands of the learned and the wise, after a thorough examination, have received as a revelation from heaven, must, surely, have at least probability in its favor. Its claims must be supported by proofs of no common strength. Taking the infidel,

then, on his own ground, it is by no means safe to reject the Scriptures. He who rejects them is far from walking safely.

2. It is safe to believe in the immortality of the soul, and in a future state of retribution. This assertion requires no proof; for it is impossible that any future evil or danger should result from believing these doctrines, even if they are not true. If the soul is not immortal, if there is no future state, they who believed, and they who disbelieved these doctrines, will alike cease to exist at death. On the other hand, it is not safe to disbelieve these doctrines. Even those who disbelieve them must allow, that they may possibly be true; nay, that there is some probability of their truth. And if they are true, the consequences of disbelieving them will be terrible; for he who does not believe that his soul is immortal, will take no care of it; and he who does not believe in a future state of retribution, will make no preparation for it, and will, of course, die unprepared. He then who disbelieves these doctrines does not walk safely.

3. It is safe to believe that men are naturally destitute of holiness, or, in other words, wholly sinful. No one, it is presumed, can point out any danger, either present or future, to which a belief of this doctrine exposes men. The Scriptures caution us against every danger to which we are exposed; but they never intimate that there is any danger of entertaining too low an opinion of ourselves. On the contrary, they give us this caution, Let no man think of himself more highly than he ought to think. It must, I conceive, be acknowledged by all, that we are far more disposed to form too high, than too low an estimate of our own characters; that we are more in danger of being too proud, than we are of becoming too humble. Even then if we were not wholly sinful, it would be erring on the safe side to believe that we are so.

But it is by no means equally safe to embrace the opposite opinion. Most awful threatenings are denounced in the Scriptures against all who do not repent of, confess, and renounce their sins. But he who does not believe that he is entirely sinful, will not feel that repentance, nor make those confessions, which a belief of this doctrine would produce, and which the Scriptures require. Besides, if it is true that men are naturally destitute of holiness, it follows, that he who disbelieves this truth, mistakes something for holiness which in fact is not holiness;

and a mistake respecting this point must be fatal. If a man thinketh himself to be something, when he is nothing, he deceiveth himself. And is there not, at least, some probability, that the doctrine is true, even its enemies themselves being judges? Do not the inspired assertions, that men are dead in trespasses and sins, that if one died for all then were all dead, that the heart of the sons of men is full of evil and madness, deceitful above all things and desperately wicked; I say, do not these, and other similar assertions, with which the Scriptures abound, seem to mean that men are entirely sinful? Do they not make it at least probable that they are so? Now if there is the least probability that such is the fact, it is safe to believe it, unsafe to deny it. To believe it, if false, can do no harm. To disbelieve it, if true, will be fatal.

4. It is safe to believe that a moral renovation, or change of heart, is necessary to salvation. No harm can result from believing this doctrine, even if it is not true. But much harm, fatal harm must result from disbelieving it, if it is true. The man who does not believe that a new heart is necessary will give himself no concern respecting its attainment. He will live and die without it. Of course, if it is necessary to salvation, he will not be saved. And is it not possible that it may be necessary? Nay, is it not probable? If any man be in Christ, he is a new creature. Verily, verily, I say unto you, except a man be born again, he cannot see the kingdom of heaven. Do not these, and the numerous other passages of the same import, which are found in the Scriptures, seem to teach that a great moral change or renovation is necessary? Do they not render it probable that it is so? Surely then, it cannot be safe to disbelieve it? He who disbelieves it cannot walk safely.

5. It is safe to believe in the proper divinity of Jesus Christ. Some may deny this assertion, on the ground that if Christ is not God, to worship him as such, will involve us in the guilt of idolatry. But whether he is or is not God, it is certainly our duty to worship him. We are commanded to honor him even as we honor the Father; and we are told that when the Father brought him into the world, he said, Let all the angels of God worship him. If it is the duty of all the angels to worship him, much more, we may conclude, is it ours. We may add, that though prophets, apostles, and angels always checked and re-

proved those who attempted to worship them, our Saviour, even during his state of humiliation on earth, frequently received worship from men as his due. Nor among all the cautions which are given us in the Scriptures, is there the least intimation that we must beware of loving and honoring Christ too much, or that there is any danger of placing him too high. Indeed, it would be strange if there were such intimation, for why should we be cautioned against worshipping one who is worshipped in heaven, and who shares with his Father the praises of its inhabitants? In fine, if it is safe to obey God, to imitate the apostles, to utter the language of heaven, then it is safe to worship Jesus Christ. And if it is safe to worship him, it cannot be unsafe to believe that he is God. You cannot suppose that any man will be condemned at the judgment day, for thinking too highly of his Saviour, or loving and honoring him too much. But if Christ is God, it is by no means equally safe to disbelieve that he is so. If the doctrine of his proper divinity is true, it must be a fundamental doctrine, a doctrine the belief of which is necessary to render us Christ's. This, Dr. Priestley, the great apostle of Unitarianism, has acknowledged. If you are right, said he to a distinguished clergyman in this country, who believed our Saviour's divinity; if you are right, we are not Christians at all, and I do not wonder in the least at the bad opinion you entertain of us. And is there not at least a probability that those who believe Christ's divinity are right? Do not many inspired passages appear to assert it in the most unequivocal terms? And since no evils can result from believing it, even though it should not prove to be true, while the most terrible evils will be the consequence of disbelieving it, if it is true, is it not the safer and wiser course to believe it? Does not he who believes it walk safely?

6. It is safe to believe that Christ has made an atonement for sin, and that we must be justified by faith in him, and not by our own works. From a belief of these doctrines rightly understood, no evil or danger can result, even if they are not true. It has indeed been asserted, that these doctrines are unfavorable to morality, but the assertion is groundless; for all who believe that we are justified by faith in Christ, believe that this faith will produce good works, and that a faith which does not produce them, cannot be genuine. They believe that good

works are as necessary to our salvation, as if we were actually justified by performing them. In fine, they believe that without holiness, no man shall see the Lord. This being the case, it is impossible that their reliance on the atonement and righteousness of Christ should make them negligent of moral duties. Nor can it be shown, that the belief of these doctrines occasions any other evil, or exposes them, either here or hereafter, to any danger. It is then safe to believe them, even if they are not true. But it is very unsafe to disbelieve them if they are true. A mistake respecting the terms of acceptance, the way of salvation, must be fatal, if any mistake can be so. Those who make the mistake, incur the guilt, and expose themselves to the fate of the Jews, who, being ignorant of God's righteousness, went about to establish their own righteousness, and thus failed of salvation. One of the most zealous advocates of the doctrine, that we are justified by our own works, after writing a large volume in support of it, concludes with this remarkable concession, "Nevertheless, since we are prone to estimate our good works too highly, and fancy that they are sufficient for our justification, when in fact they are not so, the safer way is to renounce all dependence on them, and rely on the righteousness of Christ alone."

Finally; It is safe to believe that all men will not be saved, and that without repentance, faith and holiness none will be saved. To prove this, little need be said. If the doctrine that all men will inherit salvation is true, those who deny, are as safe as those who believe it. If it is not true, those who trust in it trust to a lie, and will utterly perish in their own deceivings. And even its warmest advocates must allow, that there is at least a possibility of its proving false. No man then walks safely who ventures his soul, his all, upon its truth.

Thus have I attempted to show who pursue a safe, and who an unsafe course, so far as doctrines, or sentiments are concerned. I shall now proceed, as was proposed,

II.   To pursue the same inquiry with respect to practice. In attempting this, however, we cannot descend to particulars. The precepts of revelation, are so numerous, that it is scarcely possible, in a single discourse, to mention them all. Nor is it necessary to our present design. It will be sufficient to remark, that, with respect to practice, all who are called Christians, may

the 2 classes are:
the Saved Believing Servants of God
The Unsaved unbelieving Slaves of Satan

THE SAFETY OF RELIGION. 231

be divided into two great classes. Of these two classes, one is distinguished by a strict, the other by a lax interpretation of the divine precepts. The former suppose that these precepts are to be understood and obeyed in their plain, obvious sense. The latter contend that, understood in this sense, it is impossible to obey them; and that it is therefore, necessary to explain away much of their apparent meaning, and bring them more nearly to a level with the inclinations and pursuits of mankind. The former suppose, that we must obey them, though obedience should displease our friends, draw upon us contempt and reproach, and expose us to sufferings and losses. The latter seem to think, that we are to obey them so far only as is consistent with our temporal interest and convenience. The former consider the salvation of the soul as the one thing needful, and religion as the great business of life. They suppose that it is our duty to be continually under its influence; and whether we eat, or drink, or whatever we do, to do all to the glory of God. The latter contend, that we are not required to be so very religious, that there is no need of feeling much concern respecting our spiritual and eternal interests, and that we are not forbidden to indulge in what the world calls innocent amusements. Hence a corresponding difference is found to exist between the conduct of these two classes. The latter allow themselves in many things which the former consider as forbidden, sinful, and dangerous. The latter are conformed to this world; the former are not so. Hence they have in all ages been censured and ridiculed as precise, superstitious, bigoted, and morose; while the other class has been complimented for its liberality, and freedom from narrow views and prejudices. Now the question before us is, Which of these two classes pursues the safe course? Which is most dangerous, — to have too little religion, or too much? And on which side are we most tempted, and most prone to err? My hearers, the bare statement of these questions renders an answer needless. You all know, that we are naturally prone, not to go beyond our duty, but to fall short of it. You know, that all the temptations to which we are exposed exert their influence on the same side. There is nothing to tempt us to be too religious. There are a thousand things which tempt us to rest satisfied with too little religion. On this side, then, our danger lies. On this side only do we need a

God does not tempt us to be believers
But Satan does tempt not to

guard. Besides, how can any man be too religious? How can
any man go beyond the precepts which require him to love God
with all his heart; to do every thing to his glory; to renounce
every thing which causes him to sin; though dear as a right
hand or a right eye; to crucify the flesh with its affections and
lusts; to deny himself, take up the cross, and to be holy as God
is holy? How can any man be more humble, prayerful, thankful and heavenly-minded than the Scriptures require him to
be? And even if it were possible to do more than our duty,
could any harm result from doing it? Would God punish a
man for being too religious, for loving him too well, and serving
him too faithfully? Did you ever hear of a man who, on his
dying bed, repented of having paid so much attention to religion, or who expressed any fears that God would be displeased
with him, on account of his zeal and devotion? Did you ever
hear of a man's saying, in such circumstances, Were I to live
my life over again, I would be less strict and scrupulous than I
have been, in obeying the divine commands? On the contrary,
do not even the most pious, reproach themselves, in a dying
hour, for their deficiencies; and say, were we to pass through
the world again, we would strive to be more faithful and more
devoted to God? Surely then, there is no danger of being too
religious. Surely the strict course is the safe course. Even if
those who pursue it go farther than is absolutely necessary, yet
their salvation is sure. In a word, they are safe, even if their
opponents are right. But the same cannot be said of the opposite course. If the former are right, the latter are fatally wrong.
Though it is not easy to conceive of a man's having too much
religion, we can easily conceive of a man's having too little.
Though it is impossible to believe, that any one will be punished
for going beyond what God requires of us, it is very possible
that many may be punished for falling short of it. He only,
then, who walks strictly, walks safely.

Now of the things which we have spoken, this is the sum.
He that walks uprightly, walks safely. Of course, every one
who walks safely, walks uprightly. The safe course is the upright course. Which is the safe course, we have attempted to
show, with respect both to sentiment and practice. We think
no one will assert, we are sure no one can prove, that the course
which has been described is not safe. And if it is safe, it is

morally correct Behavior
Righteousness

right; for rectitude and safety are inseparably connected. Will you not all be persuaded then, to adopt this course? Will you not embrace sentiments which, even allowing they are not true, can expose you to no danger, but which, if true, cannot be rejected without exposing you to destruction. Does any one reply, The course which you have described, though it may be safe, is not pleasant. If it does not lead to unhappiness hereafter, it must render those who walk in it unhappy here? I answer, all who have made trial of it, deny this assertion, and those who have not, make it without any knowledge of the subject. But allowing for a moment, that this course is attended with some present unhappiness; can this afford the shadow of a reason for exposing ourselves to everlasting wretchedness? No man, who really believes that he has an immortal soul, that he is an accountable creature, will assert that it does. Indeed, every man who pays any regard to the dictates of wisdom or prudence, will say, It is folly, it is madness, to incur the smallest risk of everlasting wretchedness, for the sake of any temporal advantage whatever. If there is only a bare possibility that the threatenings of God's word will be executed, nothing shall tempt me to pursue a course which may bring them upon my head. Whatever I lose, I will not place my soul at hazard. If any course is safe, I will pursue it, cost what it may.

It has probably already occurred to you, my hearers, that the course which we have now described is the same which has often been recommended to you from this place. It is a course which we can recommend to you with full confidence. We are under no apprehensions that any of you will complain of us in the other world, or at the judgment day, for having recommended this course. We are under no apprehensions that you will then say, we required of you more than God requires, or represented the way to heaven as narrower than it really is. If you have then any cause of complaint, it will be that we did not press you with greater earnestness and importunity to walk in this way.

To you, my Christian friends, who are pursuing the course which has now been described, the preceding remarks are unnecessary. You need no additional arguments to convince you, that the course you have adopted is both right and safe. It may, however, sometimes afford you pleasure in a dark hour,

Gods words bring comfort
and assurance.

to reflect, that the system of doctrines and practice which you have adopted, includes every thing which is valuable in all other systems, together with many distinguishing excellencies peculiar to itself. If any are safe, you are so. If any religious system is right, yours is right. But if yours is right, all others are wrong. Hold fast your confidence, then to the end. Be steadfast, unmoveable, always abounding in the work of the Lord.

AMEN!
AND Amen!

CPSIA information can be obtained at www.ICGtesting.com
Printed in the USA
BVOW02s1341070715

407757BV00001B/8/P